Enhanced Recovery for Major Abdominopelvic Surgery

First Edition

Editors:

Tong Joo (TJ) Gan, MD, MHS, FRCA
Professor and Chair, Department of Anesthesiology
Stony Brook University School of Medicine

Julie K. Thacker, MD
Assistant Professor of Surgery
Duke University School of Medicine

Timothy E. Miller, MB, ChB, FRCA
Associate Professor of Anesthesiology
Duke University Medical Center

Michael J. Scott, MB, ChB
Consultant in Anaesthesia and Intensive Care Medicine
Royal Surrey County Hospital NHS Foundation Trust
Honorary Senior Lecturer University College London

Stefan D. Holubar, MD, MS
Assistant Professor of Surgery
Dartmouth Geisel School of Medicine

AMERICAN SOCIETY FOR
ENHANCED RECOVERY

PROFESSIONAL
COMMUNICATIONS, INC.

Professional Communications, Inc.
A Medical Publishing & Communications Company

400 Center Bay Drive
West Islip, NY 11795
(t) 631/661-2852
(f) 631/661-2167

1223 W. Main, #1427
Durant, OK 74702-1427
(t) 580/745-9838
(f) 580/745-9837

For orders only, please call
1-800-337-9838
or visit our Web site at
www.pcibooks.com

ISBN: 978-1-943236-02-2

Printed in the United States of America

DISCLAIMER
The opinions expressed in this publication reflect those of the editors. However, the editors make no warranty regarding the contents of the publication. The protocols described herein are general and may not apply to a specific patient. Any product mentioned in this publication should be taken in accordance with the prescribing information provided by the manufacturer.

This text is printed on recycled paper.

TABLE OF CONTENTS

■ About ASER

ASER (American Society for Enhanced Recovery) is a nonprofit organization with an international membership, which is dedicated to the practice of enhanced recovery in the perioperative patient through education and research. It is a multidisciplinary and multispecialty society with representations from the surgeons, anesthesiologists, nurses, nurse anesthetists, pharmacists, allied heath care professionals, healthcare administrators and patient advocates.

■ The ASER Mission

To advance the practice of perioperative enhanced recovery, to contribute to its growth and influences, by fostering and encouraging research, education, public policies, programs and scientific progress.

■ ASER History

The concept of enhanced recovery or fast-track surgery originated from the work of Professor Henrik Kehlet in Denmark in the 1990s. However, the adoption of the fast track concept has been relatively slow until the mid to late 2000 when several countries in Europe and the United Kingdom started to implement this strategy in surgical patients. In the United States (US) interest in enhanced recovery has been growing since the late 2000s. The Duke University Medical Center Enhanced Recovery Program in colorectal surgery started in 2010. Since then many centers around the US have started enhanced recovery protocols (ERP). The first US Enhanced Recovery Congress organized was held in Washington DC in 2013. The 2nd US Enhanced Recovery program was held in New Orleans in October 2014, and marked the official launch of the ASER.

■ ASER Education Activities

ASER has many educational programs to help clinicians and practitioners to implement ERPs. The highlight of the society's education event is the annual congress. Partnering with the United Kingdom based Evidence Based Perioperative Medicine (EBPOM), the congress covers a variety of topics on enhanced recovery and perioperative medicine. In addition, ASER is launching its enhanced recovery Leadership Forum, aimed at helping the multidisciplinary team to implement ERPs at their hospitals.

For more information, please visit the ASER website at **aserhq.org** or **enhancedrecovery.org** or contact the ASER Office (**info@aserhq.org**, **414-389-8610**).

Contributing Authors

Robin Anderson, BSN, RN
Enhanced Recovery Program Coordinator,
Duke University Health System

Joshua A. Bloomstone, MD, CSSGB, CLS
Chairman, Department of Anesthesia and Perioperative Medicine, Banner Thunderbird Medical Center, Glendale, AZ
Physician Chair, Anesthesiology Clinical Consensus Group
Banner Health, Phoenix, AZ
Valley Anesthesiology Consultants, Ltd., Phoenix, AZ

G. Bousquet-Dion, MD
Department of Anesthesia, McGill University Health Centre

Maxime Cannesson, MD, PhD
Professor of Anesthesiology and Vice Chair for Perioperative Medicine, Department of Anesthesiology and Perioperative Medicine, University of California Los Angeles

F. Carli, MD, MPhil
Department of Anesthesia, McGill University Health Centre

Robert R. Cima, MD, MA
Professor of Surgery, Mayo Clinic College of Medicine
Consultant, Division of Colon and Rectal Surgery

Ryan W. Day, MD
Division of Colon and Rectal Surgery, Mayo Clinic Arizona

Tong Joo (TJ) Gan, MD, MHS, FRCA
Professor and Chair, Department of Anesthesiology,
Stony Brook University School of Medicine

Michael P.W. Grocott, BSc, MBBS, MD, FRCA, FRCP, FFICM
Professor of Anaesthesia and Critical Care Medicine
University of Southhampton, UK

Ruchir Gupta, MD
Assistant Professor, Department of Anesthesiology
Stony Brook University School of Medicine

Traci L. Hedrick, MD, MS-CR, FACS, FACRS
Assistant Professor of Surgery, University of Virginia

Stefan D. Holubar, MD, MS
Assistant Professor of Surgery,
Dartmouth Geisel School of Medicine

Henrik Kehlet, MD, PhD
Professor, Section for Surgical Pathophysiology
Righospitalet, Copenhagen University

Clifford Y. Ko, MD
Professor of Surgery, UCLA School of Medicine
Director, National Surgical Quality Improvement Program
and Division of Research and Optimal Patient Care
American College of Surgeons

Sandhya Lagoo-Deenadayalan, MD
Associate Professor of Surgery, Duke University

David W. Larson, MD, MBA
Division of Colon and Rectal Surgery, Mayo Clinic

Kristoffer Lassen, MD, PhD
Department of Gastrointestinal Surgery
University of Tromsoslash, Norway

Elaine Ah-Gi Lo, PharmD, BCPS
Department of Pharmacy, Kwong Wah Hospital, Hong Kong

Larry Manders, MD
Anesthesiology Resident, Oakland University William Beaumont School of Medicine

Amit Merchea MD
Section of Colon and Rectal Surgery
Mayo Clinic, Jacksonville, FL

Timothy E. Miller, MB, ChB, FRCA
Associate Professor of Anesthesiology,
Duke University Medical Center

E.M. Minnella MD
Department of Anesthesia, McGill University Health Centre
School of Anesthesia and Intensive Care, University of Milan

Joshua D. Morris, MD
Resident Physician, Department of Anesthesiology,
University of Virginia

Timothy A. Rockall, MD, FRCS
Director of MATTU
Professor of Surgery, Royal Surrey County Hospital NHS Trust, Guildford, UK

Sean Ryan, MD
Orthopaedic Surgery Resident, Department of Orthopaedic Surgery, Duke University Medical Center

Bethany M. Sarosiek, RN, MSN, MPH, CNL
ERAS Development Coordinator
UVA Health System, Charlottesville, VA

Michael J. Scott, **MB**, **ChB**
Consultant in Anaesthesia and Intensive Care Medicine,
Royal Surrey County Hospital NHS Foundation Trust,
Honorary Senior Lecturer University College London

Anthony J. Senagore, **MD**, **MBA**, **FACS**, **FASCRS**
Professor of Surgery, Chief Division of
Gastrointestinal Surgery, UTMB, Galveston, TX

Lawrence Siu-Chun Law, **MD**
Duke-NUS Graduate Medical School, Singapore

Mattias Soop, **MD**, **PhD**
Manchester, UK

Roy G. Soto, **MD**
Professor of Anesthesiology
Oakland University William Beaumont School of Medicine

Martin Szafran, **MD**
Assistant Professor, Department of Anesthesiology
Stony Brook University

Julie K. Thacker, **MD**
Assistant Professor of Surgery
Duke University School of Medicine

Robert H. Thiele, **MD**
Assistant Professor of Anesthesiology, University of Virginia

Debbie Watson, **RN**, **MN**
McGill University Health Centre–Montreal General Hospital
Enhanced Recovery Program Coordinator

Malcolm A. West, **MD**, **MRCS**, **PhD**
NIHR Clinical Academic and General Surgical Registrar
Academic Unit of Cancer Sciences
Faculty of Medicine, University of Southhampton, UK

Christopher L. Wu, **MD**
Professor of Anesthesiology and Critical Care Medicine
Department of Anesthesiology and Critical Care Medicine
Division of Regional Anesthesia and Acute Pain Medicine
Division of Obstetric Anesthesiology
The Johns Hopkins Hospital

Tonia M. Young-Fadok, **MD**, **MS**, **FACS**, **FASCRS**
Professor of Surgery
Division of Colon and Rectal Surgery
Mayo Clinic Arizona

TABLES

FIGURES

During the last decade, research from many parts of the world has documented the clinical and economic benefits of introducing multimodal, enhanced recovery programs, initially with most data from colonic surgery. Despite much research on each of the many elements in these programs, regional and national surveys have shown an important "knowing–doing" gap from clinical research to clinical implementation. In this context, the American Society for Enhanced Recovery (ASER) is doing a great job to provide guidelines, postgraduate teaching, etc.

The present ASER manual provides an update on the different care elements to be considered for implementation of a successful enhanced recovery program in major abdominopelvic surgery, again emphasizing that such programs require a close collaboration between anesthesiology, surgery, and nursing. Consequently, the manual is a laudable effort to help clinicians to improve within seven important abdominopelvic operations. Although the colorectal protocols are based on the most recent data, the future challenge is to develop evidence-based and better protocols in the other major operations, but where the present protocols provide a sound basis to start.

Hopefully, this manual will stimulate the development of protocols in other types of surgery. Although preliminary data are positive, they will require a procedure-specific focus on the recovery problems based on the question "Why is the patient in the hospital today?"

Henrik Kehlet, Professor, MD, PhD
Section for Surgical Pathophysiology 4074
Rigshospitalet, Copenhagen University, Rigshospitalet
DK-2100 Copenhagen, Denmark

Overview for Surgeons

by Professor Timothy A Rockall, MD, FRCS
and Julie K Thacker, MD

It is worth considering that the father of the concept of fast-track surgery and enhanced recovery after surgery (ERAS)—Dr Henrik Kehlet—is a surgeon. There is rightly a great emphasis on a multidisciplinary approach to enhanced recovery the process in the most successful units; however, much of the research into Enhanced Recovery has been led by surgeons. Surgeons perform an essential leadership role in delivering the overall package of care, as they are the primary observers of the improved outcome that Enhanced Recovery Protocols (ERPs) deliver. The surgeon, with the goal of optimizing their outcomes, must abandon dogma, embrace evidenced-based practice, and lead the process of change.

It is well established that poor surgery impacts on surgical recovery and local cancer recurrence. Less well appreciated is that complications also have a major impact on long-term survival and systemic cancer recurrence. The ultimate goal of ERPs should be improvement in clinical and oncological outcomes, as well as better overall experience for the surgical patient. The aim of instituting ERPs is foremost a reduction in complications following surgical intervention and consequent lower morbidity and mortality. With these improvements, better long-term overall survival and disease-free survival for cancer patients are seen. Length of hospital stay, the most commonly measured surgical outcome, is of great importance to health systems and hospital administrators. In reality though, this is a reflection of the improved outcome and lower complication rate rather than a goal or an outcome in its own right. Simply put, patients who recover well and without complications and without the imposition of ill-informed dogmatic care pathways will go home quickly. There is a proviso that the early discharge philosophy is in harmony with the patients' expectations.

ERPs cannot be delivered without a multidisciplinary engagement and crucially without a partnership.

High-quality ERPs require an enthusiastic attention to detail, which must be driven from the top by people who really believe in its efficacy. Here the surgeon plays a crucial role. Recognition and partnering with patients, anaesthesia, nursing, families, and other caregivers along the continuum of recovery need to led by the surgeon. Surgeons are the only members of these teams, besides the patients themselves, who are involved from start to finish of the surgical journey.

In addition to leading the team, there are aspects of care particular to the surgeon's role. A commitment to good-quality minimally invasive surgical techniques, evidence-based fluid management and analgesia regimens and continuous audit are the keys to success. Implementing the evidence-proven details of perioperative care requires diligence in literature review, knowledge of one's hospital system, and collegial coordination with other caregivers. It is important to appreciate that excellent surgery in the operating theatre can be adversely affected by poor care at all points in the pathway from referral through to discharge from hospital and beyond. A lack of engagement or attention to detail can lead to missed opportunities for pre-operative optimization.

Lack of an intra-operative and postoperative fluid therapy and analgesia regimen can have profound effects on outcome and complications. In the development of the enhanced recovery program, the surgeon must take charge of the delivery of optimal care at all points in the pathway. Eventually, good practice becomes routine rather than something new and different. The pre-operative and postoperative phases are generally directed by the surgical team. In the intra-operative and immediate postoperative period, however, the surgeon has less control over the crucial elements of anesthesia (which critically impact the immediate postoperative period, particularly nausea, vomiting, pain control), fluid management, and analgesia. Engagement with skilled and enthusiastic anesthesiologists who have an equal interest in improved outcome is absolutely crucial.

There are a number of principals by which enhanced recovery surgeons attain good outcomes. The first is to lead by example:

- Bringing along members of the team who might be less confident in delivering changes amplifies any individual effort. Until other members of the team can see the benefits, this guidance leads change. Eventually, practice becomes normalized. However, maintaining and guiding presence is necessary through personnel changes, dips in team momentum, and system changes.
- Secondly, persistent leadership in the cooperative relationship with anesthesiology will exponentially strengthen this partnership.
- Thirdly, the surgeon is essential in research because there is always a risk that the new principals of enhanced recovery care themselves will become dogmatic principals that are resistant to change and improvement.
- Fourthly, the surgeon is best situated to constantly audit the enhanced recovery program performance. Audit is a powerful tool. Results from audits are useful in discussion with managers, especially where investment is required; in discussion with new teams or specialties considering a program; and in discussion of needed internal improvement.
- Fifthly, the surgeon can direct the timetable of implementation. Aiming to, within a relatively short time scale, establish ERPs as the normal care pathway requires the surgeon to ensure that the evidence-proven principles are embedded in every aspect of care.

Overview for the Anesthesiologist and CRNA

by Mike Scott, MB, ChB, MRCP, FRCA, FFICM

The anesthesiologist and CRNA play an important role as part of the multidisciplinary team to create and deliver an evidence-based and patient-focused pathway across the whole of ERPs. As well as delivering many of the Enhanced Recovery elements and an anesthetic with minimal residual effects, the additional clinical and practical skills to optimize fluid therapy and analgesia are unique to the anesthesiologist. Optimization of fluids and analgesia are key elements to reduce the stress response to surgery and optimize gut and cellular function, all of which improve healing, reduce secondary complications, shorten length of stay, and improves surgical outcomes.

The role of the anesthesiologist and CRNA can be categorized into five main areas in the Enhanced Recovery/perioperative care pathway:

- Patient preoperative assessment and optimization.
- Delivering an anesthetic with minimal residual side effects and ensuring compliance of all intraoperative Enhanced Recovery elements.
- Optimizing intravascular blood volume, cardiac output, oxygen delivery, and tissue perfusion using a combination of fluids and vasopressors.
- Using, where appropriate, central neuroaxial blockade, regional/truncal blocks, or local anesthetic techniques in combination with multimodal analgesia to control postoperative pain and reduce morphine requirements.
- Immediate postoperative optimization of fluids and analgesia to restore homeostasis and function at a time when there are large physiological changes for the patient.

Overall the aim is to rapidly restore function after surgery to facilitate:

- Early mobilization
- Early restoration of gut function and enteral intake
- Sleeping without pain and stress

You will know if your patient is on an ERP as intravenous fluids will be stopped and the patient will be able to take oral fluids and a light diet. Your patient should be able to mobilize the morning after surgery without discomfort.

Anesthesiologist Overview

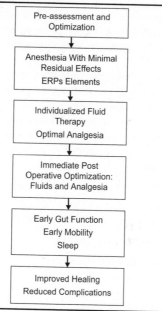

Preoperative Assessment and Optimization

Patients should be medically optimized prior to major surgery so that conditions such as hypertension, cardiac function, pulmonary function, and diabetic control are optimized. Pre-operative anemia is a predictor of poor outcome and should be investigated and attempt to correct it prior to surgery, preferably by iron supplementation using the oral or intravenous route. Reducing alcohol intake and cigarette smoking is also important.

There is growing recognition that patients should be instructed how to improve cardiopulmonary and metabolic fitness in addition to the optimization of the above coexisting medical conditions.

Although the anesthesiologist and CRNA may not be responsible for the preoperative assessment and evaluation of patients coming to the operating room, it is important that there is planned communication between the hospital provider and point of referral for surgery to ensure necessary assessment and optimization protocols.

Timing of surgery after chemotherapy is also important to ensure the patient has returned as close to baseline fitness as possible. Three weeks is usually needed, but there is variability between patients and the different chemotherapy regimens used depending on the cancer being treated.

Different healthcare systems can lead to silo management of these main components of preoperative assessment and optimization; however, it is imperative the anesthetist maintains their knowledge of the current evidence base, interacts with other healthcare professionals, and delivers the necessary evidence-based care to optimize outcomes for their patients.

Ensuring Compliance with ERP Elements

The anesthesiologist plays a major role in ensuring compliance with many ERP elements throughout the perioperative period.

Preoperative ERP Elements

- Minimize starvation times—allow food up to 6 hours pre-operatively.
- Oral carbohydrate drink up to 2 hours before surgery (if not available, allow free fluids up to 2 hours preoperatively).

Intraoperative ERP Elements

- VTE prophylaxis (graduated compression stockings, calf compression during surgery, correct dosing and timing of chemical prophylaxis).
- Antibiotic prophylaxis (give as soon as possible before incision of surgery).
- Avoid nasogastric tube insertion (or if needed to decompress the stomach, remove it at the end of surgery) unless there is a surgical indication.
- PONV prophylaxis (use two drugs together as most efficacious).

- Avoid hypothermia—consider preoperative warming, maintain temperature with warm air blowers or water-based systems, warm intravenous fluids.

Anesthesia ERP Elements

- Use short-acting induction agents.
- Use short-acting opiates.
- Rapid offset inhalational anesthetic agents or total intravenous anesthesia using target-controlled infusions (TCI).
- Anesthetic agent monitoring to reduce awareness and BIS monitoring to reduce overdosage of agent in those at risk of postoperative cognitive dysfunction (elderly, dementia).
- Avoiding nitrous oxide (N_2O) where appropriate.
- Ventilate the lungs using a protective lung strategy (5-7 mL/kg) with optimal peak end expiratory pressure (PEEP).
- Perioperative glucose control—maintain glucose level of <180 mg/dL.
- Monitor neuromuscular function using acceleromyography.
- Maintain neuromuscular block in laparoscopic surgery to facilitate lower pressure pneumoperitoneum without losing intra-abdominal space to aid surgical view/triangulation and to facilitate ventilation.
- Ensure complete reversal of neuromuscular block (NMB) prior to extubation (TOF ratio >0.9) to reduce the risk of microaspiration, which may be a risk factor for postoperative pulmonary infection.

Fluid Therapy

- The overall aim is to give the minimal amount of intravenous fluid to maintain normovolemia and optimize cardiac function throughout the perioperative period while avoiding fluid and salt excess.
- Balanced crystalloid solutions may be advantageous compared with normal saline to avoid chloride excess, but if less than 4 L of total IV fluid is given, it may not be significant.

- Additional minimally invasive monitoring devices can be used to help guide fluid responsiveness or to try and predict the need for further fluid boluses. Examples include: esophageal doppler monitoring, pulse contour wave analysis, bioimpedence, bioreactance, pleth variability index, pulse pressure variability (PPV), and stroke volume variability (SVV). These are particularly useful in patients with poor cardiorespiratory reserve or comorbidities, situations of high blood loss, long open procedures, and when the patient develops an acidosis or SIRS, or is septic. All have pros and cons in the information they can provide in different clinical settings.
- Maintain MAP with vasopressors once intravascular volume is normal to overcome the effects of anesthetic drugs and regional anesthesia.
- Measure hemoglobin, and if possible, measure or at least estimate cardiac output and oxygen delivery.
- Maintain hemoglobin >7.0 g/dL in fit patients but titrate hemoglobin up to 10 g/dL in patients who have cardiopulmonary dysfunction or patient groups that may benefit from a higher hemoglobin (eg, the elderly fractured neck of femur patient).
- Correct for clotting abnormalities and low platelets as necessary.
- Look for signs of hypoperfusion using clinical and laboratory criteria (eg, arterial blood gases) and respond appropriately.

Analgesia

- Consider central neuroaxial blockade (spinal or epidural analgesia) or truncal nerve blocks to reduce the stress response and amount of opiate needed in the postoperative period.
- Using ultrasound to guide blocks can increase efficacy.
- Several analgesic options are needed and will be procedure and patient specific, as not all patients can have the same technique and some techniques fail either due to practical aspects (obesity) or efficacy.

- Consider other adjuncts to reduce post operative opiate use such as intravenous acetaminophen or NSAIDS, dexamethasone, and gabapentinoids.

Many of the above elements and evidence base are covered in more detail in subsequent chapters.

Immediate Postoperative Recovery

The first few hours after surgery are when there are major changes to patient physiology:

- The patient's physiology changes as the effects of intermittent positive pressure ventilation (IPPV) (ventilated) change back to those of spontaneous ventilation.
- The patient's position during surgery (eg, Trendelenberg or reverse Trendelenberg) is returned to supine/slightly head up with subsequent effects on venous return.
- Anesthetic agents and vasopressors are stopped resulting in changes in arterial afterload and venous preload that affect cardiac output and blood pressure and may make the assessment of intravascular volume status more difficult.
- Fluid shifts due to surgical tissue injury can further complicate fluid management. Fluid therapy needs to keep up with the fluid shifts to avoid central hypovolemia and hypotension or cellular hypoperfusion.
- There is the possibility of tissue oxygen deficit, even if not due to reduced global oxygen delivery perhaps locally due to surgical injury, retraction, or microvascular changes.
- Pain manifests as the patient becomes conscious. This can be due to a combination of visceral and wound pain and varies according to the surgical procedure, intraoperative analgesia administered, and whether nerve blockade of any type has been utilized. It is important to address these analgesic requirements rapidly to reduce pain and stress and allow restoration of function such as respiratory function and mobility.

The anesthesiologist's care and attention in addressing these issues in a timely manner are important for the success of any major surgical enhanced recovery program. There is huge variation across different health care systems of where and by whom patients have their immediate post operative care delivered. The ERP should focus on standardized ways to address fluid and analgesia requirements in the immediate postoperative period according to operation type and patient characteristics.

Overview for Nurses

by Bethany M Sarosiek, RN, MSN, MPH, CNL

A patient's surgical journey begins during the preoperative visit, spans the course of surgery, and ends postoperatively at a defined time after discharge. Thinking through the entirety of their experience and the variety of multidisciplinary personnel that come into contact with each patient throughout this period, nurses certainly stand out as a prominent feature for every patient.

It is the nurse who sees the patient in clinic, often doing intake, assessing vital signs, reviewing medications, and providing education, among other key preoperative tasks. There is a nurse who sees the patient in the surgery evaluation clinic, drawing labs, running tests, further educating, and ensuring the patient is properly prepared and cleared for surgery. There is a nurse in the day-of-surgery area, to initiate the patient's IV, reconcile medications, administer preoperative medications, and confirm the patient is ready for his surgery. In the operating room, it is the nurse who verifies the right procedure is being performed on the right patient, calming and supporting the patient during induction, and advocating for the patient while under anesthesia.

Postoperatively, a nurse treats the patient's postoperative pain in PACU while monitoring their IV fluid status and continuously assessing vital signs. Once on the floor, nurses are responsible for a comprehensive postoperative assessment, which includes administering scheduled pain medications, walking patients as soon as they are able, transitioning their diet, and, later, educating them in preparation for discharge.

No matter what the phase of care, nurses are a consistent presence in the perioperative process. For the development, implementation, and success of an ERP, nurse buy-in, input, and support are absolutely essential. The key to a successful enhanced recovery program at any institution, large or small, is strong nursing engagement.

What Are the Barriers to Nursing Change?

Too often, the nursing-specific components to an ERP are developed and distributed from the top down. Surgeons and anesthesiologists provide key input on the "what" and the "why" behind protocol development, but the "how" of the hands-on nursing application is often overlooked. In an age when nurses feel as though more and more is being asked of them on a daily basis, a top-down approach to large-scale change can be an immediate roadblock to acceptance, support, and ultimately, programmatic success.

To encourage active participation and gain nursing support from those directly doing the work, it is important to engage active nursing leadership on the unit early on in the planning process.

In preparing for such change, it is important to identify the advanced practice nurses, strong clinician leaders, and nurse educators. These are likely the unit-based staff that nurses trust for assistance, for advice, or with questions. Engaging these core staff in the planning and implementation phases of an ERP will help to create an environment of acceptance. If their mentors are directly involved, nursing staff are more likely to feel they have the resources needed for guidance and support. Clinicians are then better situated to push through new challenges they may face as part of the process and will be more motivated to accomplish ERP goals.

Another potential nursing barrier can be the lack of rationale provided to support enhanced recovery programs. Explaining the evidence behind the key tenets of the protocols can help to provide a solid foundation for large-scale practice change. For example, multimodal pain management from an enhanced recovery perspective is very different from the traditional use of opioids in the perioperative setting. With the implementation of ERPs, we ask nurses to use alternative analgesic options including nonsteroidal anti-inflammatory drugs, *N*-methyl-D-aspartate receptor antagonists, intravenous lidocaine, acetaminophen, and glucocorticoids, among others, as safer, more effective alternatives. Administering new medications and leaving behind traditional practices can be challenging. Ensuring that nurses understand the rationale behind this change—namely, using multimodalities to achieve effective pain control while reducing opioid-related side effects—can ensure the practice is routinely adopted. With this understanding, nurses will also be better equipped to pass along this same rationale to the patients.

Lastly, one of the biggest barriers that is seen in implementing ERPs is best summed up in the aphorism, "perfect is the enemy of good." As nurses, we strive to do our best as leaders for change in any environment, and introducing an evidence-based program like enhanced recovery is no exception. ERPs require full-scale, multidisciplinary involvement, and implementation requires both time and energy. Inevitably, errors will be made, road blocks encountered, and speed bumps experienced as part of the process. Ensuring that preparedness for such mistakes is integrated into nurse training will ensure that clinicians have clear expectations for hiccups they may experience along the way. In doing so, they will not feel discouraged by small mishaps but will continue to forge ahead, staying motivated to bring change for their patients.

What Are the Key Concepts in Setting Nurses Up for Success?

One of the most important concepts in positioning nurses for success is through the use of ongoing and real-time feedback throughout the implementation process. Enhanced recovery programs can result in dramatic practice change for many clinicians. Assuring nurses that they are successful (positive feedback) or reminding them of specific areas for improvement (constructive feedback) can help to ensure they remain compliant with the protocol, particularly early on in the implementation process.

Feedback can be given indirectly through staff meetings, daily "huddle" check-ins, and unit-based white boards. Direct feedback can be delivered through electronic correspondence or one-on-one discussions, providing individualized praise for successful completion of Enhanced Recovery elements or suggestions for improving compliance. Hosting open forums to encourage dialogue in a group setting can also be particularly useful to learn directly from staff what works and what does not, in order to meet ERP goals. Finally, in the weeks and months following implementation, quarterly meetings for data review and ongoing protocol discussion are important to bring information back to the multidisciplinary group at large. After widespread ERP adoption, staff want to know what difference their practice changes have made, and presenting compelling compliance data can be the ultimate motivator.

In summary, nurses are the change agents who translate the best available evidence from the literature directly to patient care. Nurses are educators who ensure patients have the understanding needed to prepare for surgery and information available for care following discharge. Nurses are motivators who provide the extra hand to hold when walking the halls after surgery or who support a diet transition in order to return normal bowel function. Nurses are care providers and patient advocates who help to treat pain using multimodal techniques while minimizing opioid use to improve postoperative outcomes. In the complex, multidisciplinary structure of an enhanced recovery program, nurses are the common thread at every phase of the patient's perioperative experience. They are undeniably essential for planning, implementation, and success.

1

Patient Education

*by Debbie Watson, RN, MN and
Robin Anderson, RN, BSN*

Preoperative education is an essential component of an enhanced recovery program. The aim of the preoperative education session is to engage patients and families to prepare the patient for the upcoming hospitalization, and to encourage patients to become active participants. This chapter elaborates the reasons why patient education is important, defines the concept of health literacy, and explains why understanding health literacy principles is at the basis of preoperative education.

We also highlight why awareness of health literacy is crucial for all health care providers. By adopting simple actions and interventions, health professionals can increase patient understanding. Examples include the teach-back method, referral to reliable Internet sites, and use of patient educational material. Lastly, this chapter draws on personal experience and explains the many benefits of creating patient education material for patients, families, caregivers, and your organization.

The Importance of Preoperative Education

Between 1940 and 1959 preoperative teaching was introduced and nurses were encouraged to have patients take on more responsibilities for their own care.[1] The decreasing trend of the surgical length of hospital stay signifies that patients are admitted to hospital only a few hours before surgery. Patients need to be ready physically and psychologically for their surgery when they arrive. The benefits of preoperative education are numerous and have been well studied. Preoperative education has been linked to decreasing anxiety,[2] better postoperative outcomes, and improved patient and family satisfaction.[3,4] Several factors influence the quality of preoperative teaching. These influences include environment noise level, teaching skills of the health care provider, number of interruptions during the teaching session, and time restraints on staff. Nevertheless, patients and family members in general value preoperative teaching as this prepares them physically and psychologically by helping them anticipate and rehearse the events of their upcoming hospitalization.

"Knowing the plans for each hospitalized day" was ranked in the top five bedside information requirements when patients were asked what they considered important during consideration of an electronic bedside communication tool.[5] Communicating to patients about their planned hospitalization, including what to expect on each day, helps to ensure a more patient-centered care approach. Superficially there is a dichotomy between care pathways and patient-centered care.[6] Enhanced recovery care pathways or protocols aim to decrease variability, standardize practice, and integrate evidence-based research into care.

In contrast, patient-centered care aims to integrate patients' values, perceptions, and individual preferences. Increasing communication between health care providers and patients helps to bridge the gap between protocols and patient-centered care.[6] To communicate effectively with patients, health care providers must first understand the health literacy concept.

Health Literacy

Health literacy is defined as the degree to which an individual has the capacity to obtain, communicate, process, and understand basic health information and services to make appropriate health decisions.[7] Others define it as the ability to perform knowledge-based literacy tasks and possessing literacy skills required in different health contexts that can be improved with education.[8] Low health literacy within the adult population is prevalent throughout the world and suggests that many patients may be struggling to understand and act on the health information that is provided to them.

Prevalence of Low Health Literacy

In Canada, 60% of the adult population has low health literacy skills.[9] In the United States, The National Assessment of Literacy Report intended specifically to measure the health literacy of adults. Health literacy was reported using four performance levels: below basic, basic, intermediate, and proficient. The majority of adults (53%) had intermediate health literacy, whereas about 22% had basic and 14% had below basic health literacy.[10] About 80 million US adults are believed to have limited health literacy.[11]

In Europe, eight countries participated in a survey to assess health literacy skills. The results showed that nearly one out of two Europeans had limited to moderate health literacy level.[12] Numerous factors influence health literacy level. Some causes may be personal such as the patient's motivation to learn, their socioeconomic levels, and the cognitive and literacy level of the individual.[9] Other factors are related to the health care system and include the complexity of what is to be learned and the environment and time constraints of health care workers.[9] Patients with low health literacy often exhibit similar behaviors.[9]

Common Behaviors

To avoid embarrassment, patients might not admit when they do not understand. People often develop mechanisms to hide their lack of understanding. There are some behavioral clues that should raise a red flag. Patients with low health literacy may not be able to name their medications or explain why they are taking medications. They may bring someone with them to the hospital to help them read or fill out their paper work.[9] Patients might miss or be late for their appointments. They might tell you that they forgot their glasses at home and that they will read the information later. Patients might clown or use humor as a diversion or, alternatively, exhibit demanding behaviors.[9]

Increasing Patient Understanding

All health care providers should be familiar with the concept of health literacy, the prevalence of low health literacy, and the typical behaviors that are often associated with low health literacy. The role and responsibility of the preoperative staff is not only to optimize patients prior to surgery but also to provide education about the upcoming surgery. If we want patients to participate in their care and take a more active role, they must first understand how they can participate. Several approaches can help to increase patient understanding such as decreasing the amount of interruptions during teaching, repeating the information, talking slowly, and minimizing the use of acronyms and medical jargon.

Another strategy known to increase patient understanding is the teach-back method. This technique verifies understanding by asking patients to explain in their own words what they comprehended. The teach-back method ensures that all the information was conveyed correctly and that the patient understood the information. The responsibility is to the teacher not the patient. Creating a shame-free environment where patients feel comfortable asking questions is the ideal setting to provide preoperative teaching. Using a combination of methods for patient education such as referring to Internet sites and using printed material, models, and posters is best to increase patients' understanding and facilitate learning.

Electronic Technology and Referring Patients to Reliable Websites

Using electronic aids or reliable websites that display simple visuals can also increase patients' understanding and readiness to learn. Patients who completed a web-based tutorial had improved pre-operative knowledge and preparedness as well as enhanced postoperative knowledge recall regarding their surgery.[13] Internet access is growing at a fast pace, and searching for health information is considered to be the third most popular activity online.[14] However, there are some essential points to consider as the digital divide persists.

Many patients may be lacking the essential skills to navigate the Internet and to differentiate reliable websites from nonreliable ones. People with low health literacy levels, the elderly, and less-educated individuals are much less likely to utilize the Internet.[15] People with limited literacy skills may have difficulty with navigating and comprehending the information on each website.[15] Skill barriers and access to the Internet remain an obstacle for low health literacy individuals.[15]

Nonetheless, for some patients, finding health information on the Internet is easy and accessible. However, not all websites are created equal, and patients may not be able to discern which websites are reliable websites and which are from the untrustworthy. Assessing the reliability of a website should be done prior to recommending these to patients. Roberts offers a simple evaluation tool to help nurses assess website trustworthiness.[16]

Five key categories are enumerated to evaluate the websites. They are credibility, construction, clarity, content, and currency. Each of the 5C's lists key points to consider and offers guidance to the nurse for referring their patients to the most appropriate and valuable websites while ensuring that the content is trustworthy.[16] Adding reliable websites to patient education material offers patients the opportunity to seek, if they wish, additional accurate information.

Creating Patient Education Material

It takes commitment and teamwork to create patient education material. There are toolkits and a plethora of guides available to help in the creation of patient education material. These guidelines often recommend a step-by-step approach when developing patient education material. Some of the points to consider are checking for already existing material, knowing who is your intended audience, providing the information in plain language with clear design, and evaluating your material with your target audience to insure comprehension. Giving patients printed material following the verbal information about their pain made it easier for patients to assimilate the information and understand it and was very much appreciated by patients.[17] Patient education material is meant to reinforce the verbal teaching and help patients remember the information.

At our institution, patient education printed material is provided to patients once surgery is confirmed. This takes place in the surgeon's office or at the preoperative clinic appointment. Providing the material before a preoperative appointment allows patients time to read the material at their own pace, share the information with family, and reread the material when needed. Patients are asked to bring their booklet to every appointment before surgery and on the day of surgery. Instructions are written at a low literacy level. The information covers the preoperative phase such as how to get ready for surgery and offers details of specific goals or expectations for each postoperative day as well as what to expect after discharge from hospital. Multiple benefits take place when an organization creates their own patient education material.

The Benefits of Creating Patient Educational Materials

1

The organization benefits when all stakeholders revise the content of the patient education material before the final version. Reviewing the content of the patient education material increases the consistency and accuracy of the information and fosters clearer communication. This final review is an important step as it may minimize confusion not only among patients and their families but also among students, residents, and nurses. Caregivers also benefit by providing patient education material. Although the material is not meant to replace the verbal communication between caregivers and patients, it may reduce time spent repeating information at a later time. Patients may therefore have fewer questions resulting in fewer subsequent phone calls.[9]

The patient and family also benefit as the information is tailored to their needs and to the organization's specific settings and processes. Evaluating patient education material is essential to ensure comprehension of the targeted users. Modifications of the content should be made based on patients' feedback. Evaluating and modifying the education material is a vital step in the development of patient educational material.[9] Including patients in the creation of educational material helps to foster a more patient-centered care approach.

Plain Language and Clear Design

The ultimate goal when writing for patients is to enhance the patient's understanding. They should be able to remember and act on the information provided. Keeping the written material to a minimum is fundamental, allowing patients to understand the essential information without overburdening them with details. Writing in plain language is substituting complex words. It is avoiding technical language and medical jargon.[18] Plain language uses a vocabulary that is familiar with the intended users, uses a conversational style and everyday language, short sentences with simple words, and writing in an active voice. Plain language aims to increase clarity of the written content, and its main goal is to increase understanding by everyone.[18] Research shows that people, regardless of their education level, prefer to read health information that is simple and easy to understand.[19] The literacy should be kept at a low level, but more importantly, it should be evaluated by the users to ensure comprehension.[18] Other factors such as the design and the layout of your material may influence the clarity of the information.

Design is how your text appears. The clarity of design influences readability. For example, leaving plenty of white space is more appealing and inviting for the reader. Using bolded headings and subheadings to separate and highlight sections helps the reader skim to read the topics of most interest. Bolding important information to draw attention to content is recommended. Bolded text is most effective, whereas using caps, underlining, and italics makes the text more difficult to read.[9] A minimum font size of 12 points is recommended when writing patient educational material.[20] Other key points to consider are the font style, compiling the content, and prioritizing the important information first, using left justification, using bullets with lists, and utilizing visuals to facilitate learning.

Integrating Meaningful Images

Health care providers should look for ways to integrate pictures when communicating with patients.[21] The addition of visuals such as photographs, illustrations, graphics, and clip art in patient education material aims to enhance understanding. Pictures should be closely located to the written text. When compared to text alone, images increased attention to and recall of health education information.[21] Illustrations do not have to be costly or be created by artists to be meaningful and enable learning. Photographs and simple line drawings such as a matchstick diagram can be efficient in increasing comprehension.[9,21] At our institutions, we use drawings to illustrate the progress during hospitalization. For example, the colorectal pictogram aims to demonstrate the progress and daily goals during hospitalization from the day of surgery until the day of discharge, depicting different elements such as tubes and drains, nutrition, pain control, activities, and breathing exercises. The colorectal surgery pictogram is shown in **Figure 1.1**.

FIGURE 1.1 — Colorectal Surgery Pictogram

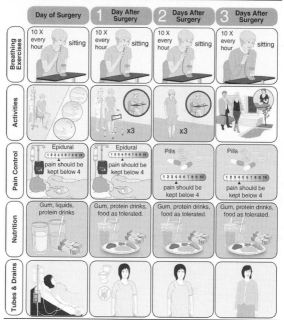

Courtesy of McGill University Health Centre Patient Education Office.

In summary, preoperative education aims to engage patients and their families in their upcoming surgery. Providing preoperative information aims to increase patients' understanding so that they can play an active role throughout the trajectory of perioperative care. Caregivers should be aware of the concept of health literacy as this may significantly influence their interactions with patients. Health care providers should use several strategies to increase patient understanding including the teach-back method and the use of plain language in all forms of communications. Creating patient education material alongside the enhanced recovery protocols is essential for promoting a more patient-centered care approach.

REFERENCES

1. Oetker-Black SL. Preoperative preparation. Historical development. *AORN J.*1993;57:1402-1410.

2. Ayyadhah Alanazi A. Reducing anxiety in preoperative patients: a systematic review. *Br J Nurs.* 2014;23:387-393.

3. Kruzik N. Benefits of preoperative education for adult elective surgery patients. *AORN J.* 2009;90:381-387.

4. Walker JA. What is the effect of preoperative information on patient satisfaction? *Br J Nurs.* 2007;16:27-32.

5. Caligtan CA, Carroll DL, Hurley AC, Gersh-Zaremski R, Dykes PC. Bedside information technology to support patient-centered care. *Int J Med Inform.* 2012;81:442-451.

6. Faber MJ, Grande S, Wollersheim H, Hermens R, Elwyn G. Narrowing the gap between organisational demands and the quest for patient involvement: the case for coordinated care pathways. *Int J Care Coord.* 2014;17:72-78.

7. Institute of Medicine. *Health Literacy: A Prescription to End Confusion.* Washington, DC: National Academies Press; 2004.

8. Nutbeam D. Defining and measuring health literacy: what can we learn from literacy studies? *Int J Public Health.* 2009;54:303-305.

9. Wizowski L, Harper T, Hutchings T. *Writing Health Information for Patients and Families.* 4th ed. Hamilton, Ontario: Hamilton Health Sciences; 2014.

10. Kutner M, Greenberg E, Jin Y, Paulsen C. The Health Literacy of America's Adults: Results from the 2003 National Assessment of Adult Literacy (NCES 2006–483). Washington, DC: National Center for Education Statistics, Institute of Education, U.S. Department of Education; 2006.

11. Berkman ND, Sheridan SL, Donahue KE, Halpern DJ, Crotty K. Low health literacy and health outcomes: an updated systematic review. *Ann Intern Med.* 2011;155:97-107.

12. Doyle G, Cafferkey K, Fullam J. The European Health Literacy Survey: results from Ireland. In: EU Health Literacy Survey. MSD/NALA Health Literacy Initiative. 2012. Available via healtliteracy.ie. http://www.healthliteracy.ie/wp-content/uploads/2010/11/EU-Health-Literacy-Full-Report.pdf. Accessed February 25, 2016.

13. Yin B, Goldsmith L, Gambardella R. Web-based education prior to knee arthroscopy enhances informed consent and patient knowledge recall: a prospective, randomized controlled study. *J Bone Joint Surg Am.* 2015;97:964-971.

14. Pew Internet: A Project of the Pew Research Center. Generations 2010. http://www.pewinternet.org/files/old-media/Files/Reports/2010/PIP_Generations_and_Tech10.pdf. Published December 16, 2010. Accessed February 25, 2016.

15. Jensen JD, King AJ, Davis LA, Guntzviller LM. Utilization of internet technology by low-income adults: the role of health literacy, health numeracy, and computer assistance. *J Aging Health*. 2010;22:804-826.

16. Roberts L. Health information and the Internet: the 5 Cs website evaluation tool. *Br J Nurs*. 2010;19:322-325.

17. Andersson V, Otterstrom-Rydberg E, Karlsson AK. The importance of written and verbal information on pain treatment for patients undergoing surgical interventions. *Pain Manag Nurs*. 2015;16:634-641.

18. Watson DJ, Davis EA. Preoperative Education. In: Feldman LS, Delaney CP, Ljungqvist O, Francesco C, eds. *The SAGES/ERAS Society Manual of Enhanced Recovery Programs for Gastrointestinal Surgery*. Cham, Switzerland: Springer International Publishing AG; 2015:13-23.

19. Weiss BD. *Health Literacy: A Manual for Clinicians*. Chicago, IL: American Medical Association and American Medical Association Foundation; 2003.

20. Doak CC, Doak LG, Root JH. *Teaching Patients with Low Literacy Skills*. 2nd ed. Philadelphia, PA: Lippincott Williams & Wilkins; 1996.

21. Houts PS, Doak CC, Doak LG, Loscalzo MJ. The role of pictures in improving health communication: a review of research on attention, comprehension, recall, and adherence. *Patient Educ Couns*. 2006;61:173-190.

Preoperative Nutrition and Prehabilitation

by Ruchir Gupta, MD

One of the main goals in enhanced recovery is to revisit the traditional dogma of nil per os (NPO) for 8 full hours prior to surgery and take steps to optimize the patient's preoperative nutritional status by instituting strategies to prevent perioperative starvation, which can lead to negative protein balance.[1] Through utilization of supplemental nutritional drinks,[2] which do not increase the risk of aspiration while still providing adequate nutritional supplementation, patients enrolled in the enhanced recovery protocol (ERP) have been shown to have a decrease in hemodynamic instability, decrease in postoperative nausea and vomiting, and decreased risk of postoperative insulin resistance.[2]

Preoperative Fasting and Carbohydrate Loading

The traditional mantra of fasting from midnight to the day of surgery and NPO has been abandoned in all recent fasting guidelines in light of ample evidence for improved insulin responsiveness in patients receiving oral intake of clear fluids up to 2 hours before induction of anesthesia.[3,4] Preoperative carbohydrate treatment is meant to replicate normal metabolic responses to eating breakfast,[3] thereby stimulating endogenous insulin release, which will switch off the overnight fasting metabolic state and decrease peripheral insulin resistance in response to surgical stress response.

Major surgical trauma can result in a transient reduction in insulin sensitivity, leading to an increase in glucose production and decrease in tissue uptake of glucose and glycogen synthesis, resulting in hyper-glycemia.[5] Not only does hyperglycemia result in an increased risk of complications,[6,7] but aggressive treatment of hyperglycemia in the postoperative period can lead to hypoglycemia with its associated negative sequelae.

Several commercially available formulations of a preoperative carbohydrate drink have been developed, but only one (Clearfast) is available in the United States. Clearfast contains 21 g of monosaccharides, 38 g of polysaccharides, and 230 calories per 12 ounces. A less-expensive alternative to Clearfast is Gatorade, which also provides monosaccharides (80 g/12 oz) and caloric replenishment (80 cal/oz) but lacks polysac-charides. Another formulation of Gatorade (Gatorade Prime) provides a more robust nourishment per 12 oz (69 g of monosaccharides, 6 g of polysaccharides, and 300 calories) and may be a suitable alternative for the ERP in centers with budgetary constraints. The differ-ences between these carbohydrate drinks have not been studied.

Metabolic Conditioning

Adequate metabolic conditioning of patients prior to surgery can lower the risk of postoperative complica-tions and hasten recovery. Metabolic conditioning can be broadly divided into two main categories: nutritional supplementation and optimization of functional physi-cal capacity. The former is indicated in patients who are malnourished either secondary to their underlying condition for which they are having surgery or from a co-existing comorbid condition. The latter is indicated in most patients who practice a sedentary lifestyle and do not engage in active exercise as defined by walking, running, or other cardiovascular activities.

The first step in nutritional optimization is accurate detection of malnourished patients and assessing the severity of the nutritional deficit.

The prevalence of malnutrition in patients undergoing surgery varies by type of surgery as well as patient population. Those patients who have advanced age, weight loss, and a lack of nutritional support are at greater risk of malnutrition.[8] The presence of malnutrition preoperatively in patients undergoing surgery has been associated with an increased risk of postoperative complications, prolonged length of hospital stay, delayed recovery of bowel function,[9,10] higher rates of re-admission,[11] and an increased incidence of postoperative death.

Malnutrition and weight loss in this population are common due to tumor-related cachexia and decreased oral food intake caused in part by gastrointestinal tract obstruction. Furthermore, malnutrition continues to be a prognostic indicator of poor outcome in terms of survival and response to surgical treatment.[1,12,13]

Although much effort has been devoted in developing tools for preoperative nutrition risk screening, it remains unclear which screening system best predicts the risk of developing nutrition-related complications. Traditional anthropometric nutritional assessment using body weight, serum nutritional factor levels (such as low serum albumin, pre-albumin, and transthyretin), skin fold thickness, and functional measurements of muscle strength have fallen out of favor due to their limited value in determining actual nutritional risk before surgery. Thus, several diverse measurements have been combined into subjective scoring systems including the SGA questionnaire,[14] the nutritional risk screening (NRS) 2002,[15] Reilly's NRS,[16] and the nutritional risk indicator (NRI) scoring systems (**Table 2.1**). A combination of objective and subjective nutritional assessment tools may be better than either alone.

TABLE 2.1 — Nutritional Scoring System

Scoring System	Indices Tested	Categorizations
Subjective Global Assessment (SGA)[1]	Medical history (weight change, dietary intake change, gastrointestinal symptoms and changes in functional capacity) and physical examination (loss of subcutaneous fat, muscle wasting, ankle or sacral edema and ascites)	SGA–A — well nourished SGA–B — moderately malnourished SGA–C — severely malnourished
Nutritional risk screening[2]	Patients are characterized by scoring the components of undernutrition and severity of disease in four categories (absent, mild, moderate, and severe). The patient can have a score of 0-3 for each component, a total score of 0-6, and any patient with a total score ≥ 3 is considered to be at nutritional risk	*Score 1* – admitted to hospital due to complications associated with a chronic disease. The patient is weak but out of bed regularly. Protein requirement is increased, but can be covered by oral diet or supplements in most cases *Score 2* – patient confined to bed due to illness, eg, following major abdominal surgery or due to severe infection. Protein requirement is substantially increased but can be covered, although artificial feeding is required in many cases. *Score 3* – intensive care patient with assisted ventilation, inotropic drugs, etc

Reilly's NRS[3]	Weight loss (amount and duration); BMI for adults (weight in kg/[height in m^2]) and percentile charts for children; food intake (appetite and ability to eat and retain food); stress factors (effect of medical condition on nutritional requirements)	7–15 — high risk 4–6 — moderate risk 0–3 — low risk
Nutritional Risk Indicator (NRI)[4]	Recent weight loss and serum albumin concentration NRI = (1.489 × serum albumin [g/L]) + (41.7 × current weight/usual weight)	>97.5 — well nourished 83.5%–97.5% — moderately malnourished <83.5% — severely malnourished

[1] Detsky AS, et al. JPEN J Parenter Enteral Nutr. 1987;11(1):8-13.
[2] Kondrup J, et al. Clin Nutr. 2003;22(3):321-336.
[3] Reilly HM, et al., Clin Nutr. 1995;14(5):269-273.
[4] Buzby GP, et al. Am J Clin Nutr. 1988;47(2 suppl):366-381.

2

Treatment of the Malnourished Patient

Once a patient is identified as nutritionally "at risk," oral nutritional supplementation should be initiated and a dietician should be involved in further nutritional care of the patient. Although there is a lack of consensus in the interval when nutritional supplementation should occur, 5 to 7 days appears to be the most commonly recommended time period.[20] If the patient is deemed to be at severe nutritional risk (ie, weight loss >10%-15%/6 months; BMI <18.5 kg/m^2; SGA Grade C [**Table 2.1**]; serum albumin <30 g/L), it would be reasonable to consider delaying surgery until the nutritional deficit is corrected, if only partially.

In circumstances where enteral nutrition is not often possible due to pre-existing gut dysfunction, supplementation with total parenteral nutrition (TPN) is often considered as an alternative. It is suggested that preoperative TPN support be administered for 7 to 10 days.[21]

TPN solutions provide complete nutritional support because they contain fat emulsion, vitamins, and trace elements. Risks associated with TPN use include pneumothorax, hemothorax, electrolyte imbalances, refeeding syndrome, and central vein catheter infection. Peripheral parenteral nutrition (PPN) has also been used due to its relative ease compared to TPN. Unfortunately, PPN solutions generally do not provide enough energy and nutrients for full nutritional support. Modified PPN solutions have been tried, where a two-in-one (dextrose + amino acids) formula or fat emulsion is utilized.[21] However, even with these formulations, multiple vitamins and trace elements are still often omitted.

Immunonutrition

Recent studies have shown that irrespective of a patient's baseline nutritional status, supplementation of preoperative oral nutritional formulations with specific immune-modulating substrates such as glutamine, arginine, and omega-3 fatty acids improves surgical outcomes.[22-24] The anabolic and immune modulatory properties of long-chain polyunsaturated fatty acids (PUFA) of the omega-3 fatty acid family have been demonstrated to be beneficial in the perioperative period.[25]

Glutamine plays a crucial role not just as a source of metabolic fuel but also as an aid for preservation of small bowel function.[26] Additionally, it aids in the preservation of T-lymphocyte responsiveness during major surgery.[27] Arginine is a nonessential amino acid that also stimulates T-cell function and improves microcirculation via the formation of nitric oxide.

Prehabilitation

Prehabilitation is defined as "the process of enhancing the functional capacity of the individual to enable him or her to withstand a stressful event."[28] Thus, a physical exercise training program preoperatively before elective surgery is an example of prehabilitation.

There is increasing evidence that good functional capacity has multiple benefits in almost every context of health and disease[29] and poor functional capacity resulting from physical inactivity is one of the most important public health issues facing our generation.[30] It has also been shown that patients who are fitter and more physically active have better outcomes as it relates to underlying conditions such as coronary artery disease,[31] heart failure,[32] hypertension, diabetes, chronic obstructive pulmonary disease (COPD), depression, dementia, chronic kidney disease, cancer, and stroke.[33] Furthermore, the evidence supports that the incidence of chronic diseases such as type 2 diabetes, osteoporosis, obesity, depression, and cancer of the breast, kidney, and colon is also reduced with increasing physical activity.

Preoperative Exercise Training

Preoperative exercise training is both feasible and safe in patients with a spectrum of severe cardiac and pulmonary disease. Indeed, physical exercise training programs have demonstrated an improvement in both physical fitness and clinical outcomes in patients with major comorbidities (ie, cardiac failure, ischemic heart disease, and COPD).[33]

Patients with malignancy often receive neoadjuvant chemotherapy and radiation therapy, which is administered weeks prior to a surgical procedures and usually require 6 to 12 weeks of recovery. This has opened up a window of opportunity to train patients prior to major cancer surgeries where previously the pressure of reducing the time between diagnosis and surgery prevented such an intervention.

Exercise Programs

Patients with increased risk may benefit from prehabilitation programs that include endurance and strength training, high-intensity training schedules, and the use of nutritional and pharmaceutical adjuncts. These programs often utilize cardiopulmonary exercise testing (CPET) to determine their effectiveness.[34] CPET integrates expired gas analysis (oxygen and carbon dioxide concentrations) with the measurement of ventilatory flow, thereby enabling calculation of oxygen uptake (VO_2) and carbon dioxide production (VCO_2) under conditions of varying physiological stress imposed by a range of defined external workloads.[33]

The incremental exercise test to the limit of tolerance using cycle ergometry (incremental ramp test) has been used extensively in both clinical practice and clinical trials. It permits the accurate determination of exercise capacity and also allows the identification of the site of exercise limitation when this is abnormal.[35] The advantages of this exercise protocol are that it evaluates the exercise response across the entire range of functional capacity, allows assessment of the normalcy or otherwise of the exercise response, permits identification of the site of functional exercise limitation, and gives an appropriate frame of reference for training or rehabilitation targets. The entire protocol consists of 8 to 12 minutes of exercise.

The typical test profile for this exercise includes 3 minutes of resting measurement, 3 minutes of unloaded cycling (cycling against no resistance), followed by a continuously increasing ramp until physical exhaustion. CPET determines perioperative aerobic capacity. This is measured by the anaerobic threshold (AT), which is the oxygen uptake at which anaerobic adenosine triphosphate (ATP) synthesis starts to supplement aerobic ATP synthesis. AT is also the point which CO_2 production increases more than oxygen uptake during gas exchange.

Consequently, it is believed that myocardial ischemia occurs at or above the AT such that patients with low AT are at risk for early ischemia. As a result, AT is useful in risk stratification of patients (**Table 2.2**).[34]

The 6MWT is a simple test that does not require expensive equipment but rather requires the patient to walk the longest distance possible in a set interval of 6 minutes, through a walking course (corridor) prefer-

TABLE 2.2 — AT Risk Stratification of Patients

AT Level (mL/min/kg)	Recommendations
>11	Perioperative mortality of <1% and unlikely to need higher level of care
≤11	Perioperative mortality of 18% and should be considered for either intensive recovery, PACU, high dependency unit or ICU
<8	Perioperative mortality of 50% and should be considered and prepared for extended ICU stay

ably 30 m long. The patient has the option of stopping or slowing down at any time and then resuming his/her walking, depending on his/her degree of fatigue. Even though other parameters can be monitored during the test, such as arterial pressure and/or heart rate, the number of times the patient has to stop during the test, the speed of walking, or even changes in respiratory gases (measured using a portable instrument) and oxygen saturation, the distance walked in 6 minutes is simple and most useful.[36]

Enright and Sherrill have developed equations to calculate the distance walked by a healthy adult during 6MWT.[37] These are:

- 6MWT distance = (7.57 × height cm)−(5.02 × age)−(1.76 × weight kg)−309 m for men
- 6MWT distance = (2.11 × height cm)−(2.29 × weight kg)− (5.78 × age)+667 m for women

Summary

Taken together, these concepts support the notion of individualized medicine whereby the right treatment is administered to the right patient at the right time. Identifying patients who are nutritionally deficient allows us to intervene preoperatively to optimize their nutritional status. In some cases, TPN therapy may be needed, either as an adjunct or exclusively, to achieve this goal. Additionally, debunking the traditional mantra of fasting for 8 hours prior to surgery, the development of a carbohydrate beverage that is considered as clear fluid has allowed patients to be brought to the operating room in a "fed" state, thereby reducing insulin resistance postoperatively and postoperative hypoglycemia.

Finally, the contribution of CPET to the evaluation of perioperative risk, the subsequent development of a training program, and the use of indices to both risk stratify as well as measure improvement after a training program allow a personalized preoperative program to be developed for each patient. Based on the available literature, it seems such a training program may need to be 6 weeks in duration, but more studies are needed to elucidate the optimal intervention duration.[38]

REFERENCES

1. Braga M, Ljungqvist O, Soeters P, Fearon K, Weimann A, Bozzetti F; ESPEN. ESPEN Guidelines on Parenteral Nutrition: surgery. *Clin Nutr*. 2009;28:378-386.

2. Lassen K, Soop M, Nygren J, et al; Enhanced Recovery After Surgery (ERAS) Group. Consensus review of optimal perioperative care in colorectal surgery: Enhanced Recovery After Surgery (ERAS) Group recommendations. *Arch Surg*. 2009;144:961-969.

3. Ljungqvist O, Søreide E. Preoperative fasting. *Br J Surg*. 2003;90:400-406.

4. Brady M, Kinn S, Stuart P. Preoperative fasting for adults to prevent perioperative complications. *Cochrane Database Syst Rev*. 2003;(4):CD004423.

5. Thorell A, Nygren J, Ljungqvist O. Insulin resistance: a marker of surgical stress. *Curr Opin Clin Nutr Metab Care*. 1999;2:69-78.

6. Doenst T, Wijeysundera D, Karkouti K, et al. Hyperglycemia during cardiopulmonary bypass is an independent risk factor formortality in patients undergoing cardiac surgery. *J Thorac Cardiovasc Surg*. 2005;130:1144.

7. Gustafsson UO, Thorell A, Soop M, Ljungqvist O, Nygren J. Haemoglobin A1c as a predictor of postoperative hyperglycaemia and complications after major colorectal surgery. *Br J Surg*. 2009;96:1358-1364.

8. Francis N, Kennedy RH, Ljungqvist O, Mythen MG. *Manual of Fast Track Recovery for Colorectal Surgery*. London, UK: Springer-Verlag London Ltd; 2012.

9. Lohsiriwat V, Chinswangwatanakul V, Lohsiriwat S, et al. Hypoalbuminemia is a predictor of delayed postoperative bowel function and poor surgical outcomes in right-sided colon cancer patients. *Asia Pac J Clin Nutr*. 2007;16:213-217.

10. Lohsiriwat V, Lohsiriwat D, Boonnuch W, Chinswangwatanakul V, Akaraviputh T, Lert-Akayamanee N. Pre-operative hypoalbuminemia is a major risk factor for postoperative complications following rectal cancer surgery. *World J Gastroenterol*. 2008;14:1248-1251.

11. Zhang JQ, Curran T, McCallum JC, et al. Risk factors for readmission after lower extremity bypass in the American College of Surgeons National Surgery Quality Improvement Program. *J Vasc Surg*. 2014;59:1331-1339.

12. Schiesser M, Kirchhoff P, Müller MK, Schäfer M, Clavien PA. The correlation of nutrition risk index, nutrition risk score, and bioimpedance analysis with postoperative complications in patients undergoing gastrointestinal surgery. *Surgery*. 2009;145:519-526.

13. Sungurtekin H, Sungurtekin U, Hanci V, Erdem E. Comparison of two nutrition assessment techniques in hospitalized patients. *Nutrition*. 2004;20:428-432.

14. Detsky AS, Baker JP, O'Rourke K, et al. Predicting nutrition-associated complications for patients undergoing gastrointestinal surgery. *JPEN J Parenter Enteral Nutr*. 1987;11:440-446.

15. Kondrup J, Allison SP, Elia M, Vellas B, Plauth M; Educational and Clinical Practice Committee, European Society of Parenteral and Enteral Nutrition (ESPEN). ESPEN guidelines for nutrition screening 2002. *Clin Nutr*. 2003;22:415-421.

16. Reilly HM, Martineau JK, Moran A, Kennedy H. Nutritional screening—evaluation and implementation of a simple Nutrition Risk Score. *Clin Nutr*. 1995;14:269-273.

17. Detsky AS, McLaughlin JR, Baker JP, et al. What is subjective global assessment of nutritional status? *JPEN J Parenter Enteral Nutr*. 1987;11:8-13.

18. Kondrup J, Rasmussen HH, Hamberg O, Stanga Z; Ad Hoc ESPEN Working Group. Nutritional risk screening (NRS 2002): a new method based on an analysis of controlled clinical trials. *Clin Nutr*. 2003;22:321-336.

19. Buzby GP, Knox LS, Crosby LO, et al. Study protocol: a randomized clinical trial of total parenteral nutrition in malnourished surgical patients. *Am J Clin Nutr*. 1988;47(2 Suppl):366-381.

20. Weimann A, Braga M, Harsanyi L, Laviano A, Ljungqvist O, Soeters P; DGEM (German Society for Nutritional Medicine), Jauch KW, Kemen M, Hiesmayr JM, Horbach T, Kuse ER, Vestweber KH; ESPEN (European Society for Parenteral and Enteral Nutrition). ESPEN Guidelines on Enteral Nutrition: Surgery including organ transplantation. *Clin Nutr*. 2006;25:224-244.

21. Liu MY, Tang HC, Hu SH, Yang HL, Chang SJ. Influence of preoperative peripheral parenteral nutrition with micronutrients after colorectal cancer patients. *Biomed Res Int*. 2015;2015:535431.

22. Braga M, Gianotti L, Nespoli L, Radaelli G, Di Carlo V. Nutritional approach in malnourished surgical patients: a prospective randomized study. *Arch Surg*. 2002;137:174-180.

23. Braga M, Gianotti L, Vignali A, Carlo VD. Preoperative oral arginine and n-3 fatty acid supplementation improves the immunometabolic host response and outcome after colorectal resection for cancer. *Surgery*. 2002;132:805-814.

24. Tepaske R, Velthuis H, Oudemans-van Straaten HM, et al. Effect of preoperative oral immune-enhancing nutritional supplement on patients at high risk of infection after cardiac surgery: a randomised placebo-controlled trial. *Lancet*. 2001;358:696-701.

25. Ryan AM, Reynolds JV, Healy L, et al. Enteral nutrition enriched with eicosapentaenoic acid (EPA) preserves lean body mass following esophageal cancer surgery: results of a double-blinded randomized controlled trial. *Ann Surg*. 2009;249:355-363.

26. Zheng YM, Li F, Zhang MM, Wu XT. Glutamine dipeptide for parenteral nutrition in abdominal surgery: a meta-analysis of randomized controlled trials. *World J Gastroenterol*. 2006;12:7537-7541.

27. O'Riordain MG, Fearon KC, Ross JA, et al. Glutamine-supplemented total parenteral nutrition enhances T-lymphocyte response in surgical patients undergoing colorectal resection. *Ann Surg*. 1994;220:212-221.

28. Ditmyer MM, Topp R, Pifer M. Prehabilitation in preparation for orthopaedic surgery. *Orthop Nurs*. 2002;21:43-51

29. Fiuza-Luces C, Garatachea N, Berger NA, Lucia A. Exercise is the real polypill. *Physiology (Bethesda)*. 2013;28:330-358.

30. Kohl HW 3rd, Craig CL, Lambert EV, et al; Lancet Physical Activity Series Working Group. The pandemic of physical inactivity: global action for public health. *Lancet*. 2012;380:294-305.

31. Thompson PD, Franklin BA, Balady GJ, et al; American Heart Association Council on Nutrition, Physical Activity, and Metabolism; American Heart Association Council on Clinical Cardiology; American College of Sports Medicine. Exercise and acute cardiovascular events placing the risks into perspective: a scientific statement from the American Heart Association Council on Nutrition, Physical Activity, and Metabolism and the Council on Clinical Cardiology. *Circulation*. 2007;115:2358-2368.

32. Belardinelli R, Georgiou D, Cianci G, Purcaro A. Randomized, controlled trial of long-term moderate exercise training in chronic heart failure: effects on functional capacity, quality of life, and clinical outcome. *Circulation.* 1999;99:1173-1182.

33. Levett DZ, Grocott MP. Cardiopulmonary exercise testing, prehabilitation, and Enhanced Recovery After Surgery (ERAS). *Can J Anaesth.* 2015;62:131-142.

34. Davies SJ, Wilson RJ. Preoperative optimization of the high-risk surgical patient. *Br J Anaesth.* 2004;93:121-128.

35. Whipp BJ, Davis JA, Torres F, Wasserman K. A test to determine parameters of aerobic function during exercise. *J Appl Physiol Respir Environ Exerc Physiol.* 1981;50:217-221.

36. Faggiano P, D'Aloia A, Gualeni A, Brentana L, Dei Cas L. The 6 minute walking test in chronic heart failure: indications, interpretation and limitations from a review of the literature. *Eur J Heart Fail.* 2004;6:687-691.

37. Enright PL, Sherrill DL. Reference equations for the six-minute walk in healthy adults. *Am J Respir Crit Care Med.* 1998;158(5 Pt 1):1384-1387.

38. The Effect of Chemotherapy and Surgery for Cancer on Exercise Capacity. Aintree University Hospitals NHS Foundation Trust. Clinical Trials.gov website. https://clinicaltrials.gov/ct2/show/NCT01325883. Updated June 25, 2015. Accessed February 24, 2016.

3 Bowel Preparation

by Traci L Hedrick, MD, MS-CR, FACS, FACRS

Introduction

Few topics conjure up more differing opinions than the use of mechanical bowel preparation (MBP) for colorectal surgery. As such, over the past decade, the MBP has been the focus of much debate. This chapter focuses initially on the evidence of MBP in colorectal surgery followed by a description of the various MBP regimens and their individual physiologic effects on the surgical patient. Finally, a summary of the studies evaluating the use of MBP specifically within an enhanced recovery protocol (ERP) is given.

Efficacy of MBP in Colorectal Surgery

Dating back to trials from the 1970s, MBP combined with oral antibiotics has been shown to reduce surgical site infection (SSI) following elective intestinal surgery.[1] In 1977, the Nichols-Condon bowel preparation (utilizing neomycin and erythromycin in addition to vigorous mechanical cleansing) was described, demonstrating a reduction in SSI from 43% to 9%. From that point forward, the Nichols-Condon bowel preparation became the standard bowel prep for the following two decades.[2] However, as a result of increasing patient dissatisfaction, the modern use of the MBP has been called into question. More recent trials and meta-analyses fail to demonstrate improvement in SSI or anastomotic leak with MBP (**Figure 3.1** and **Figure 3.2**).[3,4] Based on these studies, the unpleasant nature of the MBP itself, and the perceived detrimental

FIGURE 3.1 — Anastomotic Leakage Meta-Analysis Results for Studies Comparing OMBP (with or without enema) vs No Preparation or Enema

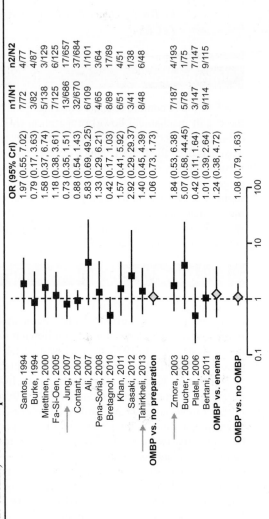

	OR (95% CrI)	n1/N1	n2/N2
Santos, 1994	1.97 (0.55, 7.02)	7/72	4/77
Burke, 1994	0.79 (0.17, 3.63)	3/82	4/87
Miettinen, 2000	1.58 (0.37, 6.74)	5/138	3/129
Fa-Si-Oen, 2005	1.18 (0.38, 3.61)	7/125	6/125
Jung, 2007	0.73 (0.35, 1.51)	13/686	17/657
Contant, 2007	0.88 (0.54, 1.43)	32/670	37/684
Ali, 2007	5.83 (0.69, 49.25)	6/109	1/101
Pena-Soria, 2008	1.33 (0.29, 6.21)	4/65	3/64
Bretagnol, 2010	0.42 (0.17, 1.03)	8/89	17/89
Khan, 2011	1.57 (0.41, 5.92)	6/51	4/51
Sasaki, 2012	2.92 (0.29, 29.37)	3/41	1/38
Tahirkheli, 2013	1.40 (0.45, 4.39)	8/48	6/48
OMBP vs. no preparation	1.06 (0.73, 1.73)		
Zmora, 2003	1.84 (0.53, 6.38)	7/187	4/193
Bucher, 2005	5.07 (0.58, 44.45)	5/78	1/75
Platell, 2006	0.42 (0.11, 1.64)	3/147	7/147
Bertani, 2011	1.01 (0.39, 2.64)	9/114	9/115
OMBP vs. enema	1.24 (0.38, 4.72)		
OMBP vs. no OMBP	1.08 (0.79, 1.63)		

54

CI, confidence interval; CrI, credible interval; OMBP, oral mechanical bowel preparation; OR, odds ratio

Note: The solid squares (and horizontal lines) indicate the point estimate of the OR (and the corresponding 95% CI) for individual studies; the diamonds (and horizontal lines) indicate the summary estimate of the OR (and the corresponding 95% central CrI). The numbers of events and the sample size of each treatment group are shown to the right of the plot. The dashed line indicates an OR of 1.

Dahabreh IJ, et al. *Dis Colon Rectum*. 2015;58(7):698-707.

3

FIGURE 3.2 — Wound Infection Meta-Analysis Results for Studies Comparing OMBP (with or without enema) vs No Preparation or Enema

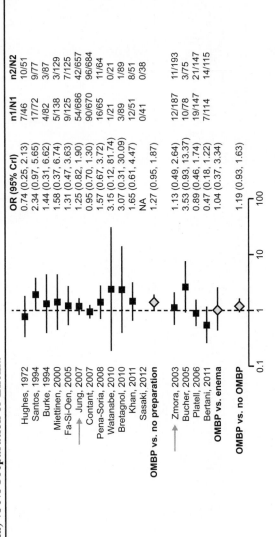

Study	OR (95% CrI)	n1/N1	n2/N2
Hughes, 1972	0.74 (0.25, 2.13)	7/46	10/51
Santos, 1994	2.34 (0.97, 5.65)	17/72	9/77
Burke, 1994	1.44 (0.31, 6.62)	4/82	3/87
Miettinen, 2000	1.58 (0.37, 6.74)	5/138	3/129
Fa-Si-Oen, 2005	1.31 (0.47, 3.63)	9/125	7/125
Jung, 2007	1.25 (0.82, 1.90)	54/686	42/657
Contant, 2007	0.95 (0.70, 1.30)	90/670	96/684
Pena-Soria, 2008	1.57 (0.67, 3.72)	16/65	11/64
Watanabe, 2010	3.15 (0.12, 81.74)	1/21	0/21
Bretagnol, 2010	3.07 (0.31, 30.09)	3/89	1/89
Khan, 2011	1.65 (0.61, 4.47)	12/51	8/51
Sasaki, 2012	NA	0/41	0/38
OMBP vs. no preparation	1.27 (0.95, 1.87)		
Zmora, 2003	1.13 (0.49, 2.64)	12/187	11/193
Bucher, 2005	3.53 (0.93, 13.37)	10/78	3/75
Platell, 2006	0.89 (0.46, 1.74)	19/147	21/147
Bertani, 2011	0.47 (0.18, 1.22)	7/114	14/115
OMBP vs. enema	1.04 (0.37, 3.34)		
OMBP vs. no OMBP	1.19 (0.93, 1.63)		

56

CI, confidence interval; CrI, credible interval; NA, not available (could not be estimated); OMBP, oral mechanical bowel preparation; OR, odds ratio

Note: The solid squares (and horizontal lines) indicate the point estimate of the OR (and the corresponding 95% CI) for individual studies; the diamonds (and horizontal lines) indicate the summary estimate of the OR (and the corresponding 95% central CrI). The numbers of events and the sample size of each treatment group are shown to the right of the plot. The dashed line indicates an OR of 1.

Dahabreh IJ, et al. *Dis Colon Rectum*. 2015;58(7):698-707.

3

effects of the MBP on fluid requirements in the perioperative period, MBP omission was an early tenet of the enhanced recovery movement.[5]

Compared with the initial efficacy trials during the 1970s, it must be noted that the majority of the recent trials included a MBP *without* the addition of oral antibiotics (trials utilizing oral antibiotics are designated with an arrow in **Figure 3.1** and **Figure 3.2**). In the absence of oral antibiotics, a mechanical cleansing theoretically results in liquid, bacteria-laden stool that is more likely to contaminate the operative field.[6] In a 2009 Cochrane review, Nelson and coworkers concluded that oral antibiotics successfully reduce the rate of SSI.[7] In addition, data from large risk-adjusted national database studies, including the National Surgical Quality Improvement Program and the Michigan Surgical Quality Collaborative-Colectomy Best Practices Project, demonstrate significant reduction in infectious morbidity associated with the use of a MBP *when combined* with oral antibiotics.[8-11]

Therefore, based on the cumulative data at hand, a MBP alone in the absence of oral antibiotics cannot be recommended. However, the data are clear that a combination of a MBP and nonabsorbable oral antibiotics may reduce infectious morbidity associated with elective colorectal surgery. This distinction in the use of MBP *with and without* oral antibiotics cannot be overemphasized given that the majority of surgeons (59%) who are currently performing MBP for elective surgery in the United States are doing so in the absence of oral antibiotics.[10-12]

What remains unclear is the efficacy of oral antibiotics in the absence of a mechanical cleansing in reducing infectious morbidity. There are some data that suggest oral antibiotics in the absence of MBP may be beneficial at reducing SSI in elective colorectal surgery, warranting further study.[13]

Types of Mechanical Bowel Preparations

A common misconception held by many perioperative care providers is that all MBPs inevitably lead to dehydration and detrimental physiologic effects. Many of the phosphate-based solutions initially described in MBP were hyperosmotic solutions, which do lead to dehydration. However, the isosmotic solutions of current standard MBP regimens are much better tolerated. **Table 3.1** describes the clinical characteristics of various MBP regimens.

The most widely used agent for MBP in elective colorectal surgery is polyethylene glycol (PEG), which is an osmotically balanced electrolyte lavage solution that is standardly administered in a 4-L preparation. Because it is a high molecular-weight, nonabsorbable polymer, PEG passes through the GI tract without net absorption or secretion thereby avoiding significant fluid and electrolyte shifts. The most common side effects associated with PEG solutions are nausea and vomiting, which affect 4% to 17% of patients on average.[3] Full-volume PEG preparations include GoLYTELY, Colyte, NuLytely, and TriLyte. The large volume and salty taste of the solution are a common source of patient dissatisfaction. As a result, low-volume PEG preparations combined with other cathartic agents have been developed including HalfLytely, MoviPrep, MiraLax, and BiPeglyte. While they seem to result in similar preparation for colonoscopy procedures, there are few data specifically evaluating the use of these low-volume preparations for colorectal surgery.

As opposed to isosmotic preparations, hyperosmotic preparations (eg, magnesium citrate, sodium phosphate) exert an osmotic effect, drawing water into the intestine. Therefore, hyperosmotic preparations are much smaller in volume and typically more satisfying to patients. However, these solutions cause significant fluid and electrolyte shifts and can be associated with

TABLE 3.1 — Clinical Characteristics of MBP Regimens

Name	Advantages	Disadvantages
Polyethylene glycol (polyethylene glycol [PEG], GoLYTELY, Colyte)	Safe	Large volume, poor taste
Sulfate-free PEG (NuLytely, TriLyte)	Safe, better taste	Large volume
Low-volume PEG and bisacodyl (HalfLytely)	Safe, lower volume	2 L solution still a sizeable volume to drink
Low-volume PEG sulfate solution (SUPREP)	Lower volume	Risk of electrolyte fluctuation and renal dysfunction
Ascorbic acid lavage (MoviPrep)	Safe, better taste	Use with caution in patients with G6PD deficiency
Sodium phosphate • Liquid form • Visicol tablets • OsmoPrep tablets	Small volume	Requires high concomitant liquid ingestion. Electrolyte and fluid shifts. Caution in cardiac/liver/renal dysfunction; elderly/dehydrated, those taking angiotensin-converting enzyme inhibitors or angiotension receptor blockers
Magnesium citrate as adjunct to PEG	Lower volume of PEG required	Caution in renal dysfunction

Adapted from Esrailian E. *Gut Instincts: A Clinician's Handbook of Digestive and Liver Diseases.* 2012: SLACK Incorporated.

renal damage. For this reason, the use of hyperosmotic bowel preparation solutions within an ERP is not recommended.

Our standard MBP protocol, which is used routinely in all patients undergoing elective colorectal surgery within our ERP at the University of Virginia, is as follows:

- 4 L of GoLytely starting at 5:00 PM
- Erythromycin (1 g administered orally at 1:00 PM, 2:00 PM, and 10:00 PM)
- Neomycin (1 g administered orally at 1:00 PM, 2:00 PM, and 10:00 PM)
- *Metronidazole if contraindication to either erythromycin or neomycin (500 mg administered orally at 1:00 PM, 2:00 PM, and 10:00 PM)*
- Regular diet ceases at 5:00 PM, after which clear liquids can be consumed *ad libidum* until 2 hours prior to surgery. A 20-oz Gatorade is consumed 2 hours prior to surgery.

Mechanical Bowel Preparation and ER Protocols

Proposed avoidance of the MBP of many ERPs is based on the questionable efficacy and perceived detrimental physiologic effects.[14] The basis for this notion is a study conducted in 12 healthy volunteers undergoing MBP with bisacodyl and sodium phosphate. As would be expected with a hypertonic preparation, the study participants demonstrated increased plasma osmolality and electrolyte abnormalities, leading the authors to conclude that bowel preparation has significant adverse physiologic effects.[15] Similarly, nearly all available studies in the literature demonstrating dehydration in the perioperative setting as the result of a MBP were conducted in patients prepped with hyperosmotic solutions.[16,17] However, as previously mentioned, isosmotic solutions such as PEG do not share these same uniformly deleterious physiologic properties.

Hendry and associates performed a feasibility study combining the use of oral carbohydrate loading with a mechanical bowel prep in patients undergoing elective left colon and rectal resections, demonstrating that 84% of patients tolerate the preoperative oral fluid/CHO loading in conjunction with the mechanical bowel prep with no untoward effects.[18]

As such, when formulating the University of Virginia ERP, the use of a MBP using GoLytely and oral antibiotics was chosen. This was combined with continued clear liquids after midnight, carbohydrate loading with 20 ounces of Gatorade 2 hours prior to induction, and goal-directed fluid resuscitation strategy based on intravascular volume status as measured by the pleth variability index. Our expectation was that patients would autoregulate their intravascular volume status and hypovolemia could be detected intraoperatively through use of the pleth variability index. Through implementation of an ERP utilizing a MBP with oral antibiotics, we reduced fluid administration by 1885 mL during surgery and by 4591 mL over the entire hospitalization resulting in a 2.2-day reduction in length of stay and a reduction in overall complications by 48.8% ($P < 0.0001$).[19]

While single-institution results of implemented enhanced recovery protocols with bowel preparation have been positive, examples of similarly improved outcomes with protocols omitting bowel preparation have also been reported.[20]

Conclusion

Despite nearly 50 years of research, the optimal preparation regimen for patients undergoing elective colorectal surgery remains elusive. Increasingly, evidence suggests that MBP in the absence of oral antibiotics is ineffective and may, in fact, be harmful. Meanwhile, MBP in combination with oral antibiotics seems to improve infectious outcomes. Whether oral antibiotics are effective in the absence of a mechanical cleansing remains to be seen.

Hypertonic solutions such as magnesium citrate or phosphate-based preparations contribute to metabolic disarray, with detrimental physiologic effects in the perioperative period. Alternatively, PEG-based solutions do not typically lead to fluid and electrolyte abnormalities and can be effectively utilized within an ERP without untoward effects on the recovery process.

3

REFERENCES

1. Nichols RL, Broido P, Condon RE, Gorbach SL, Nyhus LM. Effect of preoperative neomycin-erythromycin intestinal preparation on the incidence of infectious complications following colon surgery. *Ann Surg*. 1973;178:453-462.

2. Clarke JS, Condon RE, Bartlett JG, Gorbach SL, Nichols RL, Ochi S. Preoperative oral antibiotics reduce septic complications of colon operations: results of prospective, randomized, double-blind clinical study. *Ann Surg*. 1977;186:251-259.

3. Dahabreh IJ, Steele DW, Shah N, Trikalinos TA. Oral mechanical bowel preparation for colorectal surgery: systematic review and meta-analysis. *Dis Colon Rectum*. 2015;58:698-707.

4. Güenaga KF, Matos D, Wille-Jørgensen P. Mechanical bowel preparation for elective colorectal surgery. *Cochrane Database Syst Rev*. 2011;(9):CD001544.

5. Gustafsson UO, Scott MJ, Schwenk W, et al; Enhanced Recovery After Surgery Society. Guidelines for perioperative care in elective colonic surgery: Enhanced Recovery After Surgery (ERAS®) Society recommendations. *Clin Nutr*. 2012;31:783-800.

6. Mahajna A, Krausz M, Rosin D, et al. Bowel preparation is associated with spillage of bowel contents in colorectal surgery. *Dis Colon Rectum*. 2005;48:1626-1631.

7. Nelson RL, Glenny AM, Song F. Antimicrobial prophylaxis for colorectal surgery. *Cochrane Database Syst Rev*. 2009;(1):CD001181.

8. Englesbe MJ, Brooks L, Kubus J, et al. A statewide assessment of surgical site infection following colectomy: the role of oral antibiotics. *Ann Surg*. 2010;252:514-519.

9. Kim EK, Sheetz KH, Bonn J, et al. A statewide colectomy experience: the role of full bowel preparation in preventing surgical site infection. *Ann Surg*. 2014;259:310-314.

10. Moghadamyeghaneh Z, Hanna MH, Carmichael JC, et al. Nationwide analysis of outcomes of bowel preparation in colon surgery. *J Am Coll Surg*. 2015;220:912-920.

11. Morris MS, Graham LA, Chu DI, Cannon JA, Hawn MT. Oral antibiotic bowel preparation significantly reduces surgical site infection rates and readmission rates in elective colorectal surgery. *Ann Surg*. 2015;261:1034-1040.

12. Kiran RP, Murray AC, Chiuzan C, Estrada D, Forde K. Combined preoperative mechanical bowel preparation with oral antibiotics significantly reduces surgical site infection, anastomotic leak, and ileus after colorectal surgery. *Ann Surg*. 2015;262:416-425.

13. Atkinson SJ, Swenson BR, Hanseman DJ, et al. In the absence of a mechanical bowel prep, does the addition of pre-operative oral antibiotics to parental antibiotics decrease the incidence of surgical site infection after elective segmental colectomy? *Surg Infect (Larchmt)*. 2015;16:728-732.

14. Miller TE, Roche AM, Mythen M. Fluid management and goal-directed therapy as an adjunct to Enhanced Recovery After Surgery (ERAS). *Can J Anaesth*. 2015;62(2):158-168.

15. Holte K, Nielsen KG, Madsen JL, Kehlet H. Physiologic effects of bowel preparation. *Dis Colon Rectum*. 2004;47:1397-1402.

16. Ackland GL, Harrington J, Downie P, et al. Dehydration induced by bowel preparation in older adults does not result in cognitive dysfunction. *Anesth Analg*. 2008;106:924-929.

17. Ackland GL, Singh-Ranger D, Fox S, et al. Assessment of preoperative fluid depletion using bioimpedance analysis. *Br J Anaesth*. 2004;92:134-136.

18. Hendry PO, Balfour A, Potter MA, et al. Preoperative conditioning with oral carbohydrate loading and oral nutritional supplements can be combined with mechanical bowel preparation prior to elective colorectal resection. *Colorectal Dis*. 2008;10:907-910.

19. Thiele RH, Rea KM, Turrentine FE, et al. Standardization of care: impact of an enhanced recovery protocol on length of stay, complications, and direct costs after colorectal surgery. *J Am Coll Surg*. 2015;220:430-443.

20. Keenan JE, Speicher PJ, Nussbaum DP, et al. Improving outcomes in colorectal surgery by sequential implementation of multiple standardized care programs. *J Am Coll Surg*. 2015;221:404-414.

4

Preoperative Assessment and Optimization

*by Malcolm A West, MD, MRCS, PhD
and Michael PW Grocott, BSc, MBBS,
MD, FRCA, FRCP, FFICM*

Introduction

Preoperative medical assessment is an essential component of all patients' surgical pathways. Outcomes after surgery are dependent on both controllable factors, such as the medical care received before, during, and after surgery, as well as fixed factors, such as the patient's age and gender. Assessment of surgical risk is essential for planning perioperative care and enabling informed consent. Planning perioperative care based on estimated risk and ensuring individualized preoperative patient optimization have the potential to substantially improve surgical outcomes.

Older patients with declining physiologic reserves may particularly benefit from accurate preoperative assessment and optimization to maximize the likelihood of maintaining normal homeostasis intraoperatively. Preoperative preparation should be individualized and comprehensive, but also mindful of relevant time constraints. It is important to identify patients with known and occult comorbidities and those increasingly vulnerable to surgical stress due to limited physiologic reserve (eg, deconditioning), allowing early preoperative optimization in an attempt to improve the patients' outcome.

Preoperative Assessment

■ Clinical Acumen and Routine Tests

The preoperative interview is usually the anesthesiologist's first introduction to a patient and is the standard approach to preoperative assessment. The objectives of the interview, in patients who are presumed to be healthy, is to detect and quantify unrecognized disease that could increase surgical or anesthetic risk.[1]

Evidence suggests that 60% to 70% of preoperative testing is unnecessary, if a proper history and physical examination is done.[1] Which tests should be ordered preoperatively for elective surgery? This question, specifically for patients with no symptoms other than those relevant to the planned operation, has been repeatedly tackled by health technology assessment agencies since 1989. The UK National Institute of Clinical Excellence and the American College of Surgeons have published comprehensive reviews of the evidence on routine preoperative testing.[2,3]

■ Clinical Judgment

Probably the most frequently used approach, this has uncertain value in comparison with other approaches. In practice, the majority of patients are assessed using clinical judgment, and in a minority, an additional objective system(s) of evaluation is used. It is currently unclear what the best approach is and additional research is needed in this area to assist clinicians in the choice of preoperative assessment tools in different patient groups. Importantly, it is clear that the documentation of assessed risk is poor in a number of contexts. It is likely that, whichever system is used, mandating documentation of risk may improve care through ensuring that risk is formally evaluated through maintaining a clear record of baseline risk as well as changes in assessed risk over time.

■ Risk Stratification

Stratification of patients into "risk categories" according to their physiologic characteristics may lead perioperative physicians to modify or abandon a planned surgical intervention if the risk is seen to outweigh the benefit. As the transition from a paternalistic to a collaborative relationship with patients continues, such information is increasingly used to guide collaborative (also know as shared) decision-making discussion between clinicians and patients. Alternatively, preoperative risk stratification may allow physicians to select those patients who may benefit from specific treatment strategies, such as perioperative hemodynamic optimization or an augmented level of postoperative care (eg, intensive care). In recent years, a number of different methods of predicting perioperative risk have been developed, including predictive risk scores, measures or estimates of functional capacity, and serological markers of inflammation and cardiac function.

■ **Predictive Risk Scores**

Predictive risk scores like the American Society of Anesthesiologists physical status (ASA-PS) score, the Charlson Age-Comorbidity Index, and the Physiological and Operative Severity Score for the Enumeration of Mortality and Morbidity (POSSUM)[4] have been validated in a number of surgical cohorts.[5] These scores, and others in existence, differ in their discriminant ability and reliability, and the types of patients, procedures, and outcomes for which they are validated. Caution should be exerted when considering the use of any of these models for clinical decision making about whether to proceed with a proposed intervention because they demonstrate variable predictive precision, particularly at the extremes of age and calculated risk. Furthermore, although a direct comparison of risk stratification models revealed POSSUM to be superior to ASA-PS and Charlson for the prediction of 30-day morbidity, none of these systems was an accurate predictor of 90-day mortality.[6] **Table 4.1** compares these tools showing their validation in multiple studies.

TABLE 4.1 — Mortality Models Validated In Multiple Studies

Model	No. of Variables	Pre-, Intra-, or Postoperative Data Used	Original Derivation Cohort and Outcome	Studies (n)	Author	Patients (n)	Type of Surgery	Endpoints	AUROC (CI)
APACHE II	16	Postoperative	Critical care patients; all diagnoses (not just surgical); hospital mortality	3	Jones	117	Gastrointestinal, vascular, renal, and urology	30 day	HDU admission score: 0.539 (± 0.083)
					Osler	5322	Non cardiac	Hospital discharge	ICU admission score: 0.806
					Stachon	271	Ortho, spinal, trauma, visceral, and limb surgery	Hospital discharge	First 24 h worst score: 0.777
ASA-PS	1	Preoperative	General surgical patients	2	Sutton	1946	Gastrointestinal, vascular, trauma	Hospital discharge	0.93 (0.90–0.97)
					Donati	1849	Abdominal, vascular, orthopedic, urology, endocrine, neurology, eye	Hospital discharge	0.81 (0.79–0.83)

Charlson	17	Preoperative	Medical patients: 10-yr mortality	2	Atherly	2167	General vascular	30 day	0.52
					Sundararjan	2461830	All inpatient surgery	Hospital discharge	0.85–0.87
POSSUM	18	Pre- and intraoperative	General surgery: 30-day mortality	3	Jones	117	Gastrointestinal, vascular, renal, and urology	30 day	0.75 (±0.08)
					Donati	1849	Abdominal, vascular, orthopedic, urology, endocrine, neurology, eye	Hospital discharge	0.92 (0.88–0.95)
					Brooks	949	General, colorectal, upper gastrointestinal, urology, head and neck	30 day	0.92 (0.90–0.95)

4

TABLE 4.1 — *Continued*

70

Model	No. of Variables	Pre-, Intra-, or Postoperative Data Used	Original Derivation Cohort and Outcome	Studies (n)	Author	Patients (n)	Type of Surgery	Endpoints	AUROC (CI)
P-POSSUM	18	Pre- and intraoperative	General surgery; 30-day mortality	5	Organ	229	General, vascular, ENT, plastics, thoracic, urology	30 day	0.68 (0.57–0.78)
					Donati	1849	Abdominal, vascular, orthopedic, urology, endocrine, neurology, eye	Hospital discharge	0.91 (0.90–0.92)
					Brooks	949	General, colorectal, upper gastrointestinal, urology, ENT	30 day	0.92 (0.90–0.95)
					Neary	2349	General, vascular, ENT, urology, orthopedics	30 day / 1 year	0.90 (0.87–0.93) / 0.90 (0.80–1.0)
					Haga	5272	Gastrointestinal and hepatobiliary	30 day / Hospital discharge	0.74 (0.63–0.86) / 0.81 (0.75–0.88)

Surgical Risk Scale	3	Preoperative	General surgery: inpatient mortality	3	Sutton	1946	Gastrointestinal, vascular, trauma	Hospital discharge	0.95 (0.93–0.97)
					Brooks	949	General, colorectal, upper gastrointestinal, urology, ENT	30 day	0.89 (0.86–0.93)
					Neary	2349	General, vascular, ENT, urology, orthopedics	30 day / 1 year	0.85 (0.82–0.89) / 0.84 (0.75–0.94)
Surgical Risk Score (Donati)	3	Preoperative	General surgery: inpatient mortality	2	Donati	1849	Abdominal, vascular, orthopedics, urology, endocrine, ENT, neurosurgery, eye, gynecology, thoracic	Hospital discharge	0.89 (0.84–0.94)
					Haga	5272	Gastrointestinal, hepatobiliary	Hospital discharge	0.73 (0.63–0.83)

APACHE II, Acute Physiology and Chronic Health Evaluation II; ASA-PS, American Society of Anesthesiologists' Physical Status score; AUROC, area under receiver operating characteristic curve; HDU, high dependency unit; ICD, International Classification of Diseases; ICU, intensive care unit; (P)-POSSUM: (Portsmouth), Physiological and Operative Severity Score for enUmeration of Morbidity and mortality.

Functional Capacity as a Measure of Risk

Simple direct questioning to assess a patient's cardiorespiratory fitness has long been a part of pre-operative assessment and has been shown to correlate with postoperative outcome.[7] Formal assessment of functional capacity may be achieved by subjective categorization (eg, the Duke Activity Status Index [DASI]), by estimating the metabolic equivalent of a task (MET), or through more objective measures including the incremental shuttle walk test (ISWT) and cardiopulmonary exercise testing (CPET). The DASI[8] is a simple questionnaire that categorizes levels of exertion according to the estimated metabolic equivalent of oxygen consumption required to achieve the task. The DASI is correlated with peak oxygen uptake on exercise testing, and its use is supported in the preoperative setting by the American College of Cardiology/American Heart Association (ACC/AHA) guidelines on perioperative cardiovascular evaluation.[9] However, it is a patient-reported and, therefore, subjective measure.

One MET represents the estimated resting oxygen consumption of an adult (1 MET = approximately 3.5 mL/kg/min), and METS may be used to categorize specific activities as being equivalent to multiples of this value. For example, the effort required to read this chapter while sitting down is 1 MET. The ISWT involves a patient walking back and forth between two fixed points, typically 10 m apart, to the limit of their exertion. It is a validated and highly reproducible measure of functional capacity, and is likely to be most valuable for the screening of patients with a sufficient level of fitness to not require further investigation.[10,11] The 6-minute walk test requires walking up and down a long flat corridor for 6 minutes to see how far one can walk. The patient is instructed to walk "at their own pace" and stop and rest as many times as needed. The 6-minute walk is a measure of distance, which is considered submaximal, and perhaps more closely approximates the capacity to perform activities of daily living. Its clinical appeal also lies in the fact that it can be performed by almost all patients without the need of sophisticated equipment.[12]

CPET is a more formal method of evaluating exercise capacity and identifying causes of exercise limitation and has been shown to be a well-tolerated, noninvasive, cost-effective way to provide a global assessment of the cardiovascular, respiratory, and skeletal muscle systems under stress that mimics the stressor of major surgery.[13] Despite requiring a moderate to high level of exertion, CPET is well tolerated and safe to conduct.[14-17] CPET is usually conducted on an electromagnetically braked cycle ergometer with the patient breathing through a mouthpiece or facemask through which gas exchange is measured. The patient is continuously monitored noninvasively, but in specific very high-risk cases, invasive monitoring may be used. A typical CPET set-up is shown in **Figure 4**.1. Variables derived from CPET, include the oxygen uptake at peak exercise ($\dot{V}O_2$ at Peak), the $\dot{V}O_2$ at the anaerobic threshold/estimated lactate threshold ($\dot{V}O_2$ at θ_L), the oxygen pulse (O_2 Pulse at θ_L and Peak), and the ventilation equivalents for carbon dioxide and oxygen ($\dot{V}_E/\dot{V}CO_2$ and $\dot{V}_E/\dot{V}O_2$). Some of these variables have been shown to predict morbidity and mortality in the perioperative context especially in major abdominal surgery.[18-23]

The perioperative period is a time of physiologic stress. As the surgical stress response increases, the metabolic rate and tissue oxygen demand rise. By detecting diminished exercise capacity and consequently reduced physiologic reserve, CPET identifies patients at increased risk of complications and mortality. Furthermore, CPET can be used to detect the cause of exercise limitation and may diagnose unsuspected cardiorespiratory disease. Initially, CPET was used to assess fitness for surgery to guide the choice of location for perioperative care (intensive care or general ward)

FIGURE 4.1 — Typical CPET Setup

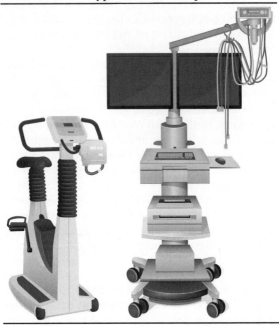

and to identify or evaluate the severity of medical comorbidity. Recently, the focus has broadened and CPET is used to guide collaborative decision making between patients and clinicians, to evaluate the impact of neoadjuvant cancer therapies (including chemotherapy and radiotherapy), and to guide prehabilitation programs. A disadvantage of CPET is the relatively high cost in comparison with other methods of evaluating fitness. Consequently, establishing effective screening tools for assessing adequate physical fitness is an important goal of current research in order to manage the number of CPETs required. The corollary of the high cost is the advantage that the test provides a comprehensive assessment of both exercise capacity and possibly limiting factors explaining exercise tolerance including ECG, and therefore it may reduce expenditure on alternative diagnostic technologies (eg, screening transthoracic echocardiogram).

Recent work suggests that the DASI and the ISWT are sensitive in the identification of patients at low risk of perioperative complications; however, they may incorrectly categorize as high risk a significant number of patients who, on CPET, would be considered low risk (that is, with a $\dot{V}_{O_2}$ at θ_L of >11 mL/kg/min or $\dot{V}_{O_2}$ at peak of >15 mL/kg/min).[7] The DASI ± ISWT have been suggested as screening tools to identify low-risk patients who warrant no further investigation; patients identified as high risk may benefit from further evaluation using CPET. Patients confirmed as high risk by CPET might benefit from perioperative hemodynamic optimization and postoperative critical care admission.[24]

Serological Markers of Risk

The biological mechanism responsible for the development of postoperative morbidity is likely to involve an inflammatory response that may clinically manifest by the systemic inflammatory response syndrome (SIRS) or milder clinical variants thereof. Perioperative levels of some pro- and anti-inflammatory markers have been found to correlate with postoperative adverse outcomes. High-sensitivity C-reactive protein (hsCRP) is well established as a marker of inflammation that may predict vascular and cardiac adverse events in the general population, independent of accepted risk factors such as smoking, hypertension, and diabetes mellitus. It has been found to inversely correlate with functional capacity as measured by $\dot{V}_{O_2}$ at peak even in symptom-free individuals, and the addition of hsCRP level to risk models for the prediction of cardiovascular risk in the general population improves predictive ability.[25]

More recent work has examined the relationship between preoperative hsCRP level and surgical outcome, and found an independent association between elevated hsCRP levels and adverse events in vascular surgical patients. Possibly the addition of biomarker assays and measures of functional capacity to risk stratification scoring systems (already generated in colorectal surgery[19,20]) will lead to improvements in accuracy of perioperative risk prediction for major surgical patients. Because biomarkers are relatively cheap, they may be a valuable means (with risk scores) of differentiating between low-risk patients who need no further assessment and higher-risk patients who may benefit from detailed evaluation using CPET.

Emerging evidence suggests that many patients sustain myocardial cardiac injury in the perioperative period that does not satisfy the criteria for myocardial infarction; however, myocardial injury due to perioperative ischemia is common and associated with substantial mortality. The Vascular Events in Noncardiac Surgery Patients Cohort Evaluation (VISION) study (26) demonstrated that after adjustment of preoperative clinical variables (eg, age), peak troponin T (TnT) values of $0.03\mu g/L$ or greater in the first 30 days after noncardiac surgery were independent predictors of 30-day mortality.[26] The high-quality evidence for acetyl-salicylic acid and statin therapy in the nonoperative setting and encouraging observational data from a large international perioperative trial (ie, PeriOperative Ischemic Evaluation) show an association with use of these drugs and decreased 30-day mortality in patients who have suffered a perioperative myocardial injury.[27] This suggests that acetyl-salicylic acid and statin therapy may benefit patients who are at high risk of myocardial injury after noncardiac surgery.

Preoperative Optimization

■ **Physiologic Function**

Postoperative complications within 30 days have been found to be an important determinant of long-term survival following surgery independent of preoperative comorbidity and intraoperative adverse events.[28,29] Avoiding or reducing complications is therefore of paramount importance. Preoperative optimization of comorbidities is central to the early stages of enhanced recovery and may reduce postoperative morbidity.

■ Cardiovascular Risk

A large body of evidence now exists that can guide the clinician in optimizing cardiovascular risk (ACC/AHA Task Force Guidelines[30]). Major abdominopelvic surgery is associated with a marked rise in tissue oxygen requirements that enforce a rise in cardiac output, elevation in heart rate and blood pressure, as well as a neuroendocrine and prothrombotic response that may unmask occult cardiovascular pathology. High-risk patients include those who are unable to spontaneously elevate their cardiac output to the required level and those who exhibit inducible ischemia. This at-risk group needs optimization both preoperatively and intraoperatively. This may be achieved through pharmacologic intervention (eg, management of hypertension), modifications to anesthesia (eg, neuraxial blockade, postoperative analgesia), and perioperative monitoring techniques to guide hemodynamic therapy (ie, fluids ± inotropes).

■ Hypertension

Treatment of hypertension is associated with a reduced mortality from stroke and coronary heart disease. In surgical patients, however, it is apparent that if a patient has a systolic blood pressure <180 mm Hg and a diastolic blood pressure <110 mm Hg (stage 1 or stage 2), then high blood pressure is not an independent risk factor for cardiovascular complications in the perioperative period. Where stage 3 hypertension is seen (systolic >180 mm Hg and diastolic >110 mm Hg), then postponing surgery to initiate or optimize antihypertensive medications may be merited if the risk of delaying surgery is acceptable.

Patients taking angiotensin-converting enzyme (ACE) inhibitors and angiotensin II (ATII) receptor antagonists are at higher risk of intraoperative hypotension, and reports vary on the effect upon cardiac and renal complications in the perioperative period.

Concerns regarding the risks of perioperative renal dysfunction in this context have prompted a (non–evidence-based) move for ACE inhibitors and ATII receptor antagonists to be withheld on the morning of surgery with the recommendation that they be restarted once a patient is deemed euvolemic and with normal renal function postoperatively.

■ **Pulmonary Risk**

Patients with co-existing pulmonary disease are at higher risk of perioperative morbidity, particularly pulmonary complications and mortality. Smokers are also at increased risk of pulmonary morbidity and the merits of short-term smoking cessation prior to surgery can be emphasized in preassessment.[31] Emphasizing the importance of postoperative mobilization in the pre-assessment clinic encourages measures to prevent atelectasis. Other actions that a patient may participate in include deep breathing and incentive spirometry exercises; these lung expansion interventions can reduce pulmonary risks postoperatively. In general, if significant pulmonary disease is suspected, then response to bronchodilators and the evaluation for the presence of carbon dioxide retention through arterial blood gas analysis may be justified. If there is evidence of infection, appropriate antibiotics are critical, and steroids and bronchodilators may need to be considered.

■ **Anemia**

A large proportion of patients undergoing elective abdominopelvic cancer are anemic and iron deficient at the time of diagnosis. A full blood count should be checked as part of the pre-assessment process, and where present, the type of anemia should be categorized and further investigations undertaken as indicated (eg, vitamin B_{12}, folate). Most patients are likely to have iron deficiency anemia. When other forms of anemia are present then, these should be managed according to appropriate local guidelines. It is recommended that elective surgery patients should receive a hemoglobin determination a minimum of 30 days before the scheduled surgical procedure.

Mild anemia is associated with a more advanced disease stage and with a higher mortality, morbidity, and length of hospital stay. More severe anemia needing blood transfusion indicates a higher-risk situation and is an independent risk factor for mortality. Optimization strategies in patients with anemia are therefore centred upon increasing hemoglobin levels preoperatively without resorting to blood transfusion and restricting intraoperative surgical blood loss to an absolute minimum. Practice guidelines from the American Society of Anesthesiology suggest transfusion at a level of 6 g/dL but not at 10 g/dL. In a patient within the range 6–10 g/dL, decisions need to be made based on individual circumstances.

■ **Nutrition**

Poor nutritional status is associated with poorer outcome after major surgery. A proportion of abdominopelvic benign and malignant surgical patients are nutritionally challenged at the time of presentation. An assessment of a patient's nutritional status is not straightforward, and currently there is a lack of standardization in the definition of nutritional depletion and there is no consensus on the best method for assessing the nutritional status of hospitalized patients. Multiple systems exist to predict nutritional "risk" including subjective global assessment (SGA), mini-nutritional assessment, the Nutrition Risk Index, and the Nutrition Risk Score (NRS).[32] When patients are identified as nutritionally at-risk, then the most suitable preoperative intervention is the initiation of oral nutritional supplements.

Preoperative oral nutritional supplements should preferably be given before admission to hospital. The evidence for how oral nutritional supplements should be given pre- and postoperatively is less clear, but it is suggested to be given 5 to 7 days before surgery and for 5 to 7 days after uncomplicated surgery. The most appropriate supplement is a standard whole protein formula for most patients, but more recently, the role of "immunonutrition" with formulas containing arginine, omega-3 fatty acids, and ribonucleic acid (RNA) has been assessed and evidence is building for a role for these products around the time of major abdominal cancer surgery and after severe trauma. Where severe nutritional risk is identified (eg, weight loss >10%-15%/6 months; BMI <18.5; Subjective Global Assessment Grade C; serum albumin <30 [with normal renal/hepatic function]), surgery should be delayed where possible and nutritional deficits corrected.

■ Obesity

Obesity is a significant problem among most patient populations and with this comes obesity-related disease. Obese patients have significantly more surgical site infections and soft tissue complications after surgery and have a greater incidence of deep venous thromboses, postoperative lung dysfunction, and metabolic disturbance postoperatively. In some cases, elective surgery can be postponed to allow weight loss by medical means or bariatric surgery; however, this is not always feasible.

■ Diabetes

It is well established that poor glucose control in the perioperative period is an independent predictor of postoperative infection and mortality independent of diabetic status. The control of blood glucose concentration is therefore more crucial than making a diagnosis of diabetes. Mortality rates in diabetic patients are estimated to be up to five times greater than in non-diabetic patients. This has been attributed to end-organ damage caused by the disease. Chronic complications resulting in microangiopathy (retinopathy, nephropathy, and neuropathy) and macroangiopathy (atherosclerosis) directly increase the need for surgical intervention and the occurrence of surgical complications due to infections and vasculopathies. In general, infections account for 66% of postoperative complications, with impaired leukocyte function, altered chemotaxis, and phagocytic activity underpinning this finding. Optimization of glucose control preoperatively is the aim and should be individualized to the patient and undertaken in cooperation with the patient's general practitioner and endocrinologist/diabetic liaison nurse. Preoperative measurement of HbA1c may identify patients at higher risk of poor glycemic control and postoperative complications.

In general, on the day of surgery, patients on oral hypoglycemic agents are advised to discontinue them owing to their potential to cause hypoglycemia. In addition, sulfonylureas have been associated with interfering with ischemic myocardial pre-conditioning and may theoretically increase the risk of perioperative myocardial ischemia and infarction. Metformin should be discontinued preoperatively because of the risk of developing lactic acidosis. For such patients, short-acting insulin may be administered subcutaneously as a sliding scale or as a continuous infusion, to maintain optimal glucose control.

■ **Smoking and Alcohol Intake**

Smoking and high alcohol intakes are important risk factors for perioperative morbidity in all elective and emergency surgery. The most common perioperative complications related to smoking are impaired wound healing, wound infection, and cardiopulmonary complications. Even in young smokers, reduced pulmonary capacity, increased mucus production, and reduced ciliary function are recorded. All patients presenting for surgery should be questioned regarding smoking and hazardous drinking as clear benefit is obtained by intensive interventions to encourage their cessation as this translates to benefit by significantly reducing the incidence of several serious postoperative complications, including wound and cardiopulmonary complications and infections.[31,33] The duration of these interventions can, however, be between 3 and 8 weeks or longer meaning that patients requiring prompt surgery may not gain this advantage.

■ Prehabilitation

A decline in physical activity as a result of aging or illness results in a significant increase in perioperative risk that may be attenuated by physical exercise interventions. Prehabilitation is defined as "the process of enhancing the functional capacity of an individual to enable them to withstand a stressful event." Physical exercise training prior to elective surgery meets this criterion. Aerobic and muscular strength training in major surgical patients has been shown to increase endurance capacity, improve objective markers of physical fitness, reduce weight gain, and improve muscle strength. Although constraints to proceeding with surgery limit the time for the initiation of prehabilitation, a 3-week period may still be sufficient to obtain a moderate gain in aerobic and muscle strength reserve. Importantly, in neoadjuvant cancer therapies, which are typically administered prior to surgery and followed by a recovery period of 6 to 12 weeks (or more), have opened up a time window to train patients prior to major cancer operations where previously the pressure of reducing the time between diagnosis and surgery precluded such an intervention.

Studies on prehabilitation before major thoracic and abdominal surgery have shown an increase in preoperative physical fitness, physical activity, decreased postoperative complications, and shorter hospital stay.[15,34-36] Prehabilitation was found to be feasible, safe, and tolerable after the additional stress of neoadjuvant cancer treatments. Whether such preoperative regimens produce long-term benefits is untested. However, in the post-treatment phase, an increase in physical activity has been associated with improved disease-specific and overall survival, regardless of pre-diagnosis activity levels.

Improved understanding of the optimal duration, pattern, intensity, and composition of such interventions will be needed to maximize efficacy. In order to maximize the effectiveness of training, a better understanding of the complex interplay between adherence, efficacy, and cost for in-hospital supervised training interventions vs self-directed outpatient approaches is needed.

■ Education and Conditioning of Expectations

The major abdominopelvic surgical patient is faced with high psychological and physical stress levels with the threat of significant life disruption. This may lead to depression and lowered self-esteem as well as placing additional strain on the social support systems that are already trying to cope with the surgery process itself. This can be reduced with patient education and conditioning of expectations. Particularly in cancer patients, it may be desirable for information to be given about perioperative care in enhanced recovery in a subsequent separate session from the appointment when the diagnosis is discussed, as an acutely distressed patient is less likely to respond to opportunities to educate and shape expectations.

The enhanced recovery consensus is that preoperative information is beneficial and patient education should describe the patient's journey and condition expectations for the period of hospitalization. Intensive preoperative patient information facilitates postoperative recovery, reduces anxiety and pain, and improves postoperative self-care and symptom management, particularly in patients who exhibit the most denial and the highest levels of anxiety. Patient education and expectation management is currently believed to be central to a successful enhanced recovery program. Patients should be engaged in their recovery by being given tasks to perform and targets to meet during their postoperative period (eg, being able to drink, eat, and mobilize on the first full day following surgery). Preparing patients for surgery using education and conditioning of expectations may therefore induce physical changes that will improve outcome.

Summary

- Preoperative assessment is essential to identify and thereby facilitate modification of patient co-morbidity prior to surgery to improve recovery and reduce complications.
- The evaluation and optimization of the high-risk patient should be a multidisciplinary exercise.
- Attention to a patient's objectively measured physical fitness and other risk factors can identify patients requiring further specialist assessment prior to surgery.
- Smoking, alcohol cessation, and optimization of nutrition should be addressed preoperatively.
- Anemia should be treated preoperatively, where possible, to reduce the need for perioperative blood transfusion.
- Prehabilitation should be introduced as an integral part of the ERP for all major surgical patients.
- Conditioning patient expectations preoperatively improves patient recovery and reduces anxiety.

REFERENCES

1. García-Miguel FJ, Serrano-Aguilar PG, López-Bastida J. Preoperative assessment. *Lancet*. 2003;362:1749-1757.

2. National Collaborating Centre for Acute Care (UK). *Preoperative Tests: The Use of Routine Preoperative Tests for Elective Surgery*. London: National Collaborating Centre for Acute Care (UK); June 2003.

3. Chow WB, Rosenthal RA, Merkow RP, Ko CY, Esnaola NF; American College of Surgeons National Surgical Quality Improvement Program; American Geriatrics Society. Optimal preoperative assessment of the geriatric surgical patient: a best practices guideline from the American College of Surgeons National Surgical Quality Improvement Program and the American Geriatrics Society. *J Am Coll Surg*. 2012;215:453-466.

4. Copeland GP, Jones D, Walters M. POSSUM: a scoring system for surgical audit. *Br J Surg*. 1991;78:355-360.

5. Moonesinghe SR, Mythen MG, Das P, Rowan KM, Grocott MP. Risk stratification tools for predicting morbidity and mortality in adult patients undergoing major surgery: qualitative systematic review. *Anesthesiology*. 2013;119:959-981.

6. Brooks MJ, Sutton R, Sarin S. Comparison of Surgical Risk Score, POSSUM and p-POSSUM in higher-risk surgical patients. *Br J Surg*. 2005;92:1288-1292.

7. Struthers R, Erasmus P, Holmes K, Warman P, Collingwood A, Sneyd JR. Assessing fitness for surgery: a comparison of questionnaire, incremental shuttle walk, and cardiopulmonary exercise testing in general surgical patients. *Br J Anaesth*. 2008;101:774-780.

8. Hlatky MA, Boineau RE, Higginbotham MB, et al. A brief self-administered questionnaire to determine functional capacity (the Duke Activity Status Index). *Am J Cardiol*. 1989;64:651-654.

9. Fleisher LA, Beckman JA, Brown KA, et al; American College of Cardiology/American Heart Association Task Force on Practice Guidelines (Writing Committee to Revise the 2002 Guidelines on Perioperative Cardiovascular Evaluation for Noncardiac Surgery); American Society of Echocardiography; American Society of Nuclear Cardiology; Heart Rhythm Society; Society of Cardiovascular Anesthesiologists; Society for Cardiovascular Angiography and Interventions; Society for Vascular Medicine and Biology; Society for Vascular Surgery. ACC/AHA 2007 guidelines on perioperative cardiovascular

evaluation and care for noncardiac surgery: a report of the American College of Cardiology/American Heart Association Task Force on Practice Guidelines (Writing Committee to Revise the 2002 Guidelines on Perioperative Cardiovascular Evaluation for Noncardiac Surgery): developed in collaboration with the American Society of Echocardiography, American Society of Nuclear Cardiology, Heart Rhythm Society, Society of Cardiovascular Anesthesiologists, Society for Cardiovascular Angiography and Interventions, Society for Vascular Medicine and Biology, and Society for Vascular Surgery. *Circulation*. 2007;116:e418-e499.

10. Nutt CL, Russell JC. Use of the pre-operative shuttle walk test to predict morbidity and mortality after elective major colorectal surgery. *Anaesthesia*. 2012;67:839-849.

11. Murray P, Whiting P, Hutchinson SP, Ackroyd R, Stoddard CJ, Billings C. Preoperative shuttle walking testing and outcome after oesophagogastrectomy. *Br J Anaesth*. 2007;99:809-811.

12. Guazzi M, Dickstein K, Vicenzi M, Arena R. Six-minute walk test and cardiopulmonary exercise testing in patients with chronic heart failure: a comparative analysis on clinical and prognostic insights. *Circ Heart Fail*. 2009;2:549-555.

13. Ridgway ZA, Howell SJ. Cardiopulmonary exercise testing: a review of methods and applications in surgical patients. *Eur J Anaesthesiol*. 2010;27:858-865.

14. American Thoracic Society; American College of Chest Physicians. ATS/ACCP Statement on cardiopulmonary exercise testing. *Am J Respir Crit Care Med*. 2003;167:211-277.

15. O'Doherty AF, West M, Jack S, Grocott MP. Preoperative aerobic exercise training in elective intra-cavity surgery: a systematic review. *Br J Anaesth*. 2013;110:679-689.

16. Skalski J, Allison TG, Miller TD. The safety of cardiopulmonary exercise testing in a population with high-risk cardiovascular diseases. *Circulation*. 2012;126:2465-2472.

17. Keteyian SJ, Isaac D, Thadani U, et al; HF-ACTION Investigators. Safety of symptom-limited cardiopulmonary exercise testing in patients with chronic heart failure due to severe left ventricular systolic dysfunction. *Am Heart J*. 2009;158(4 Suppl):S72-S77.

18. Wilson RJ, Davies S, Yates D, Redman J, Stone M. Impaired functional capacity is associated with all-cause mortality after major elective intra-abdominal surgery. *Br J Anaesth*. 2010;105:297-303.

19. West MA, Lythgoe D, Barben CP, et al. Cardiopulmonary exercise variables are associated with postoperative morbidity after major colonic surgery: a prospective blinded observational study. *Br J Anaesth*. 2014;112:665-671.

20. West MA, Parry MG, Lythgoe D, et al. Cardiopulmonary exercise testing for the prediction of morbidity risk after rectal cancer surgery. *Br J Surg*. 2014;101:1166-1172.

21. Snowden CP, Prentis JM, Anderson HL, et al. Submaximal cardiopulmonary exercise testing predicts complications and hospital length of stay in patients undergoing major elective surgery. *Ann Surg*. 2010;251:535-541.

22. Carlisle J, Swart M. Mid-term survival after abdominal aortic aneurysm surgery predicted by cardiopulmonary exercise testing. *Br J Surg*. 2007;94:966-969.

23. Hennis PJ, Meale PM, Grocott MP. Cardiopulmonary exercise testing for the evaluation of perioperative risk in non-cardiopulmonary surgery. *Postgrad Med J*. 2011;87:550-557.

24. Miller TE, Roche AM, Mythen M. Fluid management and goal-directed therapy as an adjunct to Enhanced Recovery After Surgery (ERAS). *Can J Anaesth*. 2015;62:158-168.

25. Edwards M, Whittle J, Ackland GL. Biomarkers to guide perioperative management. *Postgrad Med J*. 2011;87:542-549.

26. Botto F, Alonso-Coello P, Chan MT, et al; Vascular events In noncardiac Surgery patIents cOhort evaluatioN (VISION) Writing Group, on behalf of The Vascular events In noncardiac Surgery patIents cOhort evaluatioN (VISION) Investigators; Appendix 1. The Vascular events In noncardiac Surgery patIents cOhort evaluatioN (VISION) Study Investigators Writing Group; Appendix 2. The Vascular events In noncardiac Surgery patIents cOhort evaluatioN Operations Committee; Vascular events In noncardiac Surgery patIents cOhort evaluation VISION Study Investigators. Myocardial injury after noncardiac surgery: a large, international, prospective cohort study establishing diagnostic criteria, characteristics, predictors, and 30-day outcomes. *Anesthesiology*. 2014;120:564-578.

27. Antithrombotic Trialists' Collaboration. Collaborative meta-analysis of randomised trials of antiplatelet therapy for prevention of death, myocardial infarction, and stroke in high risk patients. *BMJ*. 2002;324:71-86.

28. Khuri SF, Henderson WG, DePalma RG, Mosca C, Healey NA, Kumbhani DJ; Participants in the VA National Surgical Quality Improvement Program. Determinants of long-term survival after major surgery and the adverse effect of postoperative complications. *Ann Surg*. 2005;242:326-341.

29. Moonesinghe SR, Harris S, Mythen MG, et al. Survival after postoperative morbidity: a longitudinal observational cohort study. *Br J Anaesth*. 2014;113:977-984.

30. Fleisher LA, Beckman JA, Brown KA, et al. 2009 ACCF/AHA focused update on perioperative beta blockade incorporated into the ACC/AHA 2007 guidelines on perioperative cardiovascular evaluation and care for noncardiac surgery: a report of the American college of cardiology foundation/American heart association task force on practice guidelines. *Circulation*. 2009;120:e169-e276.

31. Thomsen T, Villebro N, Møller AM. Interventions for preoperative smoking cessation. *Cochrane Database Syst Rev*. 2014;3:CD002294.

32. Kondrup J, Rasmussen HH, Hamberg O, Stanga Z; Ad Hoc ESPEN Working Group. Nutritional risk screening (NRS 2002): a new method based on an analysis of controlled clinical trials. *Clin Nutr*. 2003;22:321-336.

33. Oppedal K, Møller AM, Pedersen B, Tønnesen H. Preoperative alcohol cessation prior to elective surgery. *Cochrane Database Syst Rev*. 2012;7:CD008343.

34. Valkenet K, van de Port IG, Dronkers JJ, de Vries WR, Lindeman E, Backx FJ. The effects of preoperative exercise therapy on postoperative outcome: a systematic review. *Clin Rehabil*. 2011;25:99-111.

35. Mayo NE, Feldman L, Scott S, et al. Impact of preoperative change in physical function on postoperative recovery: argument supporting prehabilitation for colorectal surgery. *Surgery*. 2011;150:505-514.

36. West MA, Loughney L, Lythgoe D, et al. Effect of prehabilitation on objectively measured physical fitness after neoadjuvant treatment in preoperative rectal cancer patients: a blinded interventional pilot study. *Br J Anaesth*. 2015;114:244-251.

5

Prehabilitation for Abdominopelvic Surgery:
Helping Patients Recover Faster

by EM Minnella, MD, G Bousquet-Dion, MD, and F Carli, MD, MPhil

Preoperative Health Status and Postoperative Complications

Postoperative complications occur after abdominal surgery at a rate of 30%[1] and, even in the absence of morbid events, there is a 40% reduction in functional capacity.[2] After surgery, patients complain of physical fatigue, poor sleep, and decreased capacity of concentration. Persistent long periods of physical inactivity induce loss of muscle mass, deconditioning, pulmonary complications, and decubitus.

There is sufficient published evidence that preoperative health status, functional capacity, and muscle strength correlate with postoperative fatigue, medical complications, and postoperative cognitive disturbances, and this is particularly true in the elderly, persons with cancer, and persons with limited physiologic and mental reserve who are the most susceptible to the negative effects of surgery.[3]

Potential Benefits of Prehabilitation

Traditionally rehabilitative interventions occur after surgery; however, this is not the best period as patients are tired, anxious, and thus unwilling to be engaged. The preoperative period may in fact be a more appropriate time since patients are waiting for final tests and are more eager to be engaged in activities related to health. The process of enhancing functional capacity of the individual to enable him or her to withstand an incoming stressor has been termed *prehabilitation.*

Conventionally, patients are prepared for the stresses of surgery through education, but the use of a multimodal intervention that includes physical activity before surgery is not routinely practiced. The benefits of physical activity have been shown to prevent many chronic conditions and to decrease the incidence of ischemic heart disease, hypertension, diabetes, stroke, and fractures in the elderly. The benefits of regular physical activity include better aerobic capacity, decreased sympathetic overreactivity, improved insulin sensitivity, and increased ratio of lean body mass to body fat.

With the introduction of enhanced recovery protocols (ERP)[4] based on evidence, surgical prehabilitation has a relevant position in the preoperative clinic where the patient's risk assessment is considered and evaluated, and if necessary, the program is implemented.

Clinical Impact of Prehabilitation

The impact of physical activity has been studied in different types of surgery, and two recent meta-analyses[5,6] concluded that preoperative exercise therapy contributed to decreased postoperative complication rates and accelerated hospital discharge in patients undergoing cardiac and abdominal surgery. Also, there was a beneficial effect from inspiratory muscle training with less risk of postoperative pulmonary complications.

While physical activity remains the main part of multimodal prehabilitation, it is necessary to consider other factors such as adequate nutrition, glycemic control, smoking cessation, alcohol reduction, pharmacological and medical optimization, and strategies to allay anxiety such as imagery, relaxation, deep breathing exercises, and yoga. There is a strong evidence that prehabilitation mitigates treatment-related morbidity in cancer patients.[7] Further studies are needed to determine the impact of prehabilitation as part of preoperative optimization on clinical outcomes.

How Long Is Prehabilitation?

Although there is no evidence for a specific duration of prehabilitation, meaningful changes in functional capacity will take 4 to 5 weeks. Within this framework of time, considerations have to be made with regard to the type of surgery, the conditions of the patient, the capacity to undertake exercise, and the interaction with other factors.

Who Could Benefit?

Patients with low functional, physiological reserve such as the elderly, frail, and sarcopenic patients could benefit from the prehabilitation in preparing themselves for the stress of surgery and recovery.

Elements of Prehabilitation

■ Medical Optimization

The presence of comorbid medical conditions is an important determinant of a patient's functional reserve, which is why preoperative screening is crucial in identifying potential risk factors for surgery. Some risk factors cannot be modified, for example age, type of surgery, extent of disease, pre-existing end-organ damage, or presence of disseminated cancer.

On the other hand, there are modifiable elements, such as body mass index (BMI), comorbidities, and functional health status.[8] These factors can be influenced by the exercise and nutrition component of the prehabilitation program, but a more medical approach may be necessary to further enhance functional reserve. A central role in preoperative medicine is to optimize status of conditions that increase morbidity and mortality associated with surgery, such as cardiovascular disease, COPD, anemia, and diabetes.[9]

■ Role of Exercise

Physical fitness has benefits in almost every context of health and disease. Training interventions are related to better outcomes in coronary artery disease, heart failure, diabetes, COPD, depression, dementia, chronic kidney disease, stroke, and cancer.[10] Studies in colorectal cancer found that disease recurrence and overall mortality may be decreased with physical activity,[11] eg, 150 minutes of aerobic activity per week, and muscle-strengthening exercises up to 2 days per week. Regular exercise has been shown to cause positive changes in functional capacity in all ages and settings, and also in postoperative cancer survivors (rehabilitation).[7] Recent data have demonstrated the role of presurgical exercise training programs (prehabilitation) to enhance functional capacity before major colorectal resection for cancer,[12] even after neoadjuvant therapy.[13]

Important elements are physical assessment and subsequent training design. Medical and physical history (encompassing previous injuries and range of motion limits) must be taken and a complete functional assessment must be performed, as explained below. An individualized training program is designed on the basis of these results. Fitness goals must be realistic, specific, measurable, time-based, and easily modified. After surgery patients may experience fatigue, new medical conditions or physical limitations, and sleep disorders. Redefining the training is mandatory to guarantee compliance, and safety, and correctly evaluate the benefits of exercise. For example, maintaining baseline functional capacity after surgery rather than progressing is a realistic target. Given the above, the primary aim of this program is to increase exercise intensity during the preoperative period.

Assessment and Training Design

- Define physical fitness levels
- Anthropometric data, skinfold and body composition (bioelectrical impedance analysis or similar tools)

- Functional capacity: 6-minute walking test (6MWT), timed up-and-go test, cardio-pulmonary exercise testing (CPET)
- Strength: curl test, grip strength test
• Define goal, program, and progression
- Type of exercise, divided in three major components: aerobic exercise, resistance exercise, and static and dynamic balance and flexibility:
  • Aerobic training is moderate-intensity activity involving large muscle groups using oxygen-supplied energy. It is done to increase cardiovascular and respiratory endurance, evaluated as the ability to take in, transport, and utilize oxygen.
  • Resistance training implies that muscles work or hold against an applied force or weight. The main purpose is to prevent or even reverse the usual decline in muscle mass, strength, and functional ability of surgical patients.
  • Balance is the process of controlling the body's center of mass with respect to its base of support, whether the body is stationary or moving. Static balance refers to that ability while relatively still, such as while quietly standing; dynamic balance refers to that ability while leaning or moving through space. Joint range-of-motion (ROM) exercises could improve flexibility.

The aim of any prehabilitation exercise protocol is to promote a comprehensive improvement in physical activity. All the different modes of training are integrated and cooperative (**Figure 5**.1). An example of an exercise program is shown in **Table 5**.1.

• Exercise intensity for endurance-type activity could be defined using:
  - Maximal heart rate (HR_{max}): calculated with the traditional age-predicted equation: HR_{max}

FIGURE 5.1 — **Synergistic Effect of Exercise Program Components**

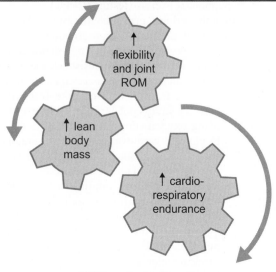

ROM — *Range of motion*

Synergistic effect of the three goals of the exercise program, which are to increase lean body mass, cardiopulmonary endurance, and flexibility and range of motion.

= 220 – age (years); or heart rate reserve (HRR) = HR_{max} – HR_{rest}.
– Borg scale (rate of perceived exertion [RPE]), a well-validated index that rates the perceived exertion, in which 6 represents resting activity with no effort, and 20 represents all-out, exhaustive exercise.
- Exercise intensity for resistance activity could be defined as a relative intensity to maximal voluntary contraction, based on the one repetition maximum (1RM), the maximum amount of force that can be generated in one maximal contraction. (See **Table 5.2** for the reference values adopted from the American College of Sport Medicine.[14])

- Duration, which is dependent on the intensity of the activity. Usually, 20 to 40 minutes of endurance-type exercise (minimum of 10 minutes) is prescribed. There are two principal types of aerobic training: a steady-state or ramped exercise (eg, continuous training at moderate intensity), and an intense intermittent endurance training (eg, 1 to 2 minutes of high-intensity exercise followed by 3 minutes of rest or light exercise)

■ Role of Nutrition

Preoperative malnutrition has independently been identified as a predictor for mortality in major abdominal surgery. The nutritional status of these patients is influenced by their age, concurrent medical therapies including radiotherapy and chemotherapy, and comorbid conditions leading to chronic inflammation such as cancer and inflammatory bowel disease. Without intervention, surgical patients already in nutritional deficit would enter the postoperative catabolic state with no macronutrients reserve.[4] An increased circulatory level of cytokines and catecholamines due to the surgical stress intensifies this catabolism. The resultant proteolysis, lipolysis, and gluconeogenesis make macronutrients more readily available in the post-stress period but at the price of muscle mass loss, impaired wound healing, and impaired glucose tolerance.

The nutrition component of the multimodal prehabilitation program aims to ensure that patients can build a nutritional reserve for the postsurgical period. Such a reserve is achieved by optimizing caloric and protein intake through nutritional counseling and supplementation and has been shown to offer gains in tissue regeneration and immunological functions.

More specifically, dietary supplementation with whey protein extract, which is rich in leucine, contributes to better muscular protein synthesis by activating the mTOR cell-signaling pathway. Whey protein has secretagogue properties at the level of the pancreatic beta islet cells. It also has anti-inflammatory properties

TABLE 5.1 — Exercise Program

Exercise	Frequency	Duration, Intensity, and RPE for Weeks 1–2	Progression
Warm Up	Before every session	30-HRR • Posture • Deep breathing • Joint range-of-motion exercises	NA
Cardiovascular Training	Mon, Wed, Thu (steady-state aerobic training)	20 min, 45% HRR, 12 RPE	Progressive up to 65% HRR, 15 RPE
	Sat (aerobic intervals)	24.5 min total or seven sets of 30 at 85% HRR, 15 RPE + 3-min rest between sets at 35% HRR, 10 RPE	Progressive up to 12 sets of 1 min at 85% HRR, 16 RPE + rest
Resistance Training	Tue	45 min, 60% of 1RM (15 reps per set), 3 sets per exercise, 14 RPE. • Lower body multi-joint: step-ups, machine hamstring curl, lunges	Progressive up to weeks 9-12: 50 min, 85% of 1RM (six reps per set), 1-min rest between sets, four sets per exercise, 17 RPE

	• Upper body multi-joint: machine incline bench press, push-ups or modified push-ups, latissimus pull-down, seated row • Upper body single-joint: triceps extension, barbell biceps curl, sit-ups (abdominal crunches)	Progressive up to weeks 9-12: 50 min, 85% of 1RM (six reps per set), 1-min rest between sets, four sets per exercise, 17 RPE
Fri	45 min, 60% of 1RM (15 reps per set), 3 sets per exercise, 14 RPE. • Lower body multi-joint: step-ups, machine hamstring curl, lunges • Upper body multi-joint: machine incline bench press, push-ups or modified push-ups, latissimus pull-down, seated row • Upper body single-joint: triceps extension, barbell biceps curl, sit-ups (abdominal crunches)	
Flexibility	Static stretches of about 20-30 s for each muscle group	

Key: HRR, maximal heart rate; RPE, rating of perceived exertion (Borg scale); 1RM, one repetition maximum.

TABLE 5.2 — Intensity Classification Based on the American College of Sports Position Stand (1998)

Intensity	Cardiorespiratory Endurance Exercise		Resistance Exercise
	HRR %	*RPE*	*% 1 RM*
Very light	<30	<9	<30
Light	30-39	9-11	30-49
Moderate	40-59	12-13	50-69
Vigorous	60-89	14-17	70-84
Near-maximal to maximal	≥90	≥18	≥85

Key: HRR, maximal heart rate; RPE, Borg scale; 1RM, one repetition maximum.

Modified from ACSM's Guidelines for Exercise Testing and Prescription. *American College of Sports Medicine*, 8th ed. 2010. Philadelphia, PA: Lippincott Williams & Wilkins:366.

by increasing glutathione (GSH) which neutralizes the reactive oxygen species (ROS) signaling during the cytokines acute phase response.[3]

In a 2014 RCT, a population of patients undergoing colorectal surgery for cancer received a 4-week nutrition-only prehabilitation program consisting of daily 1.2 to 1.5 g/kg of whey protein supplementation.[15] It was observed that the functional walking capacity (assessed by the 6MWT) increased in a clinically significant manner in more than 50% of the subjects vs 31% in the placebo group. There is also evidence supporting the use of an immunologically active nutritional formula containing arginine and omega-3 fatty acid, pre- and postoperatively in major gastrointestinal surgery. Benefits of such formulas include lower infection rates and shorter length of stay.[16]

■ Nutrition and Physical Activity Integration

The premise of the multimodal prehabilitation approach with a nutrition and physical exercise component rests on their synergy. Achieving recommended daily caloric and protein intake helps patients perform better during their exercise session, which in turn increases the efficiency of muscular protein synthesis from dietary and supplementary amino acids. The resultant increase in lean body mass, intramuscular protein stores, and overall strength and endurance helps patients to regain their baseline functionality level faster after major abdominal surgery.[12]

■ Psychological Intervention

The preoperative period is a difficult time for patients as they are afraid of the unknown. The level of psychological distress is associated with the diagnosis and required medical therapy, eg, neoadjuvant therapy for cancer. Depression and anxiety have been linked to longer hospital stay, more frequent readmissions, and longer wound healing. The physical exercise component of multimodal prehabilitation is already known to decrease emotional distress.

Involving patients in their healing process with the physical exercise and nutrition aspect as well as providing them with relaxing music and visualization exercises has had positive psychological effects noted on health-related quality of life questionnaires (SF-36).[12] Other interventions that are part of ERPs, such as giving information booklets, have been observed to decrease length of stay, decrease demand for analgesia, and increase patient satisfaction.[4]

Conclusions

Many multidisciplinary prehabilitation programs that incorporate innovative, comprehensive preoperative risk evaluation need to be developed, tested, implemented, and directed to patients, especially those at risk. The integrated role of physical exercise, adequate nutrition, and psychosocial balance, together with medical and pharmacologic optimization, within the context of an enhanced recovery program, can contribute to better quality of clinical care (**Figure 5.2**).

REFERENCES

1. Lawson EH, Wang X, Cohen ME, Hall BL, Tanzman H, Ko CY. Morbidity and mortality after colorectal procedures: comparison of data from the American College of Surgeons case log system and the ACS NSQIP. *J Am Coll Surg*. 2011;212:1077-1085.

2. Christensen T, Kehlet H. Postoperative fatigue. *World J Surg*. 1993;17:220-225.

3. Carli F, Scheede-Bergdahl C. Prehabilitation to enhance perioperative care. *Anesthesiol Clin*. 2015;33:17-33.

4. Lassen K, Soop M, Nygren J, et al; Enhanced Recovery After Surgery (ERAS) Group. Consensus review of optimal perioperative care in colorectal surgery: Enhanced Recovery After Surgery (ERAS) Group recommendations. *Arch Surg*. 2009;144:961-969.

5. Valkenet K, van de Port IG, Dronkers JJ, de Vries WR, Lindeman E, Backx FJ. The effects of preoperative exercise therapy on postoperative outcome: a systematic review. *Clin Rehabil*. 2011;25:99-111.

6. Santa Mina D, Clarke H, Ritvo P, et al. Effect of total-body prehabilitation on postoperative outcomes: a systematic review and meta-analysis. *Physiotherapy*. 2014;100:196-207.

7. Silver JK, Baima J. Cancer prehabilitation: an opportunity to decrease treatment-related morbidity, increase cancer treatment options, and improve physical and psychological health outcomes. *Am J Phys Med Rehabil*. 2013;92:715-727.

8. Parks RM, Rostoft S, Ommundsen N, Cheung KL. Peri-operative management of older adults with cancer. The roles of the surgeon and geriatrician. *Cancers (Basel)*. 2015;7:1605-1621.

9. Miller RD, Cohen NH, Eriksson LI, Fleisher LA, Wiener-Kronish JP, Young WL. *Miller's Anesthesia*. 8th ed. Vol. 1. Philadelphia, PA: Elsevier Saunders; 2015.

10. Carli F, Zavorsky GS. Optimizing functional exercise capacity in the elderly surgical population. *Curr Opin Clin Nutr Metab Care*. 2005;8:23-32.

11. Van Blarigan EL, Meyerhardt JA. Role of physical activity and diet after colorectal cancer diagnosis. *J Clin Oncol*. 2015;33:1825-1834.

12. Gillis C, Li C, Lee L, et al. Prehabilitation versus rehabilitation: a randomized control trial in patients undergoing colorectal resection for cancer. *Anesthesiology*. 2014;121:937-947.

5

FIGURE 5.2 — Interaction and Effects of the Prehabilitation Components on Functional Capacity

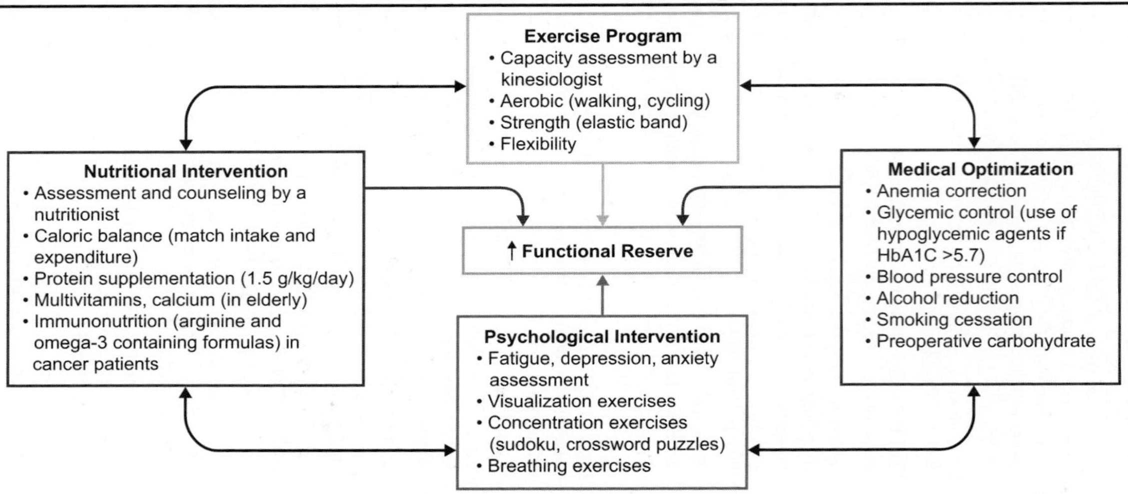

Medical Optimization
· Anemia correction
· Glycemic control (use of hypoglycemic agents if HbA1C >5.7)
· Blood pressure control
· Alcohol reduction
· Smoking cessation
· Preoperative carbohydrate

Exercise Program
· Capacity assessment by a kinesiologist
· Aerobic (walking, cycling)
· Strength (elastic band)
· Flexibility

↑ Functional Reserve

Psychological Intervention
· Fatigue, depression, anxiety assessment
· Visualization exercises
· Concentration exercises (sudoku, crossword puzzles)
· Breathing exercises

Nutritional Intervention
· Assessment and counseling by a nutritionist
· Caloric balance (match intake and expenditure)
· Protein supplementation (1.5 g/kg/day)
· Multivitamins, calcium (in elderly)
· Immunonutrition (arginine and omega-3 containing formulas) in cancer patients

Individual program components are made more efficient with the help of the other components. For example, appropriate caloric intake, protein supplementation, and anemia correction increase the benefits of the exercise program that then offer psychological advantages. Moreover, multiple components of the program can help achieve a goal. The exercise program, nutritional intervention, and use of hypoglycemic agents can help to achieve glycemic control.

5

13. West MA, Loughney L, Lythgoe D, et al. Effect of prehabilitation on objectively measured physical fitness after neoadjuvant treatment in preoperative rectal cancer patients: a blinded interventional pilot study. *Br J Anaesth.* 2015;114:244-251.

14. Thompson WR, Gordon Neil F, Pescatello LS. *ACSM's Guidelines for Exercise Testing and Prescription.* 8th ed. Baltimore, MD: American College of Sports Medicine; 2010.

15. Gillis C, Loiselle SE, Fiore JF Jr, et al. Prehabilitation with whey protein supplementation on perioperative functional exercise capacity in patients undergoing colorectal resection for cancer: a pilot double-blinded randomized placebo-controlled trial. *J Acad Nutr Diet.* 2015;pii:S2212-S2672.

16. Drover JW, Dhaliwal R, Weitzel L, Wischmeyer PE, Ochoa JB, Heyland DK. Perioperative use of arginine-supplemented diets: a systematic review of the evidence. *J Am Coll Surg.* 2011;212:385-399.

6

Preoperative Antiemetic and Analgesic Management

by Lawrence Siu-Chun Law, MD,
Elaine Ah-Gi Lo, PharmD, BCPS, and
Tong Joo Gan, MD, FRCA, MHS, LiAc

Introduction

Suboptimal management of postoperative nausea and vomiting (PONV) and pain may prolong postanesthesia care unit (PACU) and hospital stay. Reducing PONV and optimizing pain control are two key components of an enhanced recovery protocol (ERP). PONV and postoperative pain are very common. The incidences of postoperative nausea and vomiting are approximately 50% and 30%, respectively, in general.[1] Around 75% of patients experienced moderate-to-severe postoperative pain and the pain continued after discharge in 74% of these patients.[2] Instead of managing PONV and pain reactively after surgery, preoperative antiemetic and analgesic management is preferred and recommended. This chapter will discuss the assessment for the risk of PONV, treatment strategies for PONV, and analgesic regimens, in the context of enhanced recovery.

Assessment for the Risk of PONV

The assessment for the risk of PONV determines the choice of antiemetic regimen. The well-established risk factors include female sex, history of PONV or motion sickness, nonsmoker, younger age, use of inhalational agents, opioids, duration of anesthesia, and type of surgery (abdominal surgery, cholecystectomy, laparoscopic surgery, and gynecological surgery).[1]

A simplified risk score from Apfel and colleagues[3] estimates the incidence of PONV (**Figure 6.1**).

Treatment Strategies for PONV in the Context of Enhanced Recovery

Modifiable risk factor management and prophylactic antiemetic agents are equally important in preventing PONV. Strategies to minimize the baseline risk are shown in **Table 6.1**. In the context of enhanced recovery, multimodal PONV prevention strategies are preferred over the conventional "no prevention" for patients with low PONV risk. The algorithm is summarized in **Figure 6.2**. If the prophylaxis for PONV fails, a different class of antiemetics should be used. It is ineffective to re-administer the same class of antiemetic agents within 6 hours. Dexamethasone and transdermal scopolamine are long acting and do not need repeat dosing within 24 to 48 hours. The recommended dosage and timing of administering antiemetic agents are shown in **Table 6.2**.

Analgesic Regimens in the Context of Enhanced Recovery

Intraoperative and postoperative opioids are the main drugs for pain control in conventional regimens. However, the adverse effects of opioids, for instance, PONV, constipation/ileus, sedation, respiratory depression, and urinary retention, may delay the recovery of patients. In ERPs, the use of opioids should be minimized by adopting multimodal analgesic regimens. Modalities other than opioids include neuraxial/regional anesthesia, local anesthesia, acetaminophen (paracetamol), nonsteroidal anti-inflammatory drugs (NSAID), systemic lidocaine or ketamine infusion, long-acting local anesthetics, and gabapentinoids (gabapentin/pregabalin).[4] Out of these modalities, neuraxial/regional anesthesia, acetaminophen, and NSAIDs

FIGURE 6.1 — Risk Score for PONV in Adults

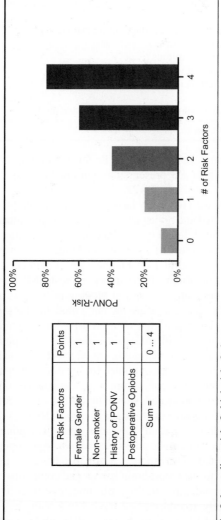

Risk Factors	Points
Female Gender	1
Non-smoker	1
History of PONV	1
Postoperative Opioids	1
Sum =	0 … 4

Low risk: 0-1, medium risk: 2, high risk: 3-4.

Adapted from Gan TJ, et al. *Anesth Analg*. 2014;118:85-113.

TABLE 6.1 — Strategies to Reduce Baseline Risk of PONV

• Avoidance of general anesthesia by the use of regional anesthesia
• Use of propofol for induction and maintenance of anesthesia
• Avoidance of nitrous oxide
• Avoidance of volatile anesthetics
• Minimization of intraoperative and postoperative opioids
• Adequate hydration, but avoid excessive fluid

Gan TJ et al. *Anesth. Analg.* 2014;118:85–113.

appear most frequently in ERPs for abdominopelvic surgery. **Table 6.3** presents the multimodal analgesic regimens in different ERPs.

ERPs with relatively large numbers of participants were selected and reviewed for the purpose of comparison between different types of abdominopelvic surgery. Although a variety of analgesic modalities were used, thoracic epidural at T7-10 is the core of pain control for open abdominopelvic surgery in most ERPs.[5] For laparoscopic surgery, spinal block and transversus abdominis plane block are the main modality for pain control.[5] On top of the neuraxial/regional blocks, systemic nonopioid analgesics, like acetaminophen, NSAIDs, and gabapentinoids are effective adjuvants. Opioids are the drugs of choice for breakthrough pain or in the case of block failure. If a neuraxial/regional block is contraindicated, wound infiltration or systemic ketamine/lidocaine infusion may be considered.

If opioids are used, peripheral opioid antagonists (eg, alvimopan) can be considered to reduce postoperative ileus and constipation.[6,7] Alvimopan has a low permeability to the blood-brain barrier and competitively binds mu-receptors in the gastrointestinal tract. It is given orally at a dose of 12 mg 0.5 to 5 hours before surgery and 12 mg every 12 hours after surgery for up to 7 days. Alvimopan is contraindicated in patients who have taken therapeutic doses of opioids for more than 7 consecutive days immediately prior to use.

Summary

To enhance the recovery process of surgical patients, proactive management of PONV and post-operative pain is crucial. Prophylactic antiemetics are advised even in the group with low risk of PONV in the context of enhanced recovery as the benefits likely outweigh the risks for most antiemetics. Thoracic epidural is recommended for open abdominal procedures unless contraindicated. **Figure 6.2** and **Figure 6.3** are flow charts for multimodal antiemetic and analgesic management summarizing this chapter.

6

REFERENCES

1. Gan TJ, Diemunsch P, Habib AS, et al; Society for Ambulatory Anesthesia. Consensus guidelines for the management of post-operative nausea and vomiting. *Anesth Analg.* 2014;118:85-113.

2. Gan TJ, Habib AS, Miller TE, White W, Apfelbaum JL. Incidence, patient satisfaction, and perceptions of post-surgical pain: results from a US national survey. *Curr Med Res Opin.* 2014;30:149-160.

3. Apfel CC, Läärä E, Koivuranta M, Greim CA, Roewer N. A simplified risk score for predicting postoperative nausea and vomiting: conclusions from cross-validations between two centers. *Anesthesiology.* 1999;91:693-700.

4. Tan M, Law LS, Gan TJ. Optimizing pain management to facilitate Enhanced Recovery After Surgery pathways. *Can J Anaesth.* 2015;62:203-218.

5. Fawcett WJ, Baldini G. Optimal analgesia during major open and laparoscopic abdominal surgery. *Anesthesiol Clin.* 2015;33:65-78.

6. Tan EK, Cornish J, Darzi AW, Tekkis PP. Meta-analysis: alvimopan vs. placebo in the treatment of post-operative ileus. *Aliment Pharmacol Ther.* 2007;25:47-57.

7. Lee CT, Chang SS, Kamat AM, et al. Alvimopan accelerates gastrointestinal recovery after radical cystectomy: a multicenter randomized placebo-controlled trial. *Eur Urol.* 2014;66:265-272.

FIGURE 6.2 — Flow Chart for Management of PONV in the Context of Enhanced Recovery

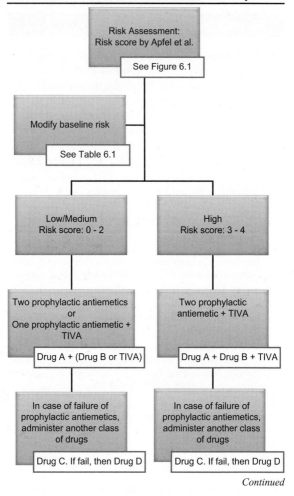

Risk Assessment:
Risk score by Apfel et al.

See Figure 6.1

Modify baseline risk

See Table 6.1

Low/Medium
Risk score: 0 - 2

High
Risk score: 3 - 4

Two prophylactic antiemetics
or
One prophylactic antiemetic +
TIVA

Drug A + (Drug B or TIVA)

Two prophylactic
antiemetic + TIVA

Drug A + Drug B + TIVA

In case of failure of
prophylactic antiemetics,
administer another class
of drugs

Drug C. If fail, then Drug D

In case of failure of
prophylactic antiemetics,
administer another class
of drugs

Drug C. If fail, then Drug D

Continued

FIGURE 6.2 — *Continued*

Example interventions: Drug A = Dexamethasone 4 mg in adults, or 0.15 mg/kg of body weight in children; Drug B = Ondansetron 4 mg in adults, or 0.1 mg/kg of body weight in children; Drug C = Promethazine 6.25 mg in adults; Drug D = Dimenhydrinate 1 mg/kg of body weight in adults, or 0.5 to 1.0 mg/kg of body weight in children. The given drug examples are used to illustrate how the algorithm may be actually implemented but may not represent the most favorable approach. The latter may be context-sensitive (children, adults or other issues). In the event of treatment failure, timely assessment is essential and an alternative antiemetic agent should be used. A multimodal treatment approach may be appropriate to increase the likelihood of success. TIVA = total intravenous anesthesia, that is, propofol induction and maintenance, no nitrous oxide. See Table 6.2 for the choices of antiemetic agents.

Adapted from Gan TJ, et al. *Anesth Analg.* 2014;118:85-113.

TABLE 6.2 — Choices of Antiemetic Agents: Dosage and Timing

Drugs	Dose	Timing
Neurokinin 1 (NK1) receptor antagonists		
Aprepitant	40 mg PO	At induction
Corticosteroids		
Dexamethasone	4–5 mg IV	At induction
Methylprednisolone	40 mg IV	
Phenothiazines		
Promethazine	6.25 - 12.5 mg IV	
Perphenazine	5 mg IV	
5-hydroxytryptamine receptor 3 (5-HT₃ receptor) antagonists		
Granisetron	0.35–3 mg IV	End of surgery
Ondansetron	4 mg IV	End of surgery
Palonosetron	0.075 mg IV	At induction
Ramosetron	0.3 mg IV	End of surgery

Dolasetron	12.5 mg IV	End of surgery; timing may not affect efficacy
Tropisetron	2 mg IV	End of surgery
Antihistamines		
Dimenhydrinate	1 mg/kg IV	
Anticholinergic agents		
Scopolamine	Transdermal patch	Prior evening or 2 h before surgery
Butyrophenones		
Droperidol	0.625–1.25 mg IV	End of surgery
Haloperidol	0.5–<2 mg IM/IV	
Sympathomimetic amine		
Ephedrine	0.5 mg/kg IM	

PO, per os/oral; IM, intramuscular; IV, intravenous.

Gan TJ, et al. *Anesth. Analg.* 2014;118:85-113.

TABLE 6.3 — Multimodal Analgesic Regimens in Enhanced Recovery Protocol for Abdominopelvic Surgery

Surgery Type	Preoperative Analgesia	Intraoperative Analgesia	Postoperative Analgesia	Outcomes
Open or laparoscopic colorectal surgery [Miller et al. 2014]	- Thoracic epidurals placed at the T8-T10 level in preoperative holding area, together with small doses of midazolam and fentanyl to facilitate epidural insertion and maintain patient comfort	- Single epidural bolus of hydromorphone at induction (0.4-0.8 mg based on body weight), followed by bupivacaine infusion (2.5 mg/mL at 3-6 mL/hr) - Generally no intraoperative IV opioids given after induction	- Epidural local anesthetic/opioid infusion (0.125% bupivacaine and hydromorphone 10 mcg/mL) for up to 72 hr - Adjunctive analgesia with acetaminophen and NSAIDs whenever possible - Transition to oral opioids after removal of epidural catheter	- Significantly less total postoperative morphine equivalents (mg) required [median (range) 29.8 (10-85) mg vs 120 (69-267) mg] - Significantly lower average (SD) pain scores throughout days 0 to 5 [3.3 (1.9) vs 4.9 (2.1)] - Significantly shorter median hospital LOS (5 vs 7 days)
Gynecologic surgery (Complex cytoreductive, staging and pelvic organ	- Celecoxib 400 mg po once - Acetaminophen 1000 mg po once - Gabapentin 600 mg po once	- IV opioids at discretion of anesthesiologist supplemented with ketamine, ketorolac, or both	- Goal: no PCA - Oxycodone 5-10 mg po q4 h prn pain [3 or greater stated comfort goal (5 mg for pain rated 4-6 or 10 mg for pain rated 7-10); for patients who	- Significantly decreased PCA opioid use (98.7% vs 33.3%) and postoperative opioid use (80% decrease in the first 48 hr) with no change in pain scores

| prolapse surgeries [Kalogera et al. 2014] | - Local anesthetic infiltration of bupivacaine at incision site after closure | received intrathecal analgesia, start 24 hr after intrathecal dose
- Acetaminophen 1 g po q6-12 h
- Ketorolac 15 mg IV q6 h for 4 doses, then ibuprofen 800 mg po q6 h. For NSAID-intolerant patients, tramadol 100 mg po q6-12 hr starting on POD 1
- For breakthrough pain (pain more than 7 more than 1 hr after receiving oxycodone, hydromorphone 0.4 mg IV once if patient did not receive intrathecal medications; may repeat once after 20 min if first dose ineffective
- Hydromorphone PCA started only if continued pain despite 2 doses of IV hydromorphone | - Significantly shorter hospital LOS (4-day reduction)
- Significantly faster return of bowel function [median (interquartile range) 3 (2-3) days vs 4 (3-5) days] and staging surgeries [2 (1-3) days vs 2 (2-3) days]
- Significantly faster return to general diet (1-5 days median difference)
- No difference in rate of severity of 30-day complications (ileus, bowel perforation, anastomotic leak, abscess) or mortality
- No difference in 30-day readmission rates or stay
- Insignificant 30-day cost savings of > $7600 USD per patient (18.8% reduction) |

Continued

TABLE 6.3 — *Continued*

Surgery Type	Preoperative/Intraoperative Analgesia	Postoperative Analgesia	Outcomes
Radical cystectomy [Xu et al. 2015; Daneshmand et al. 2014)	- IV or oral acetaminophen and/or ketorolac - Para-incisional subfascial catheters to continuously infuse local anesthestics	- Oral pain medications started on POD 1 - IV morphine or oral opioids for breakthrough pain	- Shorter LOS [mean (SD) 4 (2) days vs 8 (6.4) days] - Less postoperative ileus [7.3% vs 22.2%] - Lower estimated blood loss (400 mL vs 600 mL) - Less opioids consumption (total 24.08 mg vs 102.48 mg), but more pain (VAS 3.1/10 vs 1.14/10)
Radical cystectomy [Cerantola et al. 2013: Guidelines from ERAS society)	Thoracic epidural analgesia is superior to systemic opioids in relieving pain. It should be continued for 72 h	A multimodal postoperative analgesia should include thoracic epidural analgesia	- Evidence for cystectomy: not available - Evidence for rectal surgery: high
Pancreatic Surgery [Balzano et al. 2008)	Placement of thoracic epidural catheter (T7-T9 level) with continuous infusion of bupivacaine 0.125% with fentanyl 2 μg/mL at a rate of 4-6 mL/h until day 5, plus IV acetaminophen or NSAIDs, or,	Epidural catheter removal on POD 5	Unlikely related to the change of analgesic regime - Shorter LOS [median (range) 13 (7-110) vs 15 (7-102) days]

			- Shorter time to pass stools [median (range) 5 (1-9) vs 6 (1-10) days]
			- Shorter LOS [median (range) 4 (2-11) vs 6 (4-16) days] - Lower total number of complications (60 vs 99)
	if epidural catheter is contraindicated, patient-controlled analgesia with morphine, plus IV acetaminophen or NSAIDs		
Liver resection (Savikko et al. 2015)	Epidural at T7-8 or T8-9 level with continuous infusion of 0.2% ropivacaine + fentanyl 5-7.5mcg/mL. If epidural is contradicted or failed, inserting a wound infiltration catheter with continuous infusion of 0.2% ropivacaine into the preperitoneal space along the upper margin of the sub-costal incision before wound closure	- Epidural or wound catheter was used for 0-48 h, and was usually removed on POD 3 morning - Pregabalin 50-100 mg bd - ibuprofen 400-800 mg tds or acetaminophen 500-1000 mg tid - Extended-release tramadol 75-150 mg bd to wean off epidural - Oral oxycodone (0.1-0.2 mg/kg) for severe pain	

Key: ERAS, enhanced recovery after surgery; IQR, interquartile range; IV, intravenous; LOS, length of stay; NSAIDs, nonsteroidal anti-inflammatory drugs; PACU, postanesthesia care unit; PCA, patient-controlled analgesia; po, oral; POD, postoperative day; PONV, postoperative nausea and vomiting; VAS, visual analogue scale.

Modified from Tan M et al. *Can J Anesth.* 2014;62:203-218.

6

FIGURE 6.3 — Flow Chart of Analgesic Regimen in an ERP

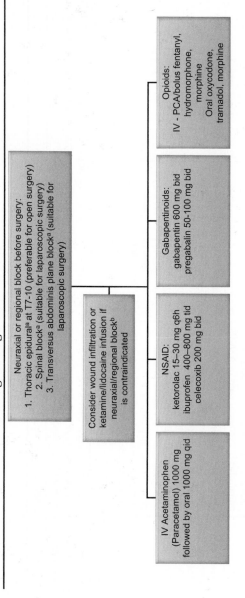

Neuraxial or regional block before surgery:
1. Thoracic epidural[a] at T7-10 (preferable for open surgery)
2. Spinal block[a] (suitable for laparoscopic surgery)
3. Transversus abdominis plane block[a] (suitable for laparoscopic surgery)

Consider wound infiltration or ketamine/lidocaine infusion if neuraxial/regional block[b] is contraindicated

IV Acetaminophen (Paracetamol) 1000 mg followed by oral 1000 mg qid

NSAID:
ketorolac 15–30 mg q6h
ibuprofen 400–800 mg tid
celecoxib 200 mg bid

Gabapentinoids:
gabapentin 600 mg bid
pregabalin 50-100 mg bid

Opioids:
IV - PCA/bolus fentanyl, hydromorphone, morphine
Oral oxycodone, tramadol, morphine

[a] Example 1: thoracic epidural with intraoperatively 0.25% bupivacaine or 0.2% ropivacaine, postoperatively 0.125% bupivacaine ± hydromorphone 10 mcg/mL up to 72 hr. Example 2: spinal block with 2.2-2.5 mL of hyperbaric bupivacaine 0.5%. Example 3: transversus abdominis plane block with 20-30 mL of bupivacaine 0.5% or ropivacaine 0.5% injected at each quadrant of the abdomen.

[b] For instance: site infection, coagulopathy, allergic to local anesthetics, patient refused.

8. Miller TE, Thacker JK, White WD, et al; Enhanced Recovery Study Group. Reduced length of hospital stay in colorectal surgery after implementation of an enhanced recovery protocol. *Anesth Analg*. 2014;118:1052-1061.

9. Kalogera, E, Bakkum-Gamez JN, Jankowski CJ. Enhanced recovery in gynecologic surgery. *Obstet Gynecol*. 2013;122 (201):319-328.

10. Xu W, Daneshmand S, Bazargani ST, et al. Postoperative pain management after radical cystectomy: comparing traditional versus enhanced recovery protocol pathway. *J Urol*. 2015;194:1209-1213.

11. Daneshmand S, Ahmadi H, Schuckman AK, et al. Enhanced recovery protocol after radical cystectomy for bladder cancer. *J Urol*. 2014;192:50-55.

12. Cerantola Y, Valerio M, Persson B, et al. Guidelines for perioperative care after radical cystectomy for bladder cancer: Enhanced Recovery After Surgery (ERAS®) society recommendations. *Clin Nutr*. 2013;32:879-887.

13. Balzano G, Zerbi A, Braga M, Rocchetti S, Beneduce AA, Di Carlo V. Fast-track recovery programme after pancreatico-duodenectomy reduces delayed gastric emptying. *Br J Surg*. 2008;95:1387-1393.

14. Savikko J, Ilmakunnas M, Mäkisalo H, Nordin A, Isoniemi H. Enhanced recovery protocol after liver resection. *Br J Surg*. 2015;102:1526-1532.

7

Prophylaxis of Postoperative Complications:
Venous Thromboembolism, Antibiotics, Diabetes, Stress-Dose Steroids

by Stefan D. Holubar, MD, MS

"The sooner patients can be removed from the depressing influence of general hospital life, the more rapid their convalescence." – Dr. Charles Mayo, circa 1940

Some components of enhanced recovery protocols (ERPs), such as VTE and antibiotic prophylaxis, represent best clinical practice, thus many programs that are implementing ERPs will already have clinical workflows for optimal VTE and ABX prophylaxis. However, implementing ERPs allows one to examine their own practices and an opportunity for improvement in other areas such as perioperative optimization of anemia, diabetes, and mitigation and avoidance of steroid-induced impaired wound healing.

VTE Prophylaxis

The most recent edition of the American College of Chest Physicians (ACCP) VTE Prevention Guidelines (Chest, 2012) represents a major revision, and readers are strongly encouraged to obtain the source document.[1] The recommendations for nonorthopedic abdominopelvic surgery are shown in **Table 7.1**. Note the new emphasis on risk stratification using validated scores such as the Rogers score and the Caprini score. In summary *all patients undergoing major abdominopelvic surgery should at a minimum receive mechanical prophylaxis* (upper extremity if lower extremity amputee as sequential compression devices release tissue

TABLE 7.1 — ACCP VTE Prophylaxis Guidelines Summary for Abdominal-Pelvic Surgery Patients

Estimated VTE Risk	Rogers Score	Caprini Score	Recommendation
<0.5%	<7	0	If **very low risk** for VTE, then no specific pharmacologic (Grade 1B) or mechanical (Grade 2C) prophylaxis other than *early ambulation*
~1.5%	7 – 10	1 – 2	If **low risk** for VTE, then IPC mechanical prophylaxis is recommended (Grade 2C)
~3.0%	>10	3 – 4	If **moderate risk** for VTE but *not* at high risk for major bleeding complications, then LMWH (Grade 2B), LDUH (Grade 2B), or IPC mechanical prophylaxis is recommended (Grade 2C).
~3.0%	>10	3 – 4	If **moderate risk** for VTE, but at *high risk for major bleeding* or those in whom consequences of bleeding are severe, then IPC mechanical prophylaxis is recommended (Grade 2C).
~6%	—	≥5	If **high risk** for VTE and *not* at high risk for major bleeding, then prophylaxis with LMWH (Grade 1B) or LDUH (Grade 1B) **plus** IPC mechanical prophylaxis (Grade 2C) is recommended.
~6%	—	—	If **high risk** for VTE, **with cancer,** who are *not otherwise at high risk for major bleeding*, then extended-duration pharmacologic prophylaxis (4 weeks) with LMWH over limited-duration prophylaxis (Grade 1B) is recommended.

Estimated VTE Risk	Rogers Score	Caprini Score	Recommendation
~6%	—	—	If **high risk** for VTE, but *high risk for major bleeding* or those in whom consequences of bleeding are severe, then IPC mechanical prophylaxis is recommended, *until risk of bleeding diminishes and pharmacologic prophylaxis may be initiated* (Grade 2C).
~6%	—	≥5	If **high risk** for VTE in whom *both LMWH and unfractionated heparin are contraindicated* or unavailable and who are not at high risk for major bleeding, then low-dose aspirin (Grade 2C), fondaparinux (Grade 2C), or IPC mechanical prophylaxis, (Grade 2C) is recommended.
—	—	—	An IVC filter should **not** be used for primary VTE prevention (Grade 2C).
—	—	—	Periodic surveillance duplex should **not** be performed (Grade 2C).

Adapted from Gould MK, et al. *Chest.* 2012;141(2 suppl):e227S-e277S.

7

factor—an endogenous anticoagulant). Outpatient surgical cases, short cases, and ambulatory the day of surgery cases in general do not need prophylaxis.

■ **Early Mobilization**

ERPs call for early mobilization after surgery. This prevents muscle atrophy, encourages patient independence, and decreases the risk of VTE and pulmonary complications. Mid-thoracic epidurals typically cover T4-T10, and can facilitate early mobilization operations that require an upper abdominal incision such as after gastrectomy, pancreatectomy, liver resection, nephrectomy, and transverse colectomy. In addition, laparoscopic modalities and intra-umbilical incisions, compared with open colectomy, have been shown in multiple studies to be protective of VTE.[2] The role of regional blocks such as one-shot spinals, transversus abdominus plane (TAP) block, or rectus sheath blocks can also facilitate early ambulation, as can multimodal narcotic-sparing analgesia. But for *most* abdominopelvic surgical patients mechanical prophylaxis and early ambulation will not be sufficient to prevent VTE, a potentially lethal complication.

■ **Chemoprophylaxis: Which Agent?**

The majority of patients who are candidates for ERPs should have VTE chemoprophylaxis in the form of BID or TID daily 5000 IU subcutaneous (SC) heparin (SQH), 40 mg of low molecular-weight heparin (LMWH, ie, enoxaparin [LVNX]) SC daily (30 mg twice daily if exceptionally high-risk patient, such as the morbidly obese), or dalteparin (also a form of LMWH). Regarding LVNX, note that for low BMI patients, specifically *for a 40 kg patient, 40 mg of LVNX is 1 mg/kg—a therapeutic dose*—thus a lower dose or a different agent should be used. Inadvertent therapeutic dosing can also result if a patient develops acute kidney injury (AKI) as LMWH is renally cleared, and in AKI, the drug serum concentration increases. Thus if a patient develops AKI, then LVNX should be stopped and the patient transitioned to SQH. LVNX, compared to SQH, results in a lower incidence of heparin-induced thrombosis and thrombocytopenia. Dalteparin (Fragmin) and fondaparinux (Arixtra) are alternatives to LMWH that can be also used for VTE prophylaxis in the setting of heparin-based thrombosis and thrombocytopenia. Timing of chemoprophylaxis before and after the insertion of central neuraxial blockade should be considered to avoid increasing the risk of vertebral canal hematoma. Timing depends on the agent and dose used but is normally 12 hours before insertion and 12 hours after removal of epidural catheters for prophylactic dosing.

■ Risk of Bleeding?

Studies quoted in the above guideline have shown that SQH and LVNX are equally effective for VTE prevention. Both SQH and LVNX are associated with an increased risk of wound hematomas, 3% and 7%, respectively. These were considered minor complications, and the risk of bleeding, which is typically minor and not life-threatening, must be weighed against that of PE, which although uncommon (roughly 1 in 200 patients) carries a 30% mortality, for 15 potentially avoidable deaths per 10,000 patients.

■ Extended Prophylaxis

The ENOXACAN-I and -II studies of LVNX for abdominopelvic cancer surgery, showed that *extended prophylaxis for a total of 28 days* resulted in a lower rate of VTE.[3,4] Recently this work has been extended to include patients with inflammatory bowel disease, especially ulcerative colitis.[5,6] The author's preference is to prescribe a total of 28 days of LVNX for all cancer and IBD patients, unless they are highly ambulatory at discharge and otherwise low risk (ie, non-pelvic surgery, no evidence of perioperative inflammation). Using this extended prophylaxis, the authors' ERP group has achieved low outlier status in NSQIP for colorectal VTE (0.78% observed vs 2.3% expected).

Patients should receive prophylactic antibiotics in the operating room prior to skin incision. The traditional practice of 1 hour prior to incision is subject to unwanted variability (ie, delays due to equipment, epidurals, etc). Optimal antibiotic selection includes assessment of the spectrum of the antibiotic(s), antibiotic pharmacokinetics including recommended re-dosing intervals, the nature of the operation and wound classification, the weight of the patient, and the length of the operation (**Table 7.2** and **Table 7.3**). We recommend not continuing doses beyond the intraoperative period, as there is no evidence to suggest increased efficacy, and extra dosing results in patient exposure to harm in the form of adverse drug reactions, and increased risk of *Clostridium difficile* colitis.

■ **Antibiotic Dose and Re-Dosing**

Traditional recommendations for elective clean cases, for example, would include a second-generation cephalosporin (1-2 g, re-dosed every 6 hours) with the

TABLE 7.2 — Preoperative Antibiotic Weight-Based Dosing for Major Surgery

Antibiotic	=80 kg (176 lb)	81–160 mg (177–352 lb)	>160 kg (352 lb)
Cefazolin	1 g	2 g	3 g
Cefuroxime	1.5 g	3 g	3 g
Ciprofloxacin	400 mg	600 mg	800 mg
Clindamycin	600 mg	900 mg	1200 mg
Gentamicin	4 mg/kg	4 mg/kg, max 420 mg	540 mg
Metronidazole	500 mg	1000 mg	1500 mg
Vancomycin	20 mg/kg	20 mg/kg, max 2500 mg)	3000 mg

Alexander JW, et al. *Ann Surg*. 2011;253(6):1082-1093.

TABLE 7.3 — Antibiotic Dosing Intervals (in hours) for Major Surgery Based on Renal Function

Antibiotic	CrCl >50 mL/min	CrCl 20–50 mL/min	CrCl <20 mL/min
Cefazolin	3 – 4	8	16
Cefuroxime	3	6	12
Ciprofloxacin	8	12	None
Ampicillin/ sulbactam	3	6	12
Clindamycin	6	6	6
Gentamicin	5	Varies	None
Metronidazole	8	8	8
Vancomycin	8	16	None

Alexander JW, et al. *Ann Surg.* 2011;253(6):1082–1093.

addition of metronidazole (500 mg, re-dosed every 6 hours) for clean contaminated (bowel) cases. However, an excellent review of best practices by Alexander and colleagues suggested more aggressive dosing and re-dosing (**Table 7.2** and **Table 7.3**).[7] Specifically, as many patients will be over 80 years of age, the initial cephalosporin should be dosed at 2-3 g (weight-based) and re-dosed every 3 hours. Traditional re-dosing of second-generation cephalosporins, given that most colorectal operations are approximately 3 to 4 hours, results in antibiotic drug levels at their nadir during closing; 3 to 4 hour re-dosing results in high drug levels during closing.

The Alexander review also suggested the initial dose of metronidazole should be 1 g, not 500 mg, for patients over 80 kg. It is the author's institutional policy to dose all patients over 40 kg with 2 g of cephazolin and 1 g of metronidazole unless they are over 125 kg, in which case 3 g and 1.5 g are used, respectively. These higher doses for colorectal operations have also resulted in a low outlier SSI status in NSQIP with a colorectal SSI rate of just 3.5% (vs expected 8.8%), 5 of 143 cases. Thus the higher dose of antibiotics does seem to be more efficacious but may be associated with increased PONV. Repeat intraoperative re-dosing should be considered if there is a large blood loss (>10 mL/kg).

■ **Antibiotic Choice**

A potential limitation of the Surgical Care Improvement Project (SCIP) is lack of broad enough coverage. Specifically, exciting basic and translational science research performed by Dr. John C. Alverdy at the University of Chicago suggests that the etiology of gastrointestinal anastomotic leakage is primarily an infectious, not ischemic phenomenon.[8] Specifically, high-collagenase *Pseudomonas* and *Enterococcus* species have been shown to "hone in on" the exposed collagen within the anastomosis, and then digest the collagen, creating an ulcer in the anastomosis, which then leaks. The authors' practice is to use Zosyn in lieu of cephazolin in patients no allergic to PCN, and to use levofloxacin in PCN-allergic patients. Levofloxacin has the added practical benefit of 12-hour re-dosing, longer than the vast majority of cases, so only a single dose is needed (both Zosyn and levofloxacin cover both *Pseudomonas* and *Enterococcus* species).

■ **Infection Prevention Bundles**

Recently, in an effort to maximally reduce postoperative SSI occurrence, infection prevention bundles, which are similar and complementary to ERPs, have been demonstrated to be effective in reducing SSI rates.[9] Specific bundles have been demonstrated in colorectal, pancreatic resection, and liver resection.[10]

Anemia

Anemic patients are at increased risk of postoperative complications, myocardial infarction, and death. A modified WHO classification of anemia is shown in **Table 7.4**.[11] *All major elective surgical patients should be screened for anemia* and, if detected, it should be

TABLE 7.4 — Preoperative Anemia Classification

Anemia Level	Hgb Level (mg/dL)	HCT Level (%)
Normal	≥13	≥38
Mild	10-12	30-37
Moderate	8-10	26-29
Severe	<8	21-25

Based on a combination of the WHO classification of anemia (Hgb <13 mg/dL) and the literature.

Leichtle SW, et al. *J Am Coll Surg.* 2011;212(2):187-194.

aggressively treated preoperatively. If mild and the operation is completely elective, then we recommend the following so-called "FIVE" therapy (**f**olate, **i**ron, **v**itamin C, **E**pogen):

- Iron: ferrous sulfate 325 mg 3× daily with vitamin C 500 mg 3× daily (ascorbic acid doubles the absorption of the ferrous moiety)
- Folic acid 1 mg daily
- Multivitamin daily
- Rarely erythropoietin (which is expensive, and can be prothrombotic)

If the operation is more urgent, then iron infusions and/or blood transfusions should be considered. Newer iron infusions with a lower allergy rate are becoming available. Autologous blood donation is generally discouraged, as it tends to make patients more anemic.

Preoperative Diabetes Management

As many as 15% of patients overall will have occult diabetes, thus we recommend preoperative screening for all major abdominopelvic surgery patients. Optimal control of diabetes, as measured by serial serum hemoglobin A1c (HbA1c) is crucial in achieving optimal postoperative outcomes. End-organ damage in the form of tissue protein glycosylation, making immunologic proteins important in heal-

129

ing "sticky" with impaired function can contribute to postoperative complications. Patients who have elevated HbA1c preoperative should be referred to their primary care physician or an endocrinology team, and for patients with poorly controlled type 2 diabetes, initiation of insulin therapy must be considered.

In addition to chronic control of elevated blood sugars preoperatively, ERP programs that utilize carbohydrate loading must inform their patients and perioperative team to anticipate hyperglycemia and treat appropriately. Evidence of its use in type 1 diabetes is currently lacking.

Perioperative Corticosteroid Management

The transplant surgery literature has shown that for those patients who are on chronic steroids, stress-dose steroids are not indicated.[12] More recently, colorectal literature in IBD confirmed that high-dose stress-dose steroids are not needed.[13] However, successful avoidance of the strategy of intentionally omitting stress-dose steroids mandate extra attention to Addisonian symptoms such as fever, tachycardia, and IV-fluid–refractory hypotension by the perioperative team. Suspicion of Addisonian crisis is an indication for empiric treatment, or metabolic testing with *cosyntropin stimulation testing*, random plasma cortisol, timed plasma cortisol, or 24-hour urinary cortisol. It is the author's strategy to rapidly "*test and treat*" in suspected cases with a single dose of 50 mg of hydrocortisone, while holding further doses until after the test results in several hours.

For patients who are on chronic steroids preoperatively, in order to optimize post-operative collagen synthesis, which is the main mechanism of steroid-induced impaired wound healing, one may consider short-term (4 weeks before and after surgery) oral supplementation with:

- Vitamin C 500 mg 2× daily
- Zinc (elemental) 50 mg (or 220 mg of zinc sulfate) 2× daily
- Vitamin A 18,000-30,000 IU 2× daily
- Daily multivitamin (including B vitamins).

Finally, some literature exists that intra-operative steroids may reduce PONV and pain scores. Specifically, a meta-analysis suggested 4 mg of dexamethasone is as effective an 8-12 mg of dexamethasone to decrease PONV and pain scores.[14]

7

REFERENCES

1. Gould MK, Garcia DA, Wren SM, et al; American College of Chest Physicians. Prevention of VTE in nonorthopedic surgical patients: Antithrombotic Therapy and Prevention of Thrombosis, 9th ed: American College of Chest Physicians Evidence-Based Clinical Practice Guidelines. *Chest.* 2012;141(2 Suppl):e227S-e277S.

2. Buchberg B, Masoomi H, Lusby K, et al. Incidence and risk factors of venous thromboembolism in colorectal surgery: does laparoscopy impart an advantage? *Arch Surg.* 2011;146:739-743.

3. Efficacy and safety of enoxaparin versus unfractionated heparin for prevention of deep vein thrombosis in elective cancer surgery: a double-blind randomized multicentre trial with venographic assessment. ENOXACAN Study Group. *Br J Surg.* 1997;84:1099-1103.

4. Bergqvist D, Agnelli G, Cohen AT, et al; ENOXACAN II Investigators. Duration of prophylaxis against venous thromboembolism with enoxaparin after surgery for cancer. *N Engl J Med.* 2002;346:975-980.

5. Wallaert JB, De Martino RR, Marsicovetere PS, et al. Venous thromboembolism after surgery for inflammatory bowel disease: are there modifiable risk factors? Data from ACS NSQIP. *Dis Colon Rectum.* 2012;55:1138-1144.

6. Gross ME, Vogler SA, Mone MC, Sheng X, Sklow B. The importance of extended postoperative venous thromboembolism prophylaxis in IBD: a National Surgical Quality Improvement Program analysis. *Dis Colon Rectum.* 2014;57:482-489.

7. Alexander JW, Solomkin JS, Edwards MJ. Updated recommendations for control of surgical site infections. *Ann Surg.* 2011;253(6):1082-1093.

8. Shogan BD, Carlisle EM, Alverdy JC, Umanskiy K. Do we really know why colorectal anastomoses leak? *J Gastrointest Surg.* 2013;17:1698-1707.

9. Keenan JE, Speicher PJ, Nussbaum DP, et al. Improving outcomes in colorectal surgery by sequential implementation of multiple standardized care programs. *J Am Coll Surg.* 2015;221:404-414.

10. Hill MV, Holubar SD, Garfield Legare CI, Luurtsema CM, Barth RJ Jr. Perioperative bundle decreases postoperative hepatic surgery infections. *Ann Surg Oncol.* 2015;22(suppl 3):1140-1146.

11. Leichtle SW, Mouawad NJ, Lampman R, Singal B, Cleary RK. Does preoperative anemia adversely affect colon and rectal surgery outcomes? *J Am Coll Surg.* 2011;212:187-194.

12. Kelly KN, Domajnko B. Perioperative stress-dose steroids. *Clin Colon Rectal Surg.* 2013;26:163-167.

13. Zaghiyan K, Melmed GY, Berel D, Ovsepyan G, Murrell Z, Fleshner P. A prospective, randomized, noninferiority trial of steroid dosing after major colorectal surgery. *Ann Surg.* 2014;259:32-37.

14. De Oliveira GS Jr, Castro-Alves LJ, Ahmad S, Kendall MC, McCarthy RJ. Dexamethasone to prevent postoperative nausea and vomiting: an updated meta-analysis of randomized controlled trials. *Anesth Analg.* 2013;116:58-74.

8

Fluid Management Strategies

by Maxime Cannesson, MD, PhD

Introduction

In the operating room, the optimization of a patient's hemodynamics is key to improving morbidity and mortality. Evidence suggests that either too little or too much fluid administration during the perioperative period can worsen tissue perfusion and oxygenation leading to organ dysfunction. Further, this impairment may not be reliably revealed by alterations in conventional hemodynamic indices such as heart rate, urine output, central venous pressure, or arterial pressure. Numerous investigative studies in a spectrum of patient populations (eg, sepsis, cardiovascular surgery, trauma, and other critical illnesses) have challenged the notion that these indicators accurately predict volume status.[1-7]

Perioperative goal-directed therapy (GDT) is the concept of using indices of continuous blood flow and/or tissue oxygen saturation to optimize end-organ function. By using the flow-related parameters such as stroke volume (SV), cardiac output (CO), and markers of fluid responsiveness such as stroke volume variation (SVV), pleth variability index (PVI), and corrected aortic flow time (FTc), one is able to precisely infer where the patient is on their Frank-Starling relationship, and thus, optimize oxygen delivery. The body of evidence in favor of GDT continues to grow; therefore, GDT is rapidly becoming the standard of care in operating rooms. However, in the context of enhanced recovery after surgery, the impact of this approach in low- to moderate-risk patients has been recently challenged,[8] and this should be considered when implementing protocols at the institutional level.

In these patients, restrictive crystalloid administration may be enough.

One of the goals of GDT is to decrease the tremendous variability in the way fluid is administered to patients during surgery. In most studies on the topic, it tends to decrease fluid administration (especially crystalloids) compared with control groups. It relies on restrictive crystalloid administration (3 mL/kg/h) and on additional fluid boluses based on rational hemodynamic endpoints described above.

GDT in the Perioperative Period

The use of flow-related indices to guide intraoperative goal-directed fluid therapy has appeal since these parameters provide a numeric representation of the patient's volume status, which can frequently be difficult to ascertain using standard hemodynamic monitors, urine output or even CVP.[9-11] In 2002, Gan and colleagues reported earlier return of bowel function, lower incidence of postoperative nausea and vomiting, and decrease in length of hospital stay in patients whose stroke volume was optimized using an esophageal Doppler.[12] Intraoperative GDT has also been reported to improve outcomes following surgery in high-risk patients, decreasing both morbidity and length of hospital stay.[13-16]

Previously published studies have shown decreased complications and hospital length of stay in high-risk patients undergoing major abdominal surgery with SVV-guided GDT therapy.[17-19] In addition, similar results have been shown in non–high-risk surgical patients undergoing elective total hip arthroplasty[20] and major abdominal surgery.[19] These studies support that the use of flow-guided parameters can aid in continuous maintenance of a euvolemic state by indicating the appropriate timing of fluid administration and improve postoperative outcome.[21-23]

Fluid Administration

Optimal fluid administration in the surgical patient is important because prior reports indicate that both hypo- and hypervolemia may deleteriously affect perioperative organ function. Given these considerations, the primary resuscitation goal in the critically ill patient is to restore tissue perfusion/cellular oxygenation and maintain end-organ function through volume resuscitation. The optimal resuscitation fluid, however, remains a subject of debate.

The decision whether to use crystalloid vs colloid as the primary resuscitation fluid in the critically ill remains contentious. Two previous meta-analyses of the numerous prospective, clinical trials in this area suggested that colloid resuscitation may be associated with increased patient mortality. A large multicenter, randomized, double-blind trial, however, documented the safety of colloid- based resuscitation using albumin, but failed to demonstrate either an economic or survival benefit to such therapy.[24] The SAFE study authors subsequently performed a post hoc analysis of their data to confirm the suggestion that albumin is associated with a higher mortality rate in patients with traumatic brain injury (TBI).[25] These studies do not refute the facts that:

- Colloids remain intravascular longer than crystalloids
- Colloids expand plasma volume to a greater extent
- Crystalloids are more likely to cause edema formation.

Protocols for Perioperative Goal-Directed Therapy

Many protocols have been proposed for GDT in the critical care setting. While they are relatively clear for the management of the septic patient, the range of protocols available for the perioperative setting is much wider and depends mainly on the patient's vascular access and the availability of the monitors. Recently, the European Society of Anaesthesiologists has released recommended protocols for perioperative goal-directed therapy during surgery.[26] These protocols as well as others are presented below.

■ GDT Protocol in the Operating Room

The first step in the operating room is to identify the patient's risk and then to define the vascular access. Then, based on the vascular access, the monitoring approach is chosen and the hemodynamic optimization protocol is applied. **Figure 8.1** is a suggestion for the choice of the hemodynamic monitoring system based on the patient's risk and vascular access. In all proposed GDT protocols, baseline crystalloid administration ranges from 1.5 to 5 mL/kg/hr and additional fluid boluses are based on physiological endpoints and driven by the protocol.

■ Protocol for Low-Risk Surgery

- Patients ASA 1 or 2, with expected blood loss less than 500 mL.
- Surgeries: breast, stomatology, ophthalmology, gynecology, endocrinology (except pheochromocytoma and carcinoid tumor), plastic surgery, minor orthopedic surgery, minor urology surgery.
- Vascular access: one or two peripheral IVs.
- Monitoring: standard ASA monitors ± respiratory variations in the plethysmographic waveform (pleth variability index [PVI]) if the conditions of applications are met (sinus rhythm, general anesthesia with mechanical ventilation, tidal volume 6 to 8 mL/kg).
- The protocol for fluid administration is shown in **Figure 8.2**. The goal is to use a baseline crystalloid administration of 3 to 5 mL/kg/h and to titrate volume expansion based on the PVI.[27]
- It has been used successfully in an ERP at the University of West Virginia.[28]

- ■ **Protocol for Moderate- and High-Risk Surgery in a Patient Who Is Not Equipped With an Arterial Line**
  - Patients ASA 2 or 3, with expected blood loss less than 1500 mL.
  - Surgeries: vascular, abdominal, peripheral angiography, head and neck, major orthopedic and gynecology surgery, urology.
  - Vascular access: one or two peripheral IV ± central venous access with or without venous oxygen saturation monitoring.
  - Monitoring: standard ASA monitors ± respiratory variations in the plethysmographic waveform (PVI) if the conditions of applications are met (sinus rhythm, general anesthesia with mechanical ventilation, tidal volume >6 mL/kg) and/or noninvasive cardiac output monitoring.
  - If a noninvasive cardiac output monitor is used, the NICE protocol can be applied (**Figure 8.3**). The goal is to titrate fluid administration in order to maximize stroke volume.

- ■ **Protocol for Moderate- and High-Risk Surgery in a Patient Equipped With an Arterial Line**
  - Monitoring: standard ASA monitors ± stroke volume variation or pulse pressure variation (sinus rhythm, general anesthesia with mechanical ventilation, tidal volume >6 mL/kg) and / or cardiac output monitoring based on arterial pressure waveform monitoring (pulse contour analysis or pulse power analysis) or noninvasive cardiac output monitor (esophageal Doppler or bioreactance).
  - In this case, stroke volume can be optimized using the NICE protocol[29] released in March 2011 by the National Health Service in the United Kingdom (**Figure 8.3**), in conjunction with SVV or PPV monitoring (**Figure 8.4**), or following the Gan and colleagues algorithm (**Figure 8.5**).[12] If only pulse pressure variation is monitored, a PPV minimization protocol aiming

FIGURE 8.1 — Proposed Algorithm Developed and Implemented at the University of California Irvine for the Choice of Hemodynamic Monitoring During Surgery

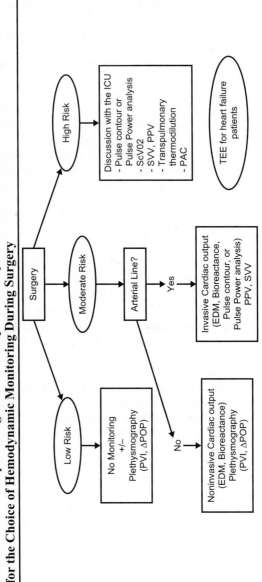

Key: PVI, pleth variability index; ΔPOP, respiratory variations in the pulse oximeter waveform; EDM, esophageal Doppler monitor; PPV, respiratory variations in pulse pressure; SVV, respiratory variations in stroke volume; ScVO$_2$, central venous oxygen saturation; PAC, pulmonary artery catheter; TEE, transesophageal echocardiography.

Courtesy of University of California Irvine.

8

FIGURE 8.2 — Goal-Directed Therapy Protocol Based on Pleth Variability Index

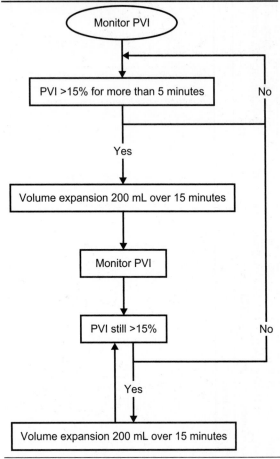

Adapted from Forget P, et al. *Anesth Analg.* 2010;111:910-914.

FIGURE 8.3 — NICE Protocol

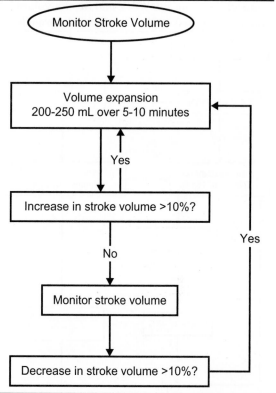

NICE draft guidance on cardiac output monitoring device published for consultation. http://www.nice.org.uk/newsroom/press-releases/DraftGuidanceOnCardiacOutputMonitoringDevice.jsp; recommended by the European Society of Anaesthesiology. Perioperative goal directed therapy protocol summary. http://html.esahq.org/patientsafetykit/resources/downloads/05_Checklists/Various_Checklists/Perioperative_Goal_Directed_Therapy_Protocols.pdf. Accessed February 25, 2016.

FIGURE 8.4 — Goal-Directed Therapy Protocol Based on PPV/SVV and Stroke Volume Monitoring Based on the Gray Zone Approach

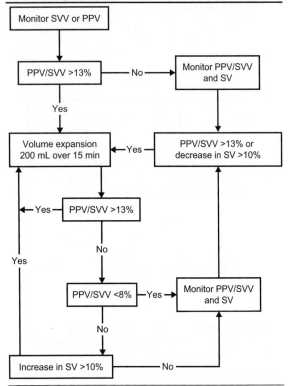

Cannesson M, et al. *Anesthesiology*. 2011;115:896-897. Protocol adapted from Gan TJ, et al. *Anesthesiology*. 2002;97(4):820-826.

**FIGURE 8.5 — Goal-Directed Therapy Protocol
Based on Esophageal Doppler Monitoring Using
Stroke Volume (SV) and Corrected Flow Time (FTc)**

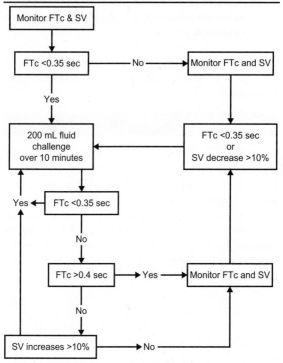

FTc, corrected flow time; SV, stroke volume

Gan TJ, et al. *Anesthesiology*. 2002;97(4):820-826.

8

at keeping PPV/SVV below 13% can be used (**Figure 8.6**).[19]

- If oxygen delivery index is monitored, a GDT protocol including this variable has been shown to improve outcome in high-risk surgery patients (**Figure 8.7**).[30]

In all cases, standard hemodynamic management for arterial pressure, urine output, and heart rate must be respected.

Conclusion

We believe that perioperative GDT is a powerful clinical approach for managing critically ill patients. Evidence supporting the role of GDT in improving patient outcomes is becoming well-established. Further implementation of protocols of GDT will likely provide consolidation and streamlining of care for patients by minimizing variability in clinical practice. This also has potential for improving resource utilization while implementing evidenced-based medicine.

FIGURE 8.6 — Goal-Directed Therapy Protocol Based on PPV/SVV Alone

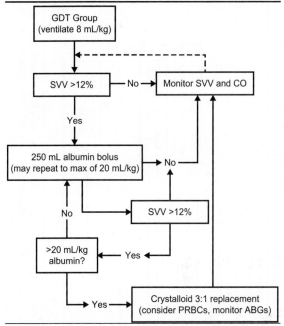

Adapted from Ramsingh DS, et al. *J Clin Monitoring Computing*. 2013;27(3):249-257; recommended by the European Society of Anaesthesiology. Perioperative goal directed therapy protocol summary. http://html.esahq.org/patientsafetykit/resources/downloads/05_Checklists/Various_Checklists/Perioperative_Goal_Directed_Therapy_Protocols.pdf. Accessed February 25, 2016.

FIGURE 8.7 — Modified Version of the St. Georges Protocol Based on Oxygen Delivery Index

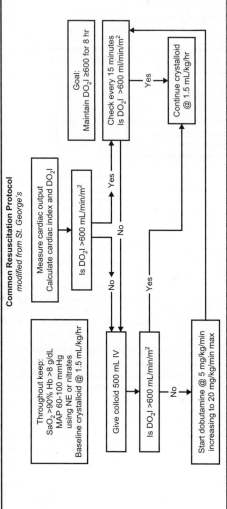

Modified from Pearse R, et al. *Crit Care*. 2005;9:R687-R693; recommended by the European Society of Anaesthesiology. Perioperative goal directed therapy protocol summary. http://html.esahq.org/patientsafetykit/resources/downloads/05_Checklists/Various_Checklists/Perioperative_Goal_Directed_Therapy_Protocols.pdf. Accessed February 26, 2016.

REFERENCES

1. Bendjelid K, Romand JA. Fluid responsiveness in mechanically ventilated patients: a review of indices used in intensive care. *Intensive Care Med*. 2003;29:352-360.

2. Diebel L, Wilson RF, Heins J, Larky H, Warsow K, Wilson S. End-diastolic volume versus pulmonary artery wedge pressure in evaluating cardiac preload in trauma patients. *J Trauma*. 1994;37:950-955.

3. Hollenberg SM, Ahrens TS, Annane D, et al. Practice parameters for hemodynamic support of sepsis in adult patients: 2004 update. *Crit Care Med*. 2004;32:1928-1948.

4. Kumar A, Anel R, Bunnell E, et al. Pulmonary artery occlusion pressure and central venous pressure fail to predict ventricular filling volume, cardiac performance, or the response to volume infusion in normal subjects. *Crit Care Med*. 2004;32:691-699.

5. Michard F, Teboul JL. Predicting fluid responsiveness in ICU patients: a critical analysis of the evidence. *Chest*. 2002;121:2000-2008.

6. Osman D, Ridel C, Ray P, et al. Cardiac filling pressures are not appropriate to predict hemodynamic response to volume challenge. *Crit Care Med*. 2007;35:64-68.

7. Tavernier B, Makhotine O, Lebuffe G, Dupont J, Scherpereel P. Systolic pressure variation as a guide to fluid therapy in patients with sepsis-induced hypotension. *Anesthesiology*. 1998;89:1313-1321.

8. Rollins KE, Lobo DN. Intraoperative goal-directed fluid therapy in elective major abdominal surgery: a meta-analysis of randomized controlled trials. *Ann Surg*. 2016;263(3):465-476.

9. Gelman S. Venous function and central venous pressure: a physiologic story. *Anesthesiology*. 2008;108:735-748.

10. Marik PE, Baram M, Vahid B. Does central venous pressure predict fluid responsiveness? A systematic review of the literature and the tale of seven mares. *Chest*. 2008;134:172-178.

11. Howell MD, Donnino M, Clardy P, Talmor D, Shapiro NI. Occult hypoperfusion and mortality in patients with suspected infection. *Intensive Care Med*. 2007;33:1892-1899.

12. Gan TJ, Soppitt A, Maroof M, et al. Goal-directed intraoperative fluid administration reduces length of hospital stay after major surgery. *Anesthesiology*. 2002;97:820-826.

13. Abbas SM, Hill AG. Systematic review of the literature for the use of oesophageal Doppler monitor for fluid replacement in major abdominal surgery. *Anaesthesia*. 2008;63:44-51.

8

147

14. Bundgaard-Nielsen M, Holte K, Secher NH, Kehlet H. Monitoring of peri-operative fluid administration by individualized goal-directed therapy. *Acta Anaesthesiol Scand.* 2007;51:331-340.

15. Giglio MT, Marucci M, Testini M, Brienza N. Goal-directed haemodynamic therapy and gastrointestinal complications in major surgery: a meta-analysis of randomized controlled trials. *Br J Anaesth.* 2009;103:637-646.

16. Rahbari NN, Zimmermann JB, Schmidt T, Koch M, Weigand MA, Weitz J. Meta-analysis of standard, restrictive and supplemental fluid administration in colorectal surgery. *Br J Surg.* 2009;96(4):331-341.

17. Lees N, Hamilton M, Rhodes A. Clinical review: goal-directed therapy in high risk surgical patients. *Crit Care.* 2009;13:231.

18. Mayer J, Boldt J, Mengistu AM, Röhm KD, Suttner S. Goal-directed intraoperative therapy based on autocalibrated arterial pressure waveform analysis reduces hospital stay in high-risk surgical patients: a randomized, controlled trial. *Crit Care.* 2010;14:R18.

19. Ramsingh DS, Sanghvi C, Gamboa J, Cannesson M, Applegate RL 2nd. Outcome impact of goal directed fluid therapy during high risk abdominal surgery in low to moderate risk patients: a randomized controlled trial. *J Clin Monit Comput.* 2013;27:249-257.

20. Cecconi M, Fasano N, Langiano N, et al. Goal-directed haemodynamic therapy during elective total hip arthroplasty under regional anaesthesia. *Crit Care.* 2011;15:R132.

21. Hamilton MA, Cecconi M, Rhodes A. A systematic review and meta-analysis on the use of preemptive hemodynamic intervention to improve postoperative outcomes in moderate and high-risk surgical patients. *Anesth Analg.* 2011;112:1392-1402.

22. Knott A, Pathak S, McGrath JS, et al. Consensus views on implementation and measurement of enhanced recovery after surgery in England: Delphi study. *BMJ Open.* 2012;2:e001878.

23. Moonesinghe SR, Mythen MG, Grocott MP. High-risk surgery: epidemiology and outcomes. *Anesth Analg.* 2011;112:891-901.

24. Finfer S, Bellomo R, Boyce N, French J, Myburgh J, Norton R; SAFE Study Investigators. A comparison of albumin and saline for fluid resuscitation in the intensive care unit. *N Engl J Med.* 2004;350:2247-2256.

25. SAFE Study Investigators; Australian and New Zealand Intensive Care Society Clinical Trials Group; Australian Red Cross Blood Service; George Institute for International Health, Myburgh J, Cooper DJ, Finfer S, et al. Saline or albumin for

fluid resuscitation in patients with traumatic brain injury. *N Engl J Med*. 2007;357:874-884.

26. Perioperative goal-directed therapy protocol summary. European Soceity of Anaesthesiology. http://html.esahq.org/patientsafetykit/resources/downloads/05_Checklists/Various_Checklists/Perioperative_Goal_Directed_Therapy_Protocols.pdf. Accessed January 27, 2016.

27. Forget P, Lois F, de Kock M. Goal-directed fluid management based on the pulse oximeter-derived pleth variability index reduces lactate levels and improves fluid management. *Anesth Analg*. 2010;111:910-914.

28. Thiele RH, Rea KM, Turrentine FE, et al. Standardization of care: impact of an enhanced recovery protocol on length of stay, complications, and direct costs after colorectal surgery. *J Am Coll Surg*. 2015;220:430-443.

29. NICE draft guidance on cardiac output monitoring device published for consultation. National Institute for Health and Clinical Excellence. https://www.nice.org.uk/guidance/mtg3/resources/nice-draft-guidance-on-cardiac-output-monitoring-device-published-for-consultation3. Issued October 4, 2010. Accessed January 27, 2016.

30. Pearse R, Dawson D, Fawcett J, Rhodes A, Grounds RM, Bennett ED. Early goal-directed therapy after major surgery reduces complications and duration of hospital stay. A randomised, controlled trial [ISRCTN38797445]. *Crit Care*. 2005;9:R687-R693.

31. Cannesson M, Le Manach Y, Hofer CK, et al. Assessing the diagnostic accuracy of pulse pressure variations for the prediction of fluid responsiveness: a "gray zone" approach. *Anesthesiology*. 2011;115:231-241.

8

9
Hemodynamic Monitoring and Goal-Directed Therapy

by Joshua D Morris, MD and
Robert H Thiele, MD

Historical Background of Goal-Directed Therapy

Infusion of intravenous fluid (IVF) is a common component of modern medical management and can at times be a life-saving intervention. The resuscitative power of IVF was clearly described almost 200 years ago by Dr. Thomas Latta, one of the pioneers of IVF therapy, during the cholera outbreak in 1832. He described a patient who was dehydrated and had "*the manifest impress of death.*" However, "*when six pints [of intravenous fluid] had been injected, she expressed in a firm voice that she was free from all uneasiness ... her extremities were warm and every feature bore the aspect of comfort and health.*"[1] Over 100 years later, the development of the pulmonary artery catheter (PAC) allowed clinicians to measure cardiac output (CO), giving them a rational, quantitative therapeutic endpoint for hemodynamic management and goal-directed therapy (GDT).[2]

Within decades, it became clear that simply maximizing CO was not necessarily helpful and could potentially be harmful.[3] A series of flawed, but nevertheless negative trials examining the use of the PAC called into question the utility of GDT for critically ill patients.[4-7] This led some investigators to focus on oxygen supply:demand matching (guided by mixed or central venous oxygen concentration), but several large trials examining the use of venous oxygen concentration as a GDT endpoint in septic patients were negative,[8-10] and even the use of IVF for the treatment of sepsis has been called into question.[11]

Perioperative Goal-Directed Therapy and Fluid Management

In contrast to the critical care patient population, the evidence supporting GDT in the perioperative patient population is positive. In 2002, Gan and colleagues demonstrated a substantial reduction in length of stay following the use of esophageal Doppler (ED) to guide fluid therapy in patients undergoing abdominal surgery (**Figure 9.1**).[12]

That said, the limitations of indiscriminate volume administration were pointed out clearly by Brandstrup and associates who demonstrated a near linear relationship between the incidence of surgical complications and total fluid balance during hospitalization for abdominal surgery.[13] The Gan and Brandstrup data were conceptually reconciled by Bellamy who proposed the "sweetspot" concept of GDT based on quantitative therapeutic endpoint allows clinicians to avoid hypoperfusion and hypervolemia, keeping their patients in an "optimized" state (**Figure 9.2**).[14]

Overall, while the perioperative GDT data consists of smaller studies (compared to the critical care literature), utilization of a structured protocol to guide hemodynamics based on quantitative metrics appears to improve outcomes in patients undergoing major surgery.[15-17]

Therapeutic Endpoints of IV Fluid Management

Traditional therapeutic endpoints include systemic arterial blood pressure, central venous pressure, and urine output, none of which have been shown, in isolation, to improve outcomes, provide meaningful information about the response to fluid administra-

FIGURE 9.1 — ED-Based Fluid Management Algorithm

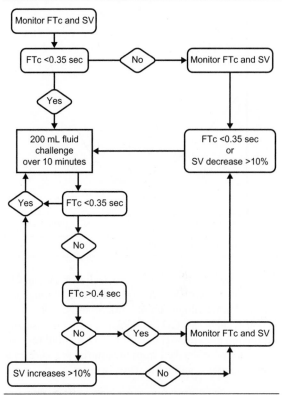

FTc, corrected flow time; SV, stroke volume

Gan TJ1, et al. *Anesthesiology*. 2002;97(4):820-826.

tion, or predict perioperative organ injury.[18-20] More modern therapeutic endpoints utilized in perioperative GDT algorithms include stroke volume (SV) or CO, and fluid responsiveness (the predicted change in SV following fluid administration) (**Figure 9.3**), but it is not clear whether one is superior to another.[15-17] The "fluid responsiveness" concept focuses on keeping patients at the peak of the Frank-Starling curve, ie,

FIGURE 9.2 — Wet, Dry, or Something Else?
Sweetspot Concept

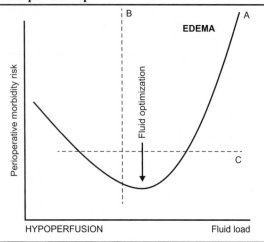

Bellamy MC. *Br J Anaesth*. 2006;97(6):755-757.

"optimizing" fluid administration such that SV and CO are maximized without driving contractility through the use of pharmacologic agents. Importantly, using fluid responsiveness as a GDT endpoint does not necessarily require the measurement of SV or CO, as fluid responsiveness can be derived from the arterial pressure and/or photoplethysmographic waveforms.

Available Devices

■ Esophageal Doppler

The ED (Deltex Medical, Chichester, UK) is capable of measuring SV, CO, stroke volume variation (SVV), and corrected flow time (FT_c), a Doppler-based volume indicator. It requires insertion of a Doppler probe that is slightly larger than a nasogastric tube, followed by manual positioning to optimize signal strength. Unlike some of the other devices, the ED may sometimes require periodic operator intervention to maintain signal strength and continuous data, due to surgical manipulation of the abdomen. That said, data suggest that the ED is more accurate than other available noninvasive CO monitors.[21] In particular, they are able to account for changes in afterload that challenge arterial waveform analyzers. Use of the ED is supported by a substantial body of outcomes data (with randomized controlled trials beginning in the 1990s),[22] and has been endorsed by both the National Institutes for Health (NIH) and National Institute of Health and Care Excellence (NICE) Group.[23,24]

■ Arterial Waveform Analyzers

Like the ED, arterial waveform analyzers attempt to measure SV, CO, and a measure of fluid responsiveness (either SVV or pulse pressure variation [PPV]). Currently available devices in the United States include the Flotrac (Edwards Lifesciences, Irvine, CA), LiDCO (LiDCO, London, UK), and PiCCO (Pulsion Medical System, Feldkirchen, Germany). These devices apply proprietary algorithms to the shape of the arterial waveform and in doing so derive an estimate of SV, which can then be used to calculate CO and SVV. Unlike the ED, they require minimal operator intervention to maintain a continuous signal, but they do require placement of an arterial catheter. They do not appear to be as accurate as the ED for the measurement of SV or CO and in particular struggle with changes in afterload.[21]

There is, however, a growing body of literature that suggests that use of arterial waveform analyzers to guide fluid therapy can improve outcomes.[22] Importantly, some arterial waveform analyzers can be calibrated using either lithium dilution or transpulmonary thermodilution. These calibrated devices appear to be more accurate than non-calibrated devices in critically ill patients, likely because of changes in afterload.[21] In the context of the intraoperative component of enhanced recovery, where SV and CO are primarily used to guide fluid administration, it is not clear whether or not there is any added value in a calibrated (as opposed to uncalibrated) device.

FIGURE 9.3 — Inter-Device Differences in Monitoring for Goal-Directed Fluid Therapy

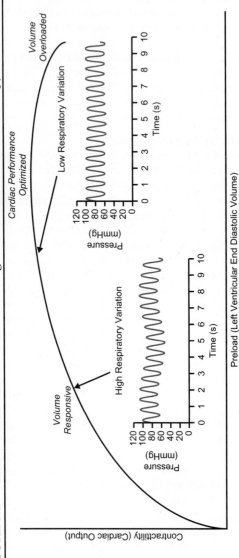

The location of the patient on the Frank-Starling curve is indicative of the likely response to fluid administration. Patients on the steep part of the curve are likely to experience an increase in SV >10% after fluid administration, while those who are on the flat part of the curve are already optimized and will not experience a 10% increase in SV. Of note, the cutoff between a "responder" and a "non-responder" is arbitrary but typically set between 10%-15%.

Thiele RH, et al. *Can J Anaesth.* 2015;62(2):169-181.

9

■ Photoplethysmography-Based Devices

Analysis of the pulse oximeter waveform (photoplethysmograph [PPG]) can provide clinicians with an estimate of fluid responsiveness (eg, Masimo PVI).[25] A recent case-control study analyzed the development of an enhanced recovery protocol that incorporated PVI for fluid management, demonstrating a significant reduction in indexed length of stay.[26]

■ Volume Clamp-Based Devices

Additionally, by combining the photoplethysmogram with a bladder cuff and a feedback loop controller, newer devices allow for the continuous measurement of blood pressure (ie, the arterial waveform), which can be utilized to estimate SV.[25] This "volume clamp" technology is relatively new and while there are no published studies on these devices in the context of GDT for enhanced recovery, such studies are ongoing. Currently, there are two variants available on the market in the United States: the Edwards Lifesciences ClearSight (Irvine, CA) and the CNSystems CNAP (Graz, Austria). Their performance (for measurement of both blood pressure and cardiac output) has been reviewed elsewhere.[27]

■ Bioreactance

Bioreactance (NICOM, Cheetah Medical, Newton Center, MA) devices analyze the resistance to the flow of electrical current across the thorax as fluid moves in and out of the thorax with each heartbeat. Because electrical resistance is a function of fluid volume, these changes can be utilized to estimate SV (and therefore CO and SVV). A direct comparison of ED vs bioreactance at Duke University found that the agreement between both devices was >60% at all time points, no significant disagreement between devices was identified at any time point, there were no differences in length of stay or any other outcomes, and, interestingly, the bioreactance device had significantly less missing data than ED.[28] The body of evidence to support these devices in the context of GDT for enhanced recovery is not as large as for ED or arterial waveform analyzers.[22]

Device vs No Device?
The Zero Balance Strategy

Recently, several investigators have asked whether or not a device is really necessary to optimize intraoperative fluid administration. They developed the "zero balance" strategy, which seeks to keep total fluid input and output equal over the course of a surgical procedure. There are now at least three randomized controlled trials comparing ED-guided perioperative GDT with either a zero balance or a restrictive strategy *within the context of an ERP*, and all three show no difference in length of stay or complication rates between groups.[29-31] Importantly, these three studies included a total of 335 patients and may not have been powered sufficiently to detect changes in complication rates. Given the large body of evidence in support of GDT, more work is needed to determine whether or not clinicians can remove advanced hemodynamic monitoring devices from their perioperative GDT algorithms without adversely affecting patient outcomes.

Conclusions

There is a large body of evidence to support the use of GDT in the perioperative environment. This is based on a large number of relatively small trials, using a variety of different therapeutic endpoints and devices designed to achieve them. Conceptually, the objective of perioperative GDT is to simultaneously avoid hypovolemia/hyperperfusion and hypervolemia/tissue edema, both of which can be harmful. Traditional metrics such as systemic arterial blood pressure, central venous blood pressure, and urine output are not helpful in that regard. Real-time SV and/or an indicator of fluid responsiveness are more up-to-date therapeutic endpoints that have been shown to improve patient outcomes when incorporated into a structured hemodynamic management protocol. The ED is probably the most accurate but can be more challenging to use and labor intensive than other GDT devices. Arterial waveform devices may not be as accurate for the measurement of SV but they have been used effectively to improve patient outcomes. More research is needed to fully assess other devices as well as to determine whether the "zero balance" or "restrictive" approach can replace GDT in certain patient populations.

REFERENCES

1. Cosnett JE. The origins of intravenous fluid therapy. *Lancet*. 1989;1:768-771.

2. Ganz W, Donoso R, Marcus HS, Forrester JS, Swan HJ. A new technique for measurement of cardiac output by thermodilution in man. *Am J Cardiol*. 1971;27:392-396.

3. Hayes MA, Timmins AC, Yau EH, Palazzo M, Hinds CJ, Watson D. Elevation of systemic oxygen delivery in the treatment of critically ill patients. *N Engl J Med*. 1994;330:1717-1722.

4. Gattinoni L, Brazzi L, Pelosi P,et al. A trial of goal-oriented hemodynamic therapy in critically ill patients. SvO2 Collaborative Group. *N Engl J Med*. 1995;333:1025-1032.

5. Sandham JD, Hull RD, Brant RF, et al; Canadian Critical Care Clinical Trials Group. A randomized, controlled trial of the use of pulmonary-artery catheters in high-risk surgical patients. *N Engl J Med*. 2003;348:5-14.

6. Richard C, Warszawski J, Anguel N, et al; French Pulmonary Artery Catheter Study Group. Early use of the pulmonary artery catheter and outcomes in patients with shock and acute respiratory distress syndrome: a randomized controlled trial. *JAMA*. 2003;290:2713-2720.

7. Harvey S, Harrison DA, Singer M, et al; PAC-Man study collaboration. Assessment of the clinical effectiveness of pulmonary artery catheters in management of patients in intensive care (PAC-Man): a randomised controlled trial. *Lancet*. 2005;366:472-477.

8. ProCESS Investigators, Yealy DM, Kellum JA, Huang DT, et al. A randomized trial of protocol-based care for early septic shock. *N Engl J Med*. 2014;370:1683-1693.

9. Mouncey PR, Osborn TM, Power GS, et al; ProMISe Trial Investigators. Trial of early, goal-directed resuscitation for septic shock. *N Engl J Med*. 2015;372:1301-1311.

10. ARISE Investigators; ANZICS Clinical Trials Group, Peake SL, Delaney A, Bailey M, et al. Goal-directed resuscitation for patients with early septic shock. *N Engl J Med*. 2014;371:1496-1506.

11. Maitland K, Kiguli S, Opoka RO, et al; FEAST Trial Group. Mortality after fluid bolus in African children with severe infection. *N Engl J Med*. 2011;364:2483-2495.

12. Gan TJ, Soppitt A, Maroof M, et al. Goal-directed intraoperative fluid administration reduces length of hospital stay after major surgery. *Anesthesiology*. 2002;97:820-826.

9

13. Brandstrup B, Tønnesen H, Beier-Holgersen R, et al; Danish Study Group on Perioperative Fluid Therapy. Effects of intravenous fluid restriction on postoperative complications: comparison of two perioperative fluid regimens: a randomized assessor-blinded multicenter trial. *Ann Surg.* 2003;238:641-648.

14. Bellamy MC. Wet, dry or something else? *Br J Anaesth.* 2006;97:755-757.

15. Hamilton MA, Cecconi M, Rhodes A. A systematic review and meta-analysis on the use of preemptive hemodynamic intervention to improve postoperative outcomes in moderate and high-risk surgical patients. *Anesth Analg.* 2011;112:1392-1402.

16. Gurgel ST, do Nascimento P Jr. Maintaining tissue perfusion in high-risk surgical patients: a systematic review of randomized clinical trials. *Anesth Analg.* 2011;112:1384-1391.

17. Pearse RM, Harrison DA, MacDonald N, et al; OPTIMISE Study Group. Effect of a perioperative, cardiac output-guided hemodynamic therapy algorithm on outcomes following major gastrointestinal surgery: a randomized clinical trial and systematic review. *JAMA.* 2014;311:2181-2190.

18. Asfar P, Meziani F, Hamel JF, et al; SEPSISPAM Investigators. High versus low blood-pressure target in patients with septic shock. *N Engl J Med.* 2014;370:1583-1593.

19. Marik PE, Baram M, Vahid B. Does central venous pressure predict fluid responsiveness? A systematic review of the literature and the tale of seven mares. *Chest.* 2008;134:172-178.

20. Alpert RA, Roizen MF, Hamilton WK, et al. Intraoperative urinary output does not predict postoperative renal function in patients undergoing abdominal aortic revascularization. *Surgery.* 1984;95:707-711.

21. Thiele RH, Bartels K, Gan TJ. Cardiac output monitoring: a contemporary assessment and review. *Crit Care Med.* 2015;43:177-185.

22. Thiele RH, Bartels K, Gan TJ. Inter-device differences in monitoring for goal-directed fluid therapy. *Can J Anaesth.* 2015;62:169-181.

23. National Institute for Health and Care Excellence (NICE). CardioQ-ODM oesophageal doppler monitor. Web site. http://www.nice.org.uk/guidance/mtg3. Updated April 2015. Accessed February 25, 2016.

24. NHS Technology Adoption Centre (NTAC). Oesophageal Doppler-guided fluid management during major surgery: reducing postoperative complications and bed days. Web site http://www.evidence.nhs.uk/Search?q=Oesophageal+Doppler+-guid

ed+fluid+management+during+major+surgery. Updated March 2012. Accessed February 25, 2016.

25. Bartels K, Thiele RH. Advances in photoplethysmography: beyond arterial oxygen saturation. *Can J Anaesth.* 2015;62:1313-1328.

26. Thiele RH, Rea KM, Turrentine FE, et al. Standardization of care: impact of an enhanced recovery protocol on length of stay, complications, and direct costs after colorectal surgery. *J Am Coll Surg.* 2015;220:430-443.

27. Bartels K, Thiele RH. Advances in photoplethysmography: beyond arterial oxygen saturation. *Can J Anaesth.* 2015;62(12):1313-1328.

28. Waldron NH, Miller TE, Thacker JK, et al. A prospective comparison of a noninvasive cardiac output monitor versus esophageal Doppler monitor for goal-directed fluid therapy in colorectal surgery patients. *Anesth Analg.* 2014;118:966-975.

29. Brandstrup B, Svendsen PE, Rasmussen M, et al. Which goal for fluid therapy during colorectal surgery is followed by the best outcome:near-maximal stroke volume or zero fluid balance? *Br J Anaesth.* 2012;109:191-199.

30. Srinivasa S, Taylor MH, Singh PP, Yu TC, Soop M, Hill AG. Randomized clinical trial of goal-directed fluid therapy within an enhanced recovery protocol for elective colectomy. *Br J Surg.* 2013;100:66-74.

31. Phan TD, D'Souza B, Rattray MJ, Johnston MJ, Cowie BS. A randomised controlled trial of fluid restriction compared to oesophageal Doppler-guided goal-directed fluid therapy in elective major colorectal surgery within an Enhanced Recovery After Surgery program. *Anaesth Intensive Care.* 2014;42:752-760.

9

10   Role of Regional Anesthesia

by Martin Szafran, MD

Introduction

Postoperative pain management is a critical component of enhanced recovery pathways (ERPs). Regional anesthetic techniques can play a role in opioid-sparing strategies by minimizing opioid-related side effects. The gold standard regional technique for major open abdominal surgery remains thoracic epidural anesthesia (TEA), with potential benefits that include shortening the length of hospital stay (LOS), as well as improving morbidity and mortality outcomes. In the setting of ERPs, more recent meta-analyses have cast some doubt on the absolute benefit of this procedure, and some of the previously known pitfalls of placing epidural catheters have resurfaced.[1] Intrathecal opioid administration and newer techniques such as the transversus abdominis plane (TAP) block have emerged as potential safer alternatives to TEA.

This chapter will focus on evaluating the current evidence for and against the use of thoracic epidurals in major abdominopelvic surgery, evaluating its role within ERPs, as well as reviewing the alternative regional techniques that can be utilized.

Thoracic Epidural Anesthesia

The decision to place an epidural for postoperative pain management is vested in several key principals. The potential benefits of placing an epidural are numerous and well documented. Many of these are listed in **Table 10.1**. On the other hand, placing an epidural is not a completely benign process, carrying several inherent concerns, as noted in **Table 10.2**. If

TABLE 10.1 — Potential Thoracic Epidural Benefits

Pulmonary	• Improved respiratory function • Decreased respiratory depression • Lower incidence of pneumonia
Cardiovascular	• Increased coronary perfusion • Decreased incidence of periop MI • Reduced postoperative arrhythmia • Decreased incidence of DVT and PE
Renal	• Improved kidney function
Gastrointestinal	• Decreased incidence of postoperative ileus
Hematologic	• Decreased transfusion requirements
Other	• Improved pain score/pain control • Decreased opioid requirement • Shortened LOS • 30-day mortality improvement

TABLE 10.2 — Thoracic Epidural Placement Limitations and Risks

Cardiovascular	• Vasodilation and hypotension
Neurologic	• Paresthesia with placement • Post dural puncture headache • Subarachnoid or intrathecal catheter placement • Nerve injury
Hematologic	• Anticoagulation restrictions on placement/removal • Epidural hematoma
Infectious	• Epidural abscess
Other	• Failed epidural/delayed analgesia • Labor/cost of epidural placement and management

a program is to adopt routine epidural placement for postoperative pain management, considerations such as cost of placing a catheter, adequate nurse education, and the availability of a designated team to manage and troubleshoot the epidural have to be taken into account.

It is important to evaluate potential benefits in detail. Earlier meta-analyses suggested that in patients undergoing major surgery, TEA could potentially improve 30-day postoperative mortality.[2] This outcome, in the presence of decreased morbidities, has been difficult to validate, with newer and larger meta-analyses suggesting minimal absolute mortality benefit of TEA.[3] With improved general anesthetic techniques, novel anesthetic medications, and advanced surgical technique, difficulty in showing TEA mortality benefits is not surprising. Nevertheless, the utility of TEA can be based on the potential morbidity benefits listed in **Table 10.1** and discussed in more detail below.

10

■ Cardiovascular Benefits

Blockade of sympathetic tone in thoracolumbar distribution can lead to arterial vasodilation, a decrease in systemic vascular resistance, and potentially drastic chronotropic and ionotropic effects on the heart.[4] These physiologic changes after TEA have translated into clinical benefits, most readily shown in sicker patient populations. In patients with known coronary artery disease undergoing coronary artery bypass grafting, TEA has been shown to have numerous benefits including decreased perioperative ischemia and improved wall motion abnormalities and left ventricular function.[5] One larger meta-analysis hints at the possibility of TEA having a larger benefit in preventing postoperative arrhythmias and pulmonary morbidity, with a smaller effect on cardiac ischemia.[6] TEA cardiovascular benefits in healthier populations and those undergoing abdominopelvic surgery are more inconclusive, and the exact cardiovascular benefits are not well defined.[7]

■ Pulmonary Effects

Similar to cardiovascular benefits, the pulmonary benefits of TEA have been determined to be most profound in sicker patients undergoing major open abdominal surgery.[8] In minimally invasive abdominal surgery, it has been difficult to show a decrease in serious pulmonary complications, such as pneumonia or worsened pulmonary function. Furthermore, in the setting of other ERPs, even in major open abdominal surgery, TEA has not shown significant difference in pulmonary morbidity.[1]

■ Gastrointestinal Effects

Improved recovery of bowel function after major open abdominal surgery with the use of TEA is well documented.[9] This is arguably one of the major benefits of TEA. It is unclear whether this benefit leads to shorter hospital stays, but in conjunction with improved pain scores, possible earlier mobility, and ability to tolerate a diet, TEA becomes an appealing option for postoperative pain control.

■ TEA and Enhanced Recovery

Several smaller trials evaluating the utility of TEA within ERPs for open abdominal surgery have been published, including a review and meta-analysis of these studies.[1] The seven trials included close to 400 patients and compared TEA with either patient-controlled analgesia (PCA) or continuous wound infiltration (CWI). The primary outcome evaluated was the incidence of any significant complication occurring within the first 30 days post-op, including pulmonary and cardiac complications, ileus, anastomotic leak, venous thromboembolism, and confusion. Although this is a small sample size and complication rates were low in all groups, **Figure 10.1** shows the forest plot for the primary outcome included in the published study, suggesting very little difference between the two groups. These outcomes need further evaluation, but the question surrounding the utility of TEA in setting of other enhanced recovery measures does arise.

FIGURE 10.1 — Forest Plot Showing Complications Within 30 Days of Surgery in Epidural and Non-Epidural Groups

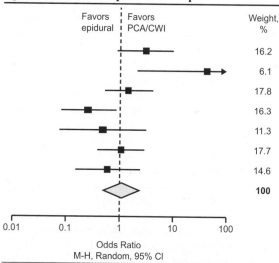

PCA, patient-controlled analgesia; CWI, continuous wound infiltration

Hughes MJ, et al. *JAMA Surg.* 2014;149(2):1224-1230.

With the advance of minimally invasive procedures and increased implementation of other opioid-sparing techniques, it is possible that the overall benefits of TEA are diminished.

Interestingly, the above meta-analysis was able to show certain secondary outcome benefits of TEA. For one, pain scores were improved. Also return to gut function was faster, although ileus rates were similar.[1] Larger sample sizes and more studies are needed to further elucidate these results, especially given that older but larger meta-analyses showed improvement in 30-day morbidity and mortality with the use of TEA.[2]

Transversus Abdominis Plane Block

The transversus abdominis plane (TAP) block is a truncal regional anesthetic technique that may be used as an alternative to TEA. TAP blocks involve identifying the neurovascular plane between the internal oblique and transversus abdominis muscles and depositing local anesthetic within that plane. There are several different approaches, and the nomenclature for the specific variations of the block has evolved in the last decade, but the purpose of blocking sensory innervation to the upper and lower abdomen has not changed. Dermatome coverage on the order of T7 to L1 is considered the target range for TAP blocks and has been verified using cadaveric studies.[10]

TAP blocks have recently undergone a transformation in how they are performed and applied clinically. Initially the blocks were performed without the use of an ultrasound. A single shot lateral TAP block technique has shown significant clinical benefit in major abdominopelvic surgery, reducing pain scores and opioid requirements.[11,12] Hebbard and colleagues went on to describe the lateral ultrasound-guided approach, where the ultrasound probe is perpendicular to the mid-axillary line between the iliac crest and subcostal margin and a needle is inserted in-plane from the antero-medial direction (**Figure 10.2**).[13] The author later described an oblique subcostal approach to the block, with the intention to cover higher dermatomes and improve analgesia for upper abdominal surgery (**Figure 10.3**).[14]

■ TAP Block vs TEA

It is important to recognize that TAP blocks are designed to block somatic pain from surgical incision in specific dermatomes, and are not expected to decrease visceral or sympathetically mediated pain. TAP blocks come with significant advantages over a central neuraxial block—they do not have the same anticoagulation restrictions and are not associated with hypotension.

FIGURE 10.2 — Ultrasound Image of Lateral TAP Block

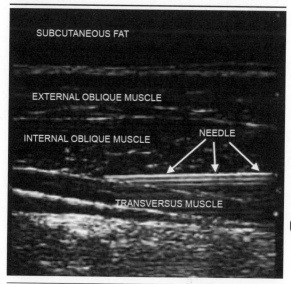

Needle placement in neurofascial plane between internal oblique and transversus abdominis muscles.

Hebbard P. *Anaesth Intensive Care*. 2007;35(4):616-617.

There is evidence that suggests TEA is superior to single shot TAP blocks for open abdominal surgery, showing improved pain scores and decreased opioid requirement in the first 24 hours after radical gastrectomy.[15] This result is not unexpected; a well-working epidural should have more analgesic benefit than the incisional pain block caused by a TAP block. Of note, improved pain scores and decreased opioid requirement are again noted in this study when comparing TAP blocks to placebo.[15]

■ TAP Block and Laparoscopic Surgery

Studies have shown TAP blocks to be beneficial compared to placebo when administered for laparoscopic abdominopelvic surgery.[16] Unfortunately when

FIGURE 10.3 — Ultrasound Probe and Needle Positioning for the Oblique Subcostal Approach to TAP Block

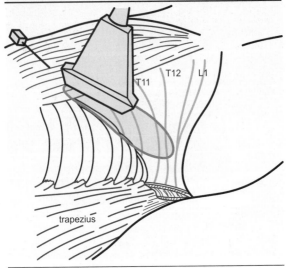

Hebbard P. *Anesth Analg*. 2008;106:674-675.

compared to wound infiltration by the surgeon, no analgesic or opioid-sparing benefits have been shown.[17] Newer, but smaller studies have aimed to show equal analgesic benefit when a combination of lateral and subcostal TAP block approaches were compared to TEA, with some success in laparoscopic colorectal surgery.[18] With the expansion of minimally invasive techniques, the utility of the TAP block as part of ERPs in not well defined but is currently being investigated. Delaney and associates have been able to show the benefit of TAPs in laparoscopic colectomy in the form of decreased hospital stay, without any increased morbidity or mortality.[19] At this time, more studies are required to make more absolute conclusions on TAP block benefits within ERPs.

Spinal Anesthesia

Spinal anesthesia as an alternative to general anesthesia has been utilized successfully in appropriate patient populations. It allows for rapid awakening, immediate postoperative pain control, modulation of the surgical stress response, and possibly improved morbidity. The strongest benefits of spinal anesthesia have been shown in orthopedic operations, such hip surgery in elderly patients.[20] Benefits such as decrease in deep vein thrombosis and a decrease in post-operative confusion in elderly patients have been noted in a large meta-analysis.[21] Currently, spinal anesthesia is employed primarily in the sub-umbilical surgery subset of open abdominopelvic surgery, especially in parturients and elderly patients.

Spinal anesthesia carries risks similar to TEA (**Table 10.2**). Additionally, the decreased sympathetic tone and subsequent hypotension may require aggressive volume expansion, challenging the anesthesia provider to adhere to ERP protocols. The timing and length of surgery also has to be taken into account when administering a single shot spinal anesthetic.

Intrathecal morphine without the use of local anesthesia can be applied as a tool to manage postoperative pain. The restrictions of using spinal anesthesia as the main anesthetic would not apply, especially intraoperative hypotension secondary to intrathecal local anesthetic administration. The opioid-sparing benefit of intrathecal morphine in major abdominal surgery has been shown to last up to 48 hours after surgery but is most pronounced in the initial 24 hours after an operation.[22] This large meta-analysis also concludes that improvement of pain scores on the visual analogue scale at 24 hours after the operation is roughly similar to that commonly reported in TEA studies, suggesting that single dose intrathecal opioid administration for major abdominal surgery is a viable alternative to TEA for postoperative pain management.

10

It is important to consider the potential increased risk of respiratory depression in patients who receive intrathecal opioids. This risk is further increased when additional opioids are administered intravenously, and in those situations, higher acuity monitoring of patients may be warranted.

Conclusions

Incorporation of any regional anesthetic technique into an ERP comes with many considerations. Navigating the wealth of evidence both for and against epidural placement is not easy. TEA remains in many ways the gold standard for open abdominopelvic surgery, with benefits that extend beyond analgesic benefits and opioid-sparing benefits. The majority of epidural benefits have been documented in sicker patients undergoing larger procedures, but the utility of TEA can extend beyond this narrow patient population. TEA benefits may diminish within ERPs, but this result again needs further investigation. Implementing TEA into routine practice requires a dedicated team that can place, manage, and troubleshoot the epidural, nursing staff on floors that is familiar with epidural complications, as well as a surgical team that is amenable to assisting in managing complications such as postoperative hypotension.

TAP blocks are an alternative to TEA, having a smaller window for analgesic benefits but also not bearing all of the risks and complications of TEA placement. The majority of TAP block benefits have been shown when compared to placebo, especially in open abdominopelvic surgery. Wound infiltration by the surgery team in minimally invasive procedures may be an equivocal opioid sparing technique. TAP blocks for abdominal surgery in concurrent ERPs are currently being investigated. Both TEA and TAP blocks can have a large role in opioid-sparing techniques as part of ERPs, but again require a strong support system in order to be incorporated successfully.

Finally, the use of intrathecal opioids is a viable alternative to TEA and, similar to TAP blocks, is not associated with hypotension, but may come with increased risk of postoperative respiratory depression.

REFERENCES

1. Hughes MJ, Ventham NT, McNally S, Harrison E, Wigmore S. Analgesia after open abdominal surgery in the setting of enhanced recovery surgery: a systematic review and meta-analysis. *JAMA Surg.* 2014; 149(12):1224-1230.

2. Rodgers A, Walker N, Schug S, et al. Reduction of postoperative mortality and morbidity with epidural or spinal anaesthesia: results from overview of randomized trials. *BMJ.* 2000; 321:1493-1497.

3. Rigg JR, Jamrozik K, Myles PS, et al. Epidural anaesthesia and analgesia and outcome of major surgery: a randomized trial. *Lancet.* 2002; 359:1276-1282.

4. Veering BT1, Cousins MJ. Cardiovascular and pulmonary effects of epidural anaesthesia. *Anaesth Intensive Care.* 2000; 28(6):620-635.

5. Berendes E, Schmidt C, Van Aken H, et al. Reversible cardiac sympathectomy by high thoracic epidural anesthesia improves regional left ventricular function in patients undergoing coronary artery bypass grafting: a randomized trial. *Arch Surg.* 2003; 138(12):1283-1290.

6. Svircevic V, van Dijk D, Nierich AP, et al. Meta-analysis of thoracic epidural anesthesia versus general anesthesia for cardiac surgery. *Anesthesiology.* 2011; 114(2):271-282.

7. Liu SS, Wu CL. Effect of postoperative analgesia on major postoperative complications: a systematic update of the evidence. *Anesth Analg.* 2007; 104(3):689-702.

8. Hanna MN, Murphy JD, Kumar K, Wu CL. Regional techniques and outcome: what is the evidence? *Curr Opin Anaesthesiol.* 2009; 22(5):672-677.

9. Jørgensen H, Wetterslev J, Møiniche S, Dahl JB. Epidural local anaesthetics versus opioid-based analgesic regimens on postoperative gastrointestinal paralysis, PONV and pain after abdominal surgery. *Cochrane Database Syst Rev.* 2000; CD001893.

10. McDonnell JG, O'Donnell BD, Farrell T, et al. Transversus abdominis plane block: a cadaveric and radiological evaluation. *Reg Anesth Pain Med.* 2007;32(5):399-404.

10

11. McDonnell JG, O'Donnell B, Curley G, et al. The analgesic efficacy of transversus abdominis plane block after abdominal surgery: a prospective randomized controlled trial. *Anesth Analg*. 2007; 104(1):193-197.

12. McDonnell JG, Curley G, Carney J, et al. The analgesic efficacy of transversus abdominis plane block after cesarean delivery: a randomized controlled trial. *Anesth Analg*. 2008;106(1):186-191.

13. Hebbard P, Fujiwara Y, Shibata Y, et al. Ultrasound-guided transversus abdominis plane (TAP) block. *Anaesth Intens Care*. 2007; 35(4):616-617.

14. Hebbard P. Subcostal transversus abdominis plane block under ultrasound guidance. *Anesth Analg*. 2008; 106:674-5.

15. Wu Y, Liu F, Tang H, Wang Q, et al. The analgesic efficacy of subcostal transversus abdominis plane block compared with thoracic epidural analgesia and intravenous opioid analgesia after radical gastrectomy. *Anesth Analg*. 2013; 117(2):507-513.

16. Walter CJ, Maxwell-Armstrong C, Pinkney TD, et al. A randomised controlled trial of the efficacy of ultrasound-guided transversus abdominis plane (TAP) block in laparoscopic colorectal surgery. *Surg Endosc*. 2013;27(7):2366-2372.

17. Ortiz J, Suliburk JW, Wu K, et al. Bilateral transversus abdominis plane block does not decrease postoperative pain after laparoscopic cholecystectomy when compared with local anesthetic infiltration of trocar insertion sites. *Reg Anesth Pain Med*. 2012; 37(2):188-192.

18. Niraj G, Kelkar A, Hart E, Horst C, Malik D, Yeow C, Singh B, Chaudhri S. Comparison of analgesic efficacy of four-quadrant transversus abdominis plane (TAP) block and continuous posterior TAP analgesia with epidural analgesia in patients undergoing laparoscopic colorectal surgery: an open-label, randomised, non-inferiority trial. *Anaesthesia*. 2014;69(4):348-355.

19. Favuzza J, Delaney CP. Outcomes of discharge after elective laparoscopic colorectal surgery with transversus abdominis plane blocks and enhanced recovery pathway. *J Am Coll Surg*. 2013;217(3):503-506.

20. Luger TJ, Kammerlander C, Gosch M, et al. Neuroaxial versus general anaesthesia in geriatric patients for hip fracture surgery: does it matter? *Osteoporos Int*. 2010;21:S555–S572.

21. Parker MJ, Handoll HH, Griffiths R. Anaesthesia for hip fracture surgery in adults. *Cochrane Database Syst Rev*. 2004;CD000521.

22. Meylan N, Elia N, Lysakowski C, Tramèr MR. Benefit and risk of intrathecal morphine without local anaesthetic in patients undergoing major surgery: meta-analysis of randomized trials. *Br J Anaesth*. 2009;102(2):156-167.

11
Maintaining Normothermia

by Larry Manders, MD and
Roy G. Soto, MD

Introduction

Enhanced recovery protocols inherently work by reducing variability in specific perioperative interventions. In 2006, the Joint Commission published a set of core measures in an attempt to reduce surgical complications based, in part, on variability reduction. These measures, known as the Surgical Care Improvement Project (SCIP), include a number of interventions primarily intended to decrease the risk of perioperative infection. Maintenance of normothermia (SCIP measure Inf-10) in particular has been shown to correlate with improved surgical outcomes,[1] and maintenance of normothermia has become an important cornerstone in enhanced recovery protocols worldwide. In this chapter, we will outline how normal thermoregulation is altered in the anesthetized surgical patient, discuss sequelae of varying degrees of hypothermia, and provide a framework for protocolizing temperature care for patients undergoing major abdominopelvic surgery.

Thermoregulation in Non-Anesthetized vs Anesthetized Patient

In the non-anesthetized patient, a normothermic set point referred to as the inter-threshold range is present. This set point corresponds to a core temperature of approximately $37^{\circ}C \pm 0.2^{\circ}C$.[2] The inter-threshold range is under tight control from the hypothalamus. When core temperatures rise to the upper level of the inter-threshold range, the hypothalamus triggers sweating and the vasodilation of peripheral blood vessels at the skin surface. These changes facilitate heat loss through radiation and convection (**Table 11.1**). In conditions where core temperatures drop to lower levels, the hypothalamus triggers vasoconstriction, which decreases heat loss via convection. Decreased temperature also triggers muscular shivering, which generates heat via thermogenesis secondary to intramuscular metabolism.[3]

TABLE 11.1 — Routes of Heat Transfer

Route	Definition	Example
Radiation	Transfer of heat from one surface to another due to photon transfer	Surrounded by cold equipment in the operating room
Convection	Transfer of heat to the surrounding air	Cold, continuously circulated room air temperatures
Conduction	Transfer of heat from one surface to another via direct contact	Operating room beds, intravenous fluids
Evaporation	Transfer of heat from vaporization of liquids to gas	Sterile surgical preparatory solution

In patients undergoing anesthesia, the use of different anesthetic drugs inhibits the body's ability to thermoregulate. General anesthetics suppress the hypothalamic response to variations in temperature. This physiological change widens the inter-threshold range to include temperatures well below the normal set point.[4,5] With this blunting of the control, the normal degree of heat conservation due to vasoconstriction is decreased and does not return until core temperature drops by 2-3°C.[6] Neuromuscular blocking agents prevent thermogenesis through muscular shivering. Regional anesthetics such as spinals, epidurals, and neuraxial blocks cause unregulated vasodilatation in the body's periphery that is uninhibited from normal hypothalamic control.[3]

Surgical Factors Affecting Normothermia

In order to provide a framework for surgical losses, we will discuss them in terms of the three routes of heat transfer: radiation, convection, and conduction. All types of heat transfer contribute to heat loss (**Table 11.1**). Radiation is the largest cause of heat loss and is the hardest to counteract in the surgical setting.[1] Heat loss through conduction and convection is controllable with certain interventions. Cold operating room temperatures, increased exposure of body surface area, and cold sterile preparatory solution are factors that provide the perfect storm of conditions to facilitate all forms of heat loss.

Pattern and Stages of Hypothermia

Hypothermia during surgery facilitated by general anesthesia follows a very specific pattern that is dependent on the type of anesthetic used, drug dosage, amount of surgical exposure, and operating room temperature[7-9] (**Figure 11.1**). During the first hour of surgery (stage 1), the body's core temperature drops on average 1-1.5°C. Afterward, temperature falls another 1-2°C over the next 3 to 4 hours (stage 2) until the point at which it reaches a final plateau and does not decrease further (stage 3).[10]

The stages of hypothermia are important to recognize for two specific reasons:

- The initial temperature drop (during stage 1) can be reduced with certain interventions but not eliminated.
- Understanding the stages of hypothermia can halt progression from stage 1 to 2 with the proper interventions.[11]

11

FIGURE 11.1 — Core Temperatures During and After Colorectal Surgery in Study Patients

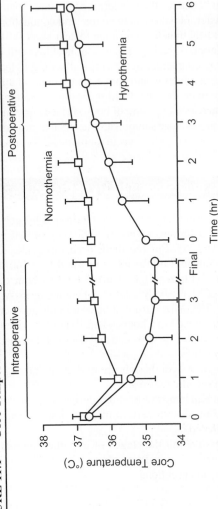

The mean (± SD) final intraoperative core temperature was 34.7 ± 0.6°C in 96 patients assigned to hypothermia who received routine thermal care and 36.6 ± 0.5°C in the 104 patients assigned to normothermia, who were given extra warming. The core temperatures in the two groups differed significantly at each measurement, except before the induction of anesthesia (first measurement) and after 6 hours of recovery.

Kurz A, et al. *N Engl J Med.* 1996;334:1209-1215.

Complications and Classifications of Hypothermia

At all stages of hypothermia, the body begins to experience difficulties with hemostasis, healing, immune function, and drug metabolism. Hypothermia inhibits the initiation phase of thrombin generation and inhibits fibrinogen synthesis.[12] In addition, hypothermia causes decreased function of both coagulation factors and platelets.[11] There is a direct correlation between patients with intraoperative hypothermia and increased surgical blood loss, even with temperature drops as little as 0.5°C.[13]

Hypothermia results in an increase in wound infections and delayed wound healing. Decreased body temperatures reduce antimicrobial effects via decreased production of oxygen free radicals within neutrophils.[14] In addition, the chemotaxis and phagocytosis of granulocytes, motility of macrophages, and production of antibodies are all decreased causing a weakened immune response.[15,16] These changes have led to delayed suture removal, wound breakdown, and prolonged hospital stays compared to patient who remained normothermic perioperatively.[17]

Intraoperative hypothermia can be subdivided into three classification groups based on core body temperature: mild, moderate, and severe. Patients within each classification demonstrate unique symptoms, physiologic derangements, and require different interventions for treatment (**Table 11.2**).

Mild hypothermia is generally classified as less than 36°C. At these temperatures, patients demonstrate signs of tachycardia, peripheral vasoconstriction, shivering, and tachypnea. These changes are not benign as the associated hypertension and tachycardia increase the risk of cardiac morbidity and mortality in elderly patients.[17] Hyperglycemia also occurs due to sympathetically mediated gluconeogenesis and a decrease in cellular insulin sensitivity. In non-anesthetized or

TABLE 11.2 — Physiologic Effects of Hypothermia

Increased

- Alterations in mentation
- Cardiac arrhythmias
- Coagulopathy (platelet dysfunction)
- Hemoglobin oxygen affinity (left shift of hemoglobin-oxygen saturation curve)
- Oxygen tissue demands
- Peripheral vascular resistance
- Protein catabolism
- Shivering

Decreased

- Drug biotransformation/metabolism
- Immune function
- Renal function
- Wound healing

sedated patients, varying degrees of mental confusion may begin to develop.

At temperatures <35°C, the body's hypothalamic thermoregulatory capacity can no longer compensate. Shivering may become more forceful to the point at which muscular miscoordination appears.[18] The degree of peripheral vasoconstriction has maximized to the point where perfusion to the periphery is reduced. Due to these effects, increasing difficulties with hemodynamic stability may arise.

Severe intraoperative hypothermia (<34°C) is usually present in patient who have undergone significant surgical changes either deliberately or inadvertently. Severe intraoperative hypothermia may also be artificially induced for cardiac or neuroprotection when concerns for ischemia exist. The protective effects from decreased metabolic demands should be weighed carefully against the previously described complications such as coagulopathy and infections.

Monitoring, Preventing, and Treating Hypothermia

Body temperatures should be monitored in all major abdominopelvic operations as clinically significant changes in body temperature are predictable. The sites for temperature monitoring are varied. Central sites such as the esophagus, nasopharynx, bladder, or blood are the most accurate reflection of core temperature but are not as easily accessible as cutaneous sites.[19] In major abdominopelvic surgery, the measurement of core temperature at central sites is absolutely necessary to accurately assess core temperature for the purpose of providing goal-directed interventions to maintain normothermia.

As previously discussed, the causes of hypothermia in the anesthetized surgical patient are multifactorial. Intraoperative strategies for reducing hypothermia focus on dampening the degree of stage 1 hypothermia and warming the patient to prevent further heat loss. There are multiple techniques and devices available to counter hypothermia, each having benefits and limitations. Heat/humidified inspired gases and low flow circle system prevent heat loss caused by ventilation.

Intravenous fluid warmers, though effective, may be of limited utility in warming a patient especially in those receiving limited amounts of goal directed fluid therapy.[20] Fluid warmers work by directly transferring heat via conduction to intravenous fluids as they pass through a series of tubes that are in contact with warmed steel rings or conductive surfaces. In order to provide any significant effect, warmed intravenous, fluids must be given quickly and in large volumes, which directly oppose current guidelines for intraoperative fluid management. Thus, the value of an intravenous fluid warmer is minimal for most patients.

Forced air warmers provide heat through convection; their effectiveness is directly related to the degree of body surface area contacted. Both upper and lower body forced air warmers have been shown

11

to be effective after 2 to 3 hours of use in returning patients undergoing major abdominal surgeries with phase 2 hypothermia to a normothermic state. Lower body forced air warmers provide a greater degree of body surface area coverage and have proven superior in increasing body temperature over a short period of time.[19] In major abdominopelvic surgery, large surgical fields sometimes restrict the use of forced air warmers to the upper body, which is suboptimal in covering a significant body surface area. Forced air warming is effective in maintaining or returning patient to normothermia but has limited ability in blunt phase 1hypothermia.

Environmental exposure and lack of attentiveness of surgical personnel are correctable contributors to hypothermia. Surgical patients are regularly brought into the cold operating rooms, disrobed, and then painted with cold preparatory solutions that are allowed to dry for an extended period of time prior to the patient being draped for surgery. During this time the anesthetized patient is exposed to all forms of heat loss, which directly combat the patient's ability to maintain normothermia and help to facilitate phase 1 hypothermia.

Simple interventions such as increasing ambient room temperatures above 79°F throughout the preoperative setting or the use of warming blankets prior to entering the operating room are extremely important as they are the only interventions that have been clinically shown to blunt phase 1 hypothermia.[7,21] Furthermore, prep solutions should be allowed to adequately dry, and damp gowns/blankets should be removed prior to surgical draping. Once the patient is properly draped and the exposed body surface area is minimized, the operative room temperature may be decreased to facilitate surgeon comfort.

It is extremely imperative to educate all surgical personnel (surgical staff, nursing, ancillary operating room staff) on the importance of providing a surgical environment that prevents hypothermia. **Table 11.3**

TABLE 11.3 — Standardized Approach for Maintaining Normothermia in an Enhanced Recovery Program

Monitoring

- Assess temperature prior, during, and post surgery
- Core temperature monitoring for all patients under general or regional anesthesia

Prewarming

- Maintain ambient room temperature to above 79°F/26°F both in preoperative and operating room prior to surgery
- Provide warming blankets prior to entering the operating room
- Do not over heat patient to point of sweat due to increased risk of evaporated heat loss
- Ensure dry surgical garments and preoperative linens

Intraoperative/Post-Op

- Continue to maintain room temperature at or above 79°F/26°F in operating room during surgical prep
- Ensure surgical prep solution properly dries. (Room temperature can be slightly decreased for surgeon comfort following drying of prep/draping of patient)
- Limit areas of exposed skin
- Provide warming blankets (forced-air/warm water) over the largest available surface area
- Implement fluid warmers
- Heat/humidify inspired gases

The education of all members of the perioperative team is important as it is everyone's responsibility to create conditions conducive to maintaining normothermia.

provides an evidence-based protocol for reducing hypothermia for abdominopelvic surgical patients.

Temperature assessment should be continued after completion of surgery and while transferring the patient to the post anesthesia care unit (PACU) or intensive care unit (ICU). Postoperative hypothermia is associated with the same decreased outcomes as intraoperative hypothermia. Previously discussed interventions should be continued postoperatively if normothermia was not achieved or maintained following completion of the surgery. As the patient continues to recover from anesthesia, their intrinsic ability to thermoregulate will return to normal, allowing for the discontinuation of the practitioner-guided warming techniques.

Conclusions

Although ideal methods of hypothermia prevention have been known for decades, implementation of these techniques is haphazard at best, leaving anesthesia providers to catch up with less useful techniques for the remainder of the case, hoping that the patient will return to a normothermic state by the time they arrive in the PACU. Normothermia upon arrival in the PACU is used as a surrogate for anesthesia quality internationally, and failure to reach specific goals will ultimately have financial/reimbursement consequences.[22,23]

Given the predictable pathophysiology of perioperative hypothermia, the understanding of best practices to maintain normothermia, as well as the existing financial pressures to comply with temperature standards, we recommend a simple, low-cost, and standardized approach for all enhanced recovery patients.

REFERENCE

1. Scott AV, Stonemetz JL, Wasey JO, et al. Compliance with surgical care improvement project for body temperature management (SCIP Inf-10) is associated with improved clinical outcomes. *Anesthesiology*. 2015;123:116-125.

2. Lopez M, Sessler DI, Walter K, Emerick T, Ozaki M. Rate and gender dependence of the sweating, vasoconstriction, and shivering thresholds in humans. *Anesthesiology*. 1994;80:780-788.

3. Sessler DI. Perioperative heat balance. *Anesthesiology*. 2000;92:578-596.

4. Xiong J, Kurz A, Sessler DI, et al. Isoflurane produces marked and nonlinear decreases in the vasoconstriction and shivering thresholds. *Anesthesiology*. 1996;85:240-245.

5. Kurz A, Ikeda T, Sessler DI, et al. Meperidine decreases the shivering threshold twice as much as the vasoconstriction threshold. *Anesthesiology*. 1997;86:1046-1054.

6. Vaughan MS, Vaughan RW, Cork RC. Postoperative hypothermia in adults:relationship of age, anesthesia, and shivering to rewarming. *Anesth Analg*. 1981;60:746-751.

7. Hart SR, Bordes B, Hart J, Corsino D, Harmon D. Unintended perioperative hypothermia. *Ochsner J*. 2011;11:259-270.

8. Morris RH, Wilkey BR. The effects of ambient temperature on patient temperature during surgery not involving body cavities. *Anesthesiology*. 1970;32:102-107.

9. Morris RH. Influence of ambient temperature on patient temperature during intraabdominal surgery. *Ann Surg*. 1971;173:230-233.

10. Kurz A, Sessler DI, Christensen R, Dechert M. Heat balance and distribution during the core-temperature plateau in anesthetized humans. *Anesthesiology*. 1995;83:491-499.

11. Sun Z, Honar H, Sessler DI, et al. Intraoperative core temperature patterns, transfusion requirement, and hospital duration in patients warmed with forced air. *Anesthesiology*. 2015;122:276-285.

12. Martini WZ. Coagulopathy by hypothermia and acidosis: mechanisms of thrombin generation and fibrinogen availability. *J Trauma*. 2009;67:202-208.

13. Winkler M, Akça O, Birkenberg B, et al. Aggressive warming reduces blood loss during hip arthroplasty. *Anesth Analg*. 2000;91:978-984.

11

14. Hohn DC, MacKay RD, Halliday B, Hunt TK. Effect of O2 tension on microbicidal function of leukocytes in wounds and in vitro. *Surg Forum*. 1976;27:18-20.

15. van Oss CJ, Absolom DR, Moore LL, Park BH, Humbert JR. Effect of temperature on the chemotaxis, phagocytic engulfment, digestion and O2 consumption of human polymorphonuclear leukocytes. *J Reticuloendothel Soc*. 1980;27:561-565.

16. Leijh PC, van den Barselaar MT, van Zwet TL, Dubbeldeman-Rempt I, van Furth R. Kinetics of phagocytosis of Staphylococcus aureus and Escherichia coli by human granulocytes. *Immunology*. 1979;37:453-465.

17. Leslie K, Sessler DI. Perioperative hypothermia in the high-risk surgical patient. *Best Pract Res Clin Anaesthesiol*. 2003;17:485-498.

18. Cheung SS, Montie DL, White MD, Behm D. Changes in manual dexterity following short-term hand and forearm immersion in 10 degrees C water. *Aviat Space Environ Med*. 2003;74:990-993.

19. Motamed C, Labaille T, Léon O, Panzani JP, Duvaldestin P, Benhamou D. Core and thenar skin temperature variation during prolonged abdominal surgery: comparison of two sites of active forced air warming. *Acta Anaesthesiol Scand*. 2000;44:249-254.

20. Raghunathan K, Singh M, Lobo DN. Fluid management in abdominal surgery: what, when, and when not to administer. *Anesthesiol Clin*. 2015;33:51-64.

21. Reynolds L, Beckmann J, Kurz A. Perioperative complications of hypothermia. *Best Pract Res Clin Anaesthesiol*. 2008;22:645-657.

22. Tillman M, Wehbe-Janek H, Hodges B, Smythe WR, Papaconstantinou HT. Surgical care improvement project and surgical site infections: can integration in the surgical safety checklist improve quality performance and clinical outcomes? *J Surg Res*. 2013;184:150-156.

23. Steelman VM, Perkhounkova YS, Lemke JH. The gap between compliance with the quality performance measure "perioperative temperature management" and normothermia. *J Healthc Qual*. 2015;37:333-341.

12 Surgical Approaches and Techniques

by Ryan W Day, MD and Tonia M Young-Fadok, MD, MS, FACS, FASCRS

Introduction

That an operation is being performed is clearly the central tenet and requirement for enhanced recovery. While the nature of the operation, the disease process, surgeon, and patient factors all have a role in outcomes, the actual technique used for the operation has a major bearing on the patient's anticipated recovery.

Historically, the introduction of laparoscopic techniques for cholecystectomy and the subsequent refinement of instrumentation and technology revolutionized the surgical world. Surgeons and especially patients readily acknowledged the marked differences in incision length, pain levels, duration of hospital stay, and overall recovery. Subsequent research interestingly showed how mini-laparotomy could achieve similar outcomes, although such approaches were only feasible on patients of normal body mass index (BMI). Other avenues of research, taking cues from laparoscopic cholecystectomy, indicated that early feeding after laparoscopic surgery was safe and well-tolerated.

Minimally invasive approaches are, however, not always feasible whether due to an emergency setting, the nature of the underlying disease process, extensive adhesions, or even lack of surgeon expertise. A considerable body of work and research has evolved, initially mainly in open colorectal cases, to show that the adoption of enhanced recovery pathways can mitigate some of the deleterious effects of the larger incisions used for open surgery, so that postoperative recovery after open surgery begins to follow the outcomes expected of minimally invasive surgery.

Communication

Similar to other aspects of enhanced recovery, the selection of surgical technique and corresponding anesthetic approach requires a partnership across disciplines and contributions from different specialties. Centers that have defined clinical care pathways and buy-in from all stakeholders will undoubtedly be more successful in coordinating care and achieving the best outcomes. Decisions made around the time of the operation by the anesthesiologist and surgeon have implications that affect the others' discipline, and maintaining open lines of communication is essential to providing timely and appropriate care.

Communication in the pre-operative period can help tailor the best anesthetic technique for a particular patient and surgical approach. During the operation, communication about the progress of the operation, deviations from planned operative approach, patient's vital signs, and intraoperative blood loss can all help to guide appropriate fluid, medication, and surgical therapy. Finally, dialogue at the conclusion of an operation can help to establish the trajectory of early postoperative recovery. This complies with current recommendations to utilize a pre-operative briefing, procedural pause, and postoperative debriefing to enhance perioperative care.

Pre-operative Considerations

Regardless of surgical approach, there are several pre-operative steps that should be standard protocol in order to reduce the frequency of adverse events after major abdominopelvic operations. Intravenous antibiotics should be administered within 60 minutes prior to any skin incision in order to reduce the frequency of postoperative infectious complications. Guidelines exist for the choice of antibiotics. In patients undergoing colorectal resection, the appropriate use of pre-operative antibiotics has been shown to reduce the rate of postoperative surgical site infection by up to 75%.[1] There may be an additional benefit from oral antibiotics as part of preoperative preparation. Thromboprophylaxis and maintenance of normothermia are also standard recommendations and components of national guidelines.

In addition to intravenous antibiotics, all patients should undergo local decontamination prior to the operation. In patients with no history of allergic reaction, chlorhexidine-alcohol–based solutions should be used to cleanse the abdomen. The use of corticosteroids administered near the time of incision to help modulate and blunt the inflammatory reaction of the operation remains controversial.[2]

Operative Approaches

There are a variety of operative approaches for major abdominopelvic operations. When all factors are equal, however, it is worth bearing in mind that there is a clear stepwise improvement in outcomes depending on the use of open laparotomy, laparoscopic techniques, without or with enhanced recovery protocols. This was clearly demonstrated in a very clean four-way randomized controlled trial of elective segmental colonic resection.[3] A nine-center study recruited 427 patients eligible for segmental colectomy. They were randomized to laparoscopic or open colectomy, and to enhanced recovery (ER) or standard care, resulting in four groups. The primary outcome was total length of stay (TLOS). The median TLOS in the laparoscopic/ ER group was 5 (interquartile range: 4-8) days; open/ ER 7 (5-11) days; laparoscopic/standard 6 (4.5-9.5) days; and open/standard 7 (6-13) days (P <0.001). Regression analysis revealed that laparoscopy was the only independent predictive factor to reduce hospital stay and morbidity. Hence, the combination of laparoscopic and enhanced recovery protocols had the shortest LOS without compromised outcomes.[3]

12

While most operations can be approached in a minimally invasive fashion in major colorectal centers, the penetration of laparoscopic approaches overall in colorectal surgery remains hovering around the 30% to 40% rate. There are many considerations regarding the choice between laparoscopic and open procedures, which are tempered by the surgeon's experience, the procedure being performed, the diagnosis, and the patient's characteristics (including comorbidities and prior abdominal operations).

There is in essence a hierarchy of operative approaches, depending on the size of the incision(s). Open laparotomy typically is considered the most invasive, with the largest incision, followed by hand-assisted laparoscopic techniques, robotic approaches (as the adjuvant ports are 8 mm rather than the commonly used 5 mm in non-robotic cases), multiport laparoscopy, and single-incision laparoscopy.

Minimally invasive approaches to abdominopelvic operations have resulted in patient benefits including decreased pain, decreased rates of postoperative complications, reduced hospital length of stay, and also cost savings, which have all been demonstrated by multiple studies.[3-5] Such improved outcomes, after a minimally invasive approach are further magnified when utilized as part of a perioperative enhanced recovery clinical care pathway.

There are several factors that the facile surgeon will need to consider when opting for a minimally invasive approach. The first consideration for a minimally invasive approach is which manifestation will be deployed. There are many options including a completely laparoscopic approach, single-incision laparoscopic approaches, robotic approaches, and hand-assisted approaches. In the authors' opinion, hand-assisted laparoscopic approaches reflect a learning curve in true laparoscopic experience and exhibit intermediate outcomes when compared with either open approaches or total laparoscopic approaches (consistent with the intermediate size of the incision) and will not be detailed further.

The ability to position laparoscopic ports appropriately and triangulate the areas of the operation is of paramount importance, unless the surgeon has experience with single-incision techniques. The first decision with regards to port placement should be the question of abdominal access. Most of the time access can be obtained utilizing a direct cut down approach. While some favor utilizing the closed-entry needle and transparent trocar method,[6] many patients who have undergone a prior major colorectal procedure are not candidates for this approach. Unique options for access are also available in some operations where the patient has a pre-existing access point such as an ileostomy or colostomy site that is being reversed as part of the surgical procedure. The stoma can be taken down, the adjacent area of the abdomen digitally swept for adhesions, and a decision made regarding proceeding laparoscopically. The location of the port, size of the port, patient's surgical history, and body habitus will all factor into the final decision on the best approach to abdominal access.

The pneumoperitoneum can have drastic physiologic effects, and surgeons should maintain open communication with the anesthesia team around the time of insufflation. Additionally, laparoscopy often utilizes extreme table and patient positioning in order to provide adequate exposure. For the patient's safety, if extreme positioning is anticipated, the patient should be secured to the operating room table securely and monitored for hemodynamic consequences.

In addition to total laparoscopic approaches, robotic approaches have become popular, particularly for pelvic operations. The hemodynamics and positioning considerations are similar to the total laparoscopic approaches; however, there is increased visualization, particularly in patients with a narrow pelvic inlet and many platforms provide three-dimensional rende,ring of the working space. These aspects and ergonomic ease come at the price of increased costs, a separate learning curve, the need to utilize 8-mm trocars as opposed to 5-mm trocars in pure laparoscopic approaches, and especially delayed intervention if the patient should require emergent laparotomy access to the abdominal cavity.

Open surgical approaches to major abdomino-pelvic operations are an integral part of any surgeon's armament when minimally invasive approaches are not feasible, not part of the surgeon's expertise, or have failed. Similar to laparoscopy, surgical planning is of paramount importance. Open surgical approaches have the benefit of allowing the surgeon to assess tissues with manual palpation. Laparoscopic approaches, while providing some feedback through instruments to the surgeon, do not afford the same level of tactile response. Robotic approaches provide very little in the way of feedback to the surgeon. When deployed as part of a clinical care pathway, open approaches have also seen a reduction in postoperative length of hospital stay.[7]

Lines and Tubes

In addition to surgical approach, the decision to place lines and tubes at the time of the operation can affect postoperative recovery. Leaving nasogastric tubes in place after major abdominopelvic operations can have several deleterious effects including dehydration and electrolyte abnormalities, patient discomfort, and delays in postoperative feeding and mobilization.[8] Whenever possible, the routine use of postoperative nasogastric tubes should be avoided. The routine use of abdominal and pelvic drains without clear indications should be avoided for similar reasons. Some operations including pancreatic resections and liver resections have evidence that routine drainage improves perioperative outcomes; outside of these settings, abdominal drains should be avoided whenever possible.

Pain Management

The management of pain in the preoperative and intraoperative period can help to determine the trajectory of pain in the postoperative period. Postoperative pain control starts preoperatively. Current enhanced recovery protocols utilize a preoperative "cocktail" of acetaminophen, a nonsteroidal anti-inflammatory drug (NSAID), and a neuromodulator. We currently use acetaminophen, gabapentin, and celecoxib, tailored to the patient's age and glomerular filtration rate. Previously we widely used epidural anesthesia to transition to postoperative pain control particularly after open operations. However, movement of patients from the operating room to the recovery room and subsequently to the floor resulted in many nonfunctioning epidurals. Other institutions have used the long-acting narcotic diamorphine in a preoperative spinal injection for analgesia in the first 24 hours.

We have moved to surgeon-administered transverse abdominis plane (TAP) blocks with liposomal bupivacaine, which has recently been approved by the FDA for multiple indications (including TAP) beyond the initial indications of hemorrhoidectomy and bunionectomy. Initially this was performed postoperatively by the anesthesia team using abdominal wall ultrasound after the completion of the operation. Intraoperatively this can be performed very simply by the surgeon at the beginning of the case using laparoscopic visualization or open palpation and the technique of "two clicks" when passing a blunted needle across the abdominal wall.[9] Utilizing this analgesic approach can help to minimize the intraoperative use of narcotics.

Conclusion

There are numerous surgical and anesthetic approaches and techniques that can be deployed in clinical care pathways to accelerate a patient's postoperative recovery. It is essential that clinicians maintain open lines of communication with regard to periopera-tive planning in order to provide a coordinated care plan that is tailored to each patient.

The take-home message is that in the absence of enhanced recovery practices minimally invasive approaches offer the best outcomes. The addition of enhanced recovery protocols to open approaches produces postoperative outcomes that parallel the trajectory of laparoscopic cases. The best outcomes are obtained with the melding of minimally invasive techniques under the auspices of an enhanced recovery program.

1. Nelson RL, Gladman E, Barbateskovic M. Antimicrobial prophylaxis for colorectal surgery. *Cochrane Database Syst Rev.* 2014;5:CD001181.

2. Orci LA, Toso C, Mentha G, Morel P, Majno PE. Systematic review and meta-analysis of the effect of perioperative steroids on ischaemia-reperfusion injury and surgical stress response in patients undergoing liver resection. *Br J Surg.* 2013;100(5):600-609.

3. Vlug MS, Wind J, Hollmann MW, et al. Laparoscopy in combination with fast track multimodal management is the best perioperative strategy in patients undergoing colonic surgery: a randomized clinical trial (LAFA-study). *Ann Surg.* 2011;254(6):868-875.

4. Kennedy GD, Heise C, Rajamanickam V, Harms B, Foley EF. Laparoscopy decreases postoperative complication rates after abdominal colectomy: results from the national surgical quality improvement program. *Ann Surg.* 2009;249(4):596-601.

5. Keller DS, Champagne BJ, Reynolds HL Jr, Stein SL, Delaney CP. Cost-effectiveness of laparoscopy in rectal cancer. *Dis Colon Rectum.* 2014;57(5):56456-56459.

6. Ahmad G, O'Flynn H, Duffy JM, Phillips K, Watson A. Laparoscopic entry techniques. *Cochrane Database Syst Rev.* 2012;2:CD006583.

7. Varadhan KK, Neal KR, Dejong CH, Fearon KC, Ljungqvist O, Lobo DN. The enhanced recovery after surgery (ERAS) pathway for patients undergoing major elective open colorectal surgery: a meta-analysis of randomized controlled trials. *Clin Nutr.* 2010;29(4):434-440.

8. Nelson R, Edwards S, Tse B. Prophylactic nasogastric decompression after abdominal surgery. *Cochrane Database Syst Rev.* 2007;(3):CD004929.

9. Keller DS, Ermlich BO, Delaney CP. Demonstrating the benefits of transversus abdominis plane blocks on patient outcomes in laparoscopic colorectal surgery: review of 200 consecutive cases. *J Am Coll Surg.* 2014;219(6):1143-1148.

12

13

Surgical Stress Response and Enhanced Recovery

by Mattias Soop, MD, PhD

Is the Surgical Stress Response Beneficial or Detrimental in Contemporary Surgery?

The term "surgical stress response" has traditionally referred to the neuroendocrine response to injury and associated changes in oxygen consumption, local inflammation, and whole-body balance of nitrogen and other elements.[1] Cuthbertson's well-known description of a biphasic response, with an initial "ebb" or hypometabolic phase and a subsequent "flow" or hypermetabolic phase, remains relevant in emergency surgery and trauma. In elective surgery, the increased urinary losses of nitrogen that characterize his "flow" phase are still observed, but the physiologic instability associated with the "ebb" phase is no longer a feature.

The development of Enhanced Recovery has focused attention on the causes of the postoperative state that prevents patients from returning to normal function after surgery. This renewed focus on perioperative physiology has brought an understanding that the surgical stress response consists of a much wider range of physiologic responses in a multitude of tissues and organs.

Importantly, it has also become clear that these responses are triggered not only by the surgical injury, but by a whole range of physiological challenges to the patient undergoing elective abdominopelvic surgery, starting days before surgery and often ending long after discharge from hospital. Indeed, the concept of enhanced-recovery surgery originated with Kehlet's suggestion that "stress free anesthesia and surgery" may be possible by combining evidence-based treat-

199

ments that blunt or, in some cases, eliminate these perioperative physiologic challenges.[2]

It was not always clear whether surgical stress responses are beneficial or detrimental to the patient undergoing major elective surgery. After all, those responses have developed during evolution and must carry a survival benefit to the injured, immobilized, and starving organism. For instance, the immediate increase of cardiac output that improves skeletal muscle perfusion and function, the preservation of water and sodium by the kidneys, and the rapid development of insulin resistance directing scarce glucose to glucose-dependent tissues all help the body to avoid or overcome injury. Intuitively, it could be suggested that such responses are beneficial also to patients undergoing elective surgery, and should not be modified.

High-grade data over the past 15 years, however, have shown that in the context of contemporary surgical care, where physiologic requirements such as oxygenation, perfusion, fluids, and nutrition can be artificially supported, many aspects of the surgical stress response are detrimental. Examples of interventions that directly reduce the surgical stress responses, rather than minimize the magnitude of surgery or other perioperative physiologic challenges, include thoracic epidural analgesia (when compared to parenteral opioid analgesia),[3] high-dose corticosteroids,[4] and intensive insulin therapy[5]; these have all been shown to improve outcomes after major surgery.

Thus, physiological responses occur in most tissues and organs before, during, and after major surgery. These are caused by activation of a multitude of endocrine, paracrine, and neural mediators. The key interventions in ERPs minimize the magnitude of the physiologic challenges to the surgical patient, such as minimizing tissue trauma, avoiding unnecessary fasting, and effectively controlling pain (**Figure 13.1**).

FIGURE 13.1 — Conceptual Framework of Mechanisms of the Surgical Stress Responses

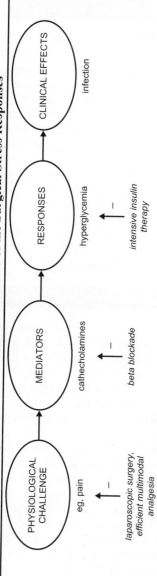

Conceptual framework of mechanisms of the surgical stress responses, showing potential opportunities for intervention for the example of pain, catecholamines, and hyperglycemia. Experience has shown that the most successful and feasible interventions aim to blunt the physiologic challenge in the first place (eg, nociception), rather than blunt release of the mediators (eg, beta adrenergic receptor blockade) or the response itself (eg, hyperglycemia). Successful ERPs consist of a series of interventions that target mainly the physiologic challenges.

Perioperative Physiologic Challenges and Their Management

Although the tissue injury associated with all surgery is the most obvious physiologic challenge to the patient undergoing surgery, there are many additional challenges to homeostasis during the perioperative course. Importantly, all of these are subject to modification by specific evidence-based interventions. As described, ERPs originated as an attempt to blunt or eliminate those challenges.[2] Experience has shown that the most successful interventions, in terms of improving clinical outcomes, are those that target these physiologic challenges directly, rather than therapies designed to blunt the subsequent stress responses. It is therefore important to understand the nature of the series of physiologic challenges in the perioperative period, and the therapies that blunt or minimize those challenges and their effects (**Table 13.1**).

Preoperative Challenges

Days before surgery starts, there are significant challenges to homeostasis. Patients are traditionally fasting overnight, and studies reveal significant degrees of anxiety for many hours prior to surgery. These challenges by themselves have been shown to cause specific endocrine and metabolic responses, most importantly an increased cortisol release and insulin resistance.

In addition, many patients take oral bowel preparation, which can cause fluid and electrolyte derangements. Avoidance of unnecessary preoperative fasting and bowel preparation by implementation of contemporary guidelines minimizes preoperative dehydration. Administration of oral preoperative carbohydrate treatment attenuates the metabolic detrimental effects of undergoing surgery in the fasted state, resulting in a shorter length of hospital stay.[6]

TABLE 13.1 — Physiologic Changes in Perioperative Period

Perioperative Physiologic Challenge	Management
Anxiety	Preoperative patient education
	Same-day admission
Preoperative dehydration	Adherence to modern preoperative fasting guidelines
	Avoidance of oral bowel preparation
Preoperative fasting	Preoperative oral carbohydrate treatment
Preoperative transfusion	Preoperative iron infusion
Tissue injury and contamination	Minimally invasive surgical approaches
	Short incisions
	Atraumatic technique
Nociception and pain	Effective analgesia
	Regional analgesia
	Multimodal analgesia
Hypothermia	Active and passive warming
Intravenous fluid overloading	Protocol-driven, balanced fluid therapy
Intra- and postoperative transfusion	Red-cell saving techniques
	Strict transfusion triggers
Postoperative fasting	Early oral diet
	Technique to avoid or minimize ileus
Postoperative lack of physical activity	Protocol-driven postoperative mobilization

13

Intraoperative Challenges

Surgery by definition involves tissue injury and manipulation, as well as a breach of sterile barriers such as the skin and the bowel wall. The first response to localized tissue injury is a local inflammatory response initiated by activation of epithelial and endothelial cells and resident leukocytes. Systemic cytokine release, if substantial, then leads to multiple systemic metabolic and other physiologic responses. These are directly proportional to the magnitude and approach of surgery; for instance, both open inguinal hernia repair[7] and laparoscopic cholecystectomy[8] result in decreased responses when compared to open cholecystectomy.

Pain is by itself a potent trigger of neuroendocrine stress signaling and results in profound physiologic responses.[9] During general anesthesia, nociception is likely to trigger similar responses. Unless intra- and postoperative pain is well controlled, this will add significantly to the stress responses.

Intra- and postoperative fluid balance remains characterized by marked water and sodium excesses, despite a significant literature identifying fluid overloading as perhaps the most important modifiable and iatrogenic cause of excess morbidity in contemporary surgery. Implementation of contemporary, evidence-based fluid guidelines, by itself, should result in a marked reduction of postoperative morbidity.[10]

Transfusion of red blood cells is another important potential trigger of inflammation and transfusion-related immunomodulation, responses that have been shown to be associated with increased risks of postoperative surgical site infections and, in the case of oncological surgery, cancer recurrence. Numerous strategies have evolved to limit perioperative transfusions, most important of which may be adoption of stricter transfusion triggers.

Postoperative Challenges

After surgery, relative or absolute starvation for several days is a major challenge to the maintenance of homeostasis. Fasting causes profound and adaptive alterations in metabolism within days, characterized by a resistance to the normally anabolic effects of insulin and a subtle increase of catecholamine and glucagon release. The result is glucose intolerance and breakdown of fat stores.[11] These effects are avoided if normal oral or enteral diet is administered.

Lack of physical activity, common in all hospitalized patients, is another significant factor, the effects of which have been little studied. In studies in healthy subjects, however, it is well established that short-term (5-10 days) bed rest leads to insulin resistance and significant reductions of lean tissue mass, isokinetic muscle strength, and exercise capacity.[12] These effects are likely to be accelerated in postoperative patients, and postoperative mobilization would counteract these effects.

13

Key Surgical Stress Responses

■ Mediators of Surgical Stress Responses

The series of challenges discussed above cause a range of physiological responses by activating mediators that affect local and distant tissues by paracrine, endocrine, and neural pathways. There is a substantial literature on the mediator pathways involved, much of it aiming at identifying pharmacologic methods of blockade or modification. This literature is too large to summarize here, but it is fair to say that such mediator blockade has so far been disappointing in improving clinical outcomes in surgery, sepsis, and trauma. Thus, blockade of paracrine mediators (for example, by nitrous oxide synthase inhibition) and endocrine factors (for example, by beta adrenergic or cytokine receptor blockade) has so far not emerged as standard therapy. This apparent lack of efficacy is likely due to a redundancy in the number of mediator pathways triggered.

Paracrine mediators include complement, the coagulation system, mediators of inflammation (including vasoactive amines, cytokines, chemokines, and eicosanoids) and nitrous oxide. Endocrine mediators include the classic stress hormones cortisol, epinephrine, norepinephrine, and glucagon, but also ACTH, growth hormone, antidiuretic hormone, and prolactin. Neural mediation of the surgical stress responses occurs through an increased sympathetic tone resulting in rapid systemic changes including key cardiovascular, renal, respiratory, central nervous, and gastrointestinal functions.

Hence, most tissues and functions in the body are affected by the stress mediators. The most important responses in relation to postoperative recovery are discussed below.

■ Metabolic Responses

The initial descriptions of the surgical stress responses focused on the metabolic responses, and specifically the increases of nitrogen excretion, energy expenditure, and glycemia that characterize Cuthbertson's flow phase.[1]

■ Responses of Protein Metabolism

The increase in urinary nitrogen losses seen in injured subjects[1] is caused by an increased release of amino acids mainly from skeletal muscle. Turnover studies in stressed states have shown that both muscle protein breakdown and synthesis are increased in stress, with a larger increase in breakdown resulting in net loss.[13] The released amino acids are needed for synthesis of proteins in the wound and acute phase proteins, and furthermore, their carbon skeletons are substrates for gluconeogenesis.

Although there is a strong and well-known association between preoperative malnutrition and poor outcome after surgery, there are little data to support a link between acute perioperative nitrogen balance and clinical outcome.[14] Protein sparing nevertheless remains a frequent endpoint in nutritional and metabolic research.

■ Responses of Carbohydrate Metabolism

Carbohydrate metabolism after surgery is characterized by hepatic and peripheral insulin resistance, leading to increased gluconeogenesis as well as decreased glucose uptake in skeletal muscle and other tissues. This so-called pseudodiabetes of injury persists for several weeks after elective surgery[15] and causes an osmotic shift of fluid into the vascular space, as well as an increased availability of glucose for (initially) glucose-dependent tissues such as the brain and white blood cells.

Although hyperglycemia was reported in postoperative patients in 1934, it was not until 2001 that the clinical consequences of perioperative hyperglycemia were fully appreciated. This year marked the publication of a large randomized study comparing permissive hyperglycemia with strict glycemic control by intensive insulin therapy.[5] Morbidity and mortality were decreased in the intervention group in this landmark trial, which predominantly included patients who had planned admission to an intensive care unit after elective cardiac and noncardiac surgery. No further trials specifically in surgical patients have been published, although a subgroup analysis of trauma patients in a multicenter trial shows similar results.[16]

Intensive insulin therapy, therefore, cannot be recommended in routine noncardiac surgery, but the cited trials do highlight the clinical risks posed by perioperative hyperglycemia. Importantly, in elective surgery, there are several opportunities to prevent insulin resistance from developing in the first place. Interventions that blunt insulin resistance include thoracic epidural analgesia, laparoscopic surgery, and oral preoperative carbohydrate treatment.

Oral preoperative carbohydrate treatment is a metabolic manipulation rather than a nutritional intervention, with the aim of converting the overnight fasting catabolic state to a postprandial anabolic state, which is known to blunt further catabolic responses to surgery.[17] A carbohydrate load (approximately 50 g) is needed and given in a limited volume (400 mL)

2 hours prior to anesthesia. In order to allow gastric emptying during this time, osmolality needs to be low (285 mOsm/L), and this is accomplished by including complex carbohydrates rather than glucose or sucrose. Meta-analysis of randomized trial shows that this treatment significantly blunts the development of insulin resistance and, in major abdominal surgery, decreases the postoperative hospital stay by 1.7 days.[6]

■ Immunological Responses

While humoral immunity (mediated by immunoglobulins and complement) is relatively unaffected, cell-mediated immunity is known to be significantly suppressed after surgery. Derangements include impairments in neutrophil chemotaxis, monocyte antigen presentation, and cell killing. This is associated with an increased susceptibility to bacterial infection[18] and, in cancer surgery, decreased control of minimal residual disease, increasing the risk of early tumor recurrence.[19] Mechanisms may include anti-inflammatory cytokines such as IL-10 and glucose toxicity.

Laparoscopic surgery attenuates the postoperative immunosuppression when compared to open surgery.[20] Intensive insulin therapy is associated with a marked reduction in infectious complications, highlighting the importance of minimizing insulin resistance.[5]

■ Cardiovascular Responses

Rapid increases in heart rate, myocardial contractility, and peripheral vasoconstriction are perhaps the most immediate and obvious physiological responses to a number of perioperative challenges, including anxiety and nociception.

These responses are unlikely to be beneficial in patients undergoing elective surgery, in contrast to trauma patients who may have significant hemorrhage. The extra cardiac workload may provoke cardiac events. Recent data indicate that as many as 8% of patients undergoing major noncardiac surgery suffer myocardial injury, as measured by biomarkers, and that this is often subclinical and easily missed.[21]

Patients with known ischemic heart disease should therefore remain on prophylactic medications perioperatively unless contraindicated for surgical reasons. The current challenge is to identify patients with previously undiagnosed cardiac and other functional limitations that may manifest only during major surgery. Medical, or even surgical, optimization of cardiovascular and respiratory function can then be considered. Cardiopulmonary exercise testing is increasingly used to screen patients prior to elective high-risk surgery.[22]

Postoperative orthostatic intolerance is a less life-threatening cardiovascular response that nevertheless poses a considerable impediment to optimal postoperative recovery. This response occurs in approximately 50% of patients undergoing major pelvic surgery without epidural analgesia.[23] It is caused by an insufficient increase in peripheral vascular resistance and a drop in cardiac output when standing upright. It thus appears that surgery causes an autonomic dysregulation that lasts for several days. In addition to impeding postoperative mobilization, this may trigger additional fluid administration resulting in fluid and electrolyte overloading.

■ Renal

It has long been known that a decreased diuresis is a physiologic response to surgery, preserving sodium and water.[24] This response is mediated by antidiuretic hormone, renin-angiotensin II-aldosterone activation, as well as an increased sympathetic nerve action on tubular cells. In particular, the ADH response is a primitive, strong reflex that cannot easily be blunted by excess fluid administration.[25]

Although oliguria is defined by the nephrology literature as a urine output <200 mL/day, in the perioperative setting, any patient with a urine output <0.5 mL/kg/h or approximately 900 mL per day is considered oliguric. This considerably higher target in perioperative patients is based on principles in trauma surgery hailing from the Korean conflict in the early 1950s.

No data exist on the relevance of such a high target for urine output in contemporary, elective surgery.

Empirical observation suggests that administration of significant additional fluid volumes is required to maintain such a high urine output in order to overcome the physiologic response of fluid sparing and reach the higher target of 0.5 mL/kg/h. Whether this is necessary, beneficial, or even harmful is currently unknown.

The Surgical Stress Response Within ERAS

Enhanced recovery after surgery programs are integrated pathways of a series of perioperative interventions, each of which has proven clinical benefits as sole interventions. As most of those interventions work through minimizing or eliminating perioperative physiologic challenges, as we have seen, full ERPs could be expected to significantly blunt the surgical stress responses.

Two studies have shown that contemporary surgery within an ERP is associated with partial or complete attenuation of key stress responses. Thus, open major colorectal surgery within an early ERP in the United Kingdom was associated with no increase in postoperative nitrogen losses, minimal insulin resistance, preserved normoglycemia during feeding, and a minor increase in energy expenditure.[26] A standard amount of protein delivered through enteral feeding resulted in a neutral nitrogen balance. Thus, the classic metabolic responses to surgery were absent or insignificant within ERPs (**Figure 13.2**).

A recent four-way randomized study of laparoscopic vs open surgery and ERPs vs traditional care assessed the independent effects of laparoscopic surgery and ERPs.[27,28] Laparoscopic surgery was associated with an improved postoperative immune function (measured as monocyte HLA-DR presentation), and Enhanced Recovery with a lower stress mediator response (measured as growth hormone).

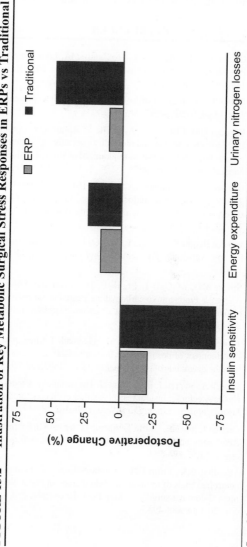

FIGURE 13.2 — Illustration of Key Metabolic Surgical Stress Responses in ERPs vs Traditional Care

Soop M, et al. *Am J Physiol Endocrinol Metab.* 2001;280:E576-E583.

13

These results confirm that optimal outcomes of major abdominopelvic surgery are achieved by a combination of a well-implemented ERP and, in suitable patients, minimally invasive surgical approaches.

REFERENCES

1. Cuthbertson DP, Angeles Valero Zanuy MA, León Sanz ML. Post-shock metabolic response. 1942. *Nutr Hosp*. 2001;16:176-182.

2. Kehlet H. The surgical stress response: should it be prevented? *Can J Surg*. 1991;34:565-567.

3. Pöpping DM, Elia N, Van Aken HK, et al. Impact of epidural analgesia on mortality and morbidity after surgery: systematic review and meta-analysis of randomized controlled trials. *Ann Surg*. 2014;259:1056-1067.

4. Srinivasa S, Kahokehr AA, Yu TC, Hill AG. Preoperative glucocorticoid use in major abdominal surgery: systematic review and meta-analysis of randomized trials. *Ann Surg*. 2011;254:183-191.

5. van den Berghe G, Wouters P, Weekers F, et al. Intensive insulin therapy in critically ill patients. *N Engl J Med*. 2001;345:1359-1367.

6. Smith MD, McCall J, Plank L, Herbison GP, Soop M, Nygren J. Preoperative carbohydrate treatment for enhancing recovery after elective surgery. *Cochrane Database Syst Rev*. 2014;8:CD009161.

7. Thorell A, Efendic S, Gutniak M, Häggmark T, Ljungqvist O. Development of postoperative insulin resistance is associated with the magnitude of operation. *Eur J Surg*. 1993;159:593-599.

8. Thorell A, Nygren J, Essén P, et al. The metabolic response to cholecystectomy: insulin resistance after open compared with laparoscopic operation. *Eur J Surg*. 1996;162:187-191.

9. Greisen J, Juhl CB, Grøfte T, Vilstrup H, Jensen TS, Schmitz O. Acute pain induces insulin resistance in humans. *Anesthesiology*. 2001;95:578-584.

10. Varadhan KK, Lobo DN. A meta-analysis of randomised controlled trials of intravenous fluid therapy in major elective open abdominal surgery: getting the balance right. *Proc Nutr Soc*. 2010;69:488-498.

11. Svanfeldt M, Thorell A, Brismar K, Nygren J, Ljungqvist O. Effects of 3 days of "postoperative" low caloric feeding with or without bed rest on insulin sensitivity in healthy subjects. *Clin Nutr*. 2003;22:31-38.

12. Kortebein P, Ferrando A, Lombeida J, Wolfe R, Evans WJ. Effect of 10 days of bed rest on skeletal muscle in healthy older adults. *JAMA*. 2007;297:1772-1774.

13. Khan AS, Gibson JM, Carlson GL, Rooyackers O, New JP, Soop M. Protein kinetics in human endotoxaemia and their temporal relation to metabolic, endocrine and proinflammatory cytokine responses. *Br J Surg*. 2015;102:767-775.

14. Wilmore DW. Postoperative protein sparing. *World J Surg*. 1999;23:545-552.

15. Thorell A, Efendic S, Gutniak M, Häggmark T, Ljungqvist O. Insulin resistance after abdominal surgery. *Br J Surg*. 1994;81:59-63.

16. NICE-SUGAR Study Investigators, Finfer S, Chittock DR, Su SY, et al. Intensive versus conventional glucose control in critically ill patients. *N Engl J Med*. 2009;360:1283-1297.

17. Soop M, Nygren J, Myrenfors P, Thorell A, Ljungqvist O. Preoperative oral carbohydrate treatment attenuates immediate postoperative insulin resistance. *Am J Physiol Endocrinol Metab*. 2001;280:E576-E583.

18. Christou NV, McLean AP, Meakins JL. Host defense in blunt trauma:interrelationships of kinetics of anergy and depressed neutrophil function, utritional status, and sepsis. *J Trauma*. 1980;20:833-841.

19. van der Bij GJ, Oosterling SJ, Beelen RH, Meijer S, Coffey JC, van Egmond M. The perioperative period is an underutilized window of therapeutic opportunity in patients with colorectal cancer. *Ann Surg*. 2009;249:727-734.

20. Whelan RL, Franklin M, Holubar SD, et al. Postoperative cell mediated immune response is better preserved after laparoscopic vs open colorectal resection in humans. *Surg Endosc*. 2003;17:972-978.

21. Botto F, Alonso-Coello P, Chan MT, et al; Vascular events In noncardiac Surgery patIents cOhort evaluatioN (VISION) Writing Group, on behalf of The Vascular events In noncardiac Surgery patIents cOhort evaluatioN (VISION) Investigators; Appendix 1. The Vascular events In noncardiac Surgery patIents cOhort evaluatioN (VISION) Study Investigators Writing Group; Appendix 2. The Vascular events In noncardiac Surgery patIents cOhort evaluatioN Operations Committee;

13

Vascular events In noncardiac Surgery patIents cOhort evaluation VISION Study Investigators. Myocardial injury after noncardiac surgery: a large, international, prospective cohort study establishing diagnostic criteria, characteristics, predictors, and 30-day outcomes. *Anesthesiology*. 2014;120:564-578.

22. Wilson RJ, Davies S, Yates D, Redman J, Stone M. Impaired functional capacity is associated with all-cause mortality after major elective intra-abdominal surgery. *Br J Anaesth.* 2010;105:297-303.

23. Bundgaard-Nielsen M, Jørgensen CC, Jørgensen TB, Ruhnau B, Secher NH, Kehlet H. Orthostatic intolerance and the cardiovascular response to early postoperative mobilization. *Br J Anaesth.* 2009;102:756-762.

24. Pringle H, Maunsell RC, Pringle S. Clinical effects of ether anaesthesia on renal activity. *Br Med J.* 1905;2:542-543.

25. Sinnatamby C, Edwards CR, Kitau, Irving MH. Antidiuretic hormone response to high and conservative fluid regimes in patients undergoing operation. *Surg Gynecol Obstet.* 1974;139:715-719.

26. Soop M, Carlson GL, Hopkinson J, et al. Randomized clinical trial of the effects of immediate enteral nutrition on metabolic responses to major colorectal surgery in an enhanced recovery protocol. *Br J Surg.* 2004;91:1138-1145.

27. Vlug MS, Wind J, Hollmann MW, et al; LAFA study group. Laparoscopy in combination with fast track multimodal management is the best perioperative strategy in patients undergoing colonic surgery: a randomized clinical trial (LAFA-study). *Ann Surg.* 2011;254:868-875.

28. Veenhof AA, Vlug MS, van der Pas MH, et al. Surgical stress response and postoperative immune function after laparoscopy or open surgery with fast track or standard perioperative care: a randomized trial. *Ann Surg.* 2012;255:216-221.

14

Postoperative Oral Nutrition and Ileus Prevention

by Julie K Thacker, MD and
Kristoffer Lassen, MD, PhD

Postoperative Oral Nutrition

■ Introduction

Eating activates all digestive reflexes, probably stimulates gut motility, and is associated with pleasure and well-being. Eating is a volitional process that leaves the patient in control, and it has never been shown to cause any harm.

Early food after surgery was dogmatically ignored throughout the "enteral vs parenteral" controversy. In the clash of the two industrially sponsored titans, few paid notice to the qualities of food. And when the tide started to turn, misconceptions arose and little distinction was made between enteral feeding and eating. To artificially tube-feed the gut was wrongly perceived as equal to eating and not as an extension of the nil-by-mouth dogma. This chapter will recommend that you allow your well-informed patients to eat at will postoperatively in almost all cases.

■ Background

The nasogastric (NG) decompression tubes and a "nil-by-mouth" prescription are among the most die-hard dogmas of traditional postoperative care. The original concerns were risk of aspiration caused by emesis and gastric distension, and intraluminal pressure from fluids or solid matter on a freshly created suture line. Early attempts to challenge this in the 1960s were sidetracked by the appearance of industrially produced solutions for parenteral and enteral feeding along with improved catheters that shifted the focus onto artificial feeding.

When you make your rounds on the patients operated earlier in the day, consider this:

- The presence of fluid and some semi-digested matter in the gut is not more hazardous to a fresh anastomosis that the natural contents, such as enzymes, bile juices, and stomach acids.
- A nasogastric tube (NGT) increases patient discomfort and risk of aspiration, as well as precludes eating and impedes mobilization. Use of an NGT is not of proven value following uncomplicated abdominal resections.
- Eating is the only process that elicits all natural gut-stimulating reflexes via sight, smell, taste, salivation, mastication, and swallowing. Eating real food is cheap, volitional, safe, and associated with "a host of pleasurable phenomena."[1] Eating food is about much more than just counting calories.
- Parenteral or enteral feeding is artificial, non-volitional processes with inherent risks from tubes or catheters and from salt or water overload. Industrial products only provide the contents we know to be important, not those we have not yet identified.
- Enteral feeding is in every respect fundamentally different from eating normal food.
- Oral sip feeds and chewing gum may not have been shown beneficial in all trials, but they are cheap interventions with no known adverse effects.

■ **Recommendations**

These are general recommendations aimed at all abdominal resections that follow an uncomplicated course. There are a few exceptions (see below), and all patients must be managed individually. Patients must be informed that their gut is not working properly in the immediate period following surgery and that they must begin oral intake with some caution and increase step wise according to tolerance. If there are no special considerations, this is a map to steer by:

- In all patients operated in the abdomen, avoid long-acting sedatives and remove the NGT at end of surgery.
- As soon as patients are fully awake, they should be encouraged to drink. When some drink is tolerated, they can start to eat a normal diet.
- For resections of liver, pancreatic tail, adrenals, small bowel, colon, rectum, urinary system, and female reproductive organs, eat according to tolerance.[2-8]
- For pancreatic head resections (Whipple procedures), resumption of gastric function is generally slower. Patients should be cautioned to begin eating small volumes of easily digested food and increase according to tolerance.[9-11]
- In total gastrectomies, there is no gastric pouch left to accommodate solid matter, and these patients also should begin eating small volumes and increase according to tolerance.[12]
- Routine use of parenteral or enteral tube feeding is not indicated. If patients reach half their nutritional need by day 4 postoperatively, they will generally not need any artificial feeding. (This does not take into account any pre-existing cachectic disease, wasting, or sarcopenia that might require special attention and nutritional interventions as such.)
- Provide the best environment for rapid resumption of gastric and gut function.[13]
- Use minimally invasive surgery (laparoscopy) whenever feasible.
- Avoid fluid and sodium imbalance from IV infusions.
- Use local anesthetic nerve blocks to reduce opioid consumption.
- Provide early and enforced mobilization. Move television and food buffet to a separate part of the ward.

14

- Avoid unnecessary wound drains.
- Provide normal drink and normal diet.

■ Special Considerations When Considering Immediate Postoperative Feeding

There are four exceptions to the general recommendations:

- NGT in esophageal resections. The vagotomized intrathoracic gastric conduit has a tendency to dilate and to empty poorly in the early phase. Risk of aspiration is greater than following abdominal resections. Most centers advocate prolonged decompression by NGT. Ask for dedicated protocol in your center.
- Nutritional support in esophageal resections. It follows from the above that patients undergoing esophageal resections will frequently need artificial nutritional support. A needle-catheter jejunostomy is a much-favored solution to deliver enteral nutrition. This technique is not without its hazards,[14] and these must be viewed against the need for feeding, but it may be the one remaining indication for routine use.[15] Also, these patients are the ones at highest risk to have long-term nutritional problems, and they will need dedicated follow-up.
- Patients suffering a mental disability and who have undergone a fundoplication are at risk for a potentially life-threatening gastric distension that they cannot relieve by vomiting. Many centers will advocate an NGT for some days.
- Some patients who have had a Whipple's procedure (about 10%) might need an NGT on demand for the first few days. It should be removed as soon as nausea has improved, and diet attempted cautiously again. If it appears the patients will not cover half their nutritional needs by postoperative day 4, artificial nutritional support should be considered.

Postoperative Ileus

This section discusses the 11% to 29% of post gastrointestinal surgery patients who suffer from postoperative ileus and are unable to eat. Postoperative ileus (POI) is an abnormal pattern of gastrointestinal motility characterized by nausea, vomiting, abdominal distension, and/or delayed passage of flatus or stool. POI can occur after any injury or operation, as a result of other illness, or, most commonly, after an abdominal operation (**Figure 14.1**).

POI slows recovery, increases postoperative complications, and confers a significant financial burden on healthcare institutions. As teams attempt to implement enhanced recovery efforts, often with the goal of shorter hospital stays, POI is an important consideration. The effect of POI, causing inability to tolerate food and medications by mouth, prolongs the expected hospital stay by days to weeks. POI is also associated with significant abdominal distention with pain and wound complications, risk of aspiration, and risk of catheter-associated complications.

To prevent or manage POI, understanding the cause is essential. Herein lies the difficulty, as an exact cause of POI is not clear. The recovery, or lack of recovery, of normal GI function after abdominal surgery is multifactorial. Identified aspects of deranged bowel function after surgery, include inflammatory cell activation, autonomic dysfunction (both primarily and as part of the surgical stress response), activation of gut opioid receptors, modulation of gastrointestinal hormone activity, and electrolyte derangements. A final common pathway for these effectors is impaired contractility and motility and gut wall edema.

In short, we need to solve the complex interaction of:
- Autonomic dysfunction to stress response
- Activation of gut opioid receptors
- GI hormone imbalance
- Electrolyte derangements
- Impaired contractility and gut wall edema.

FIGURE 14.1 — Proposed Mechanism for Postoperative Ileus

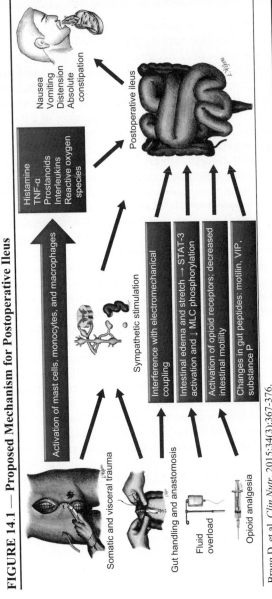

Bragg D, et al. *Clin Nutr*. 2015;34(3):367-376.

■ Enhanced Recovery and Postoperative Ileus

Several causes of postoperative ileus are addressed by the management of perioperative physiologic stress as defined by enhanced recovery principles. While there is no evidence that enhanced recovery efforts decrease the incidence of POI, the indirect evidence of decreased LOS for total populations, and the presumed decrease in stress factors leading to ileus, support the use of enhanced recovery principles towards decreasing POI incidence.

■ Specific Interventions to Prevent Postoperative Ileus

- Minimizing preoperative fasting decreases the autonomic response to surgery and decreases the amount of intravenous fluid necessary at the time of induction of anaesthesia
  - Use bowel preparations only as indicated
  - Recommend clear liquids until 2 hours prior to operation
- Optimize preoperative health to avoid the need for intravenous electrolyte infusions or blood transfusion. Maximize patient's mobility to ensure movement around the time of surgery
  - Correct anemia and nutritional deficits
  - Prehabilitate
- Minimize insulin resistance to help balance perioperative hormones and optimize healing. Particularly important is to be aware of diabetic gastroparesis as a different entity, but similar presentation to ileus
  - Recommend CHO-rich drink 2 to 3 hours prior to operation
  - Follow postoperative blood sugars and treat to keep blood sugars normal
- Minimize fluid shifts
  - Use bowel preparation only as indicated and select an iso-osmolar preparation
  - Optimize electrolytes preoperatively
  - Encourage fluids until 2 hours preoperative and encourage the CHO-rich drink

14

- Use intentional intraoperative fluid strategies to minimize intravascular fluid overload, bowel edema, and fluid shifts
- Use minimally invasive surgical techniques
  - Lesser surgical stress results in lesser physiologic response to surgery
  - Smaller incisions and less bowel manipulation result in less hormonal response to surgery and faster recovery
- Multimodal pain management
  - Non-opioid adjuncts: as opioids are presumed to be a major cause of POI, the avoidance of opioids is key to prevention of POI
    - Acetaminophen for musculoskeletal pain
    - Gabapentin acting as calcium channel antagonist to block the transmission of pain pathway
    - Regional blocks
      · Reduce the autonomic response to surgery
      · Reduce the systemic narcotics necessary during and after operation
  - Preoperative education
    - Intentional dialogue regarding the intent of pain management strategies and the patient's involvement is essential
    - Use of perioperative opioid is regionally highly variable. This observation suggests that routine use of less opioid is possible
    - Use of perioperative opioids in the United States is much higher than in other counties. This again suggests that our routine use of opioid could be challenged. This requires preoperative discussion with the patient to set expectations and elicit plans for pain management
- Avoidance of opioid exposure at the level of the gut
  - Minimizing systemic narcotics, including the preoperative dose for relaxation or set doses intraoperatively or postoperatively without signs or complaints of pain

- Use of gut-specific mu-opioid receptor antagonists
  - Alvimopan is available in the United States
    · Decreases the time to return of GI function
    · Results in lower rate of postoperative ileus
    · Results in shorter length of hospital stay
- In summary, the Duke approach to prevention of postoperative ileus, takes into account aspects of each phase of care

■ Duke Postoperative Ileus Prevention Strategy
- Preoperative optimization
- Minimize fluid shifts
  - Avoidance of bowel preparation when indicated
  - Preoperative fluids until 2 hours before induction
  - Preoperative carbohydrate drink
- Intentional intraoperative fluid management
  - Minimize opioid use
- Regional blocks
- Adjunct non-narcotic pain management modality
  - Combat opioid effect on the gut
- Gut-specific mu-opioid receptor antagonist
- Early postoperative food by mouth

14

REFERENCES

1. Lipman TO. The chicken soup paradigm and nutrition support: rethinking terminology. *JPEN J Parenter Enteral Nutr.* 2003;27:93-94.

2. Lassen K, Soop M, Nygren J, et al; Enhanced Recovery After Surgery (ERAS) Group. Consensus review of optimal perioperative care in colorectal surgery: Enhanced Recovery After Surgery (ERAS) Group recommendations. *Arch Surg.* 2009;144:961-969.

3. Cerantola Y, Valerio M, Persson B, et al. Guidelines for perioperative care after radical cystectomy for bladder cancer: Enhanced Recovery After Surgery (ERAS(®)) society recommendations. *Clin Nutr.* 2013;32:879-887.

4. van Dam RM, Hendry PO, Coolsen MM, et al; Enhanced Recovery After Surgery (ERAS) Group. Initial experience with a multimodal enhanced recovery programme in patients undergoing liver resection. *Br J Surg.* 2008;95:969-975.

5. Gustafsson UO, Scott MJ, Schwenk W, et al; Enhanced Recovery After Surgery (ERAS) Society, for Perioperative Care; European Society for Clinical Nutrition and Metabolism (ESPEN); International Association for Surgical Metabolism and Nutrition (IASMEN). Guidelines for perioperative care in elective colonic surgery: Enhanced Recovery After Surgery (ERAS(®)) Society recommendations. *World J Surg.* 2013;37:259-284.

6. Gustafsson UO, Scott MJ, Schwenk W, et al; Enhanced Recovery After Surgery Society. Guidelines for perioperative care in elective colonic surgery: Enhanced Recovery After Surgery (ERAS®) Society recommendations. *Clin Nutr.* 2012;31:783-800.

7. Nygren J, Thacker J, Carli F, et al; Enhanced Recovery After Surgery Society. Guidelines for perioperative care in elective rectal/pelvic surgery: Enhanced Recovery After Surgery (ERAS®) Society recommendations. *Clin Nutr.* 2012;31:801-816.

8. Nygren J, Thacker J, Carli F, et al; Enhanced Recovery After Surgery (ERAS) Society, for Perioperative Care; European Society for Clinical Nutrition and Metabolism (ESPEN); International Association for Surgical Metabolism and Nutrition (IASMEN). Guidelines for perioperative care in elective rectal/pelvic surgery: Enhanced Recovery After Surgery (ERAS(®)) Society recommendations. *World J Surg.* 2013;37:285-305.

9. Lassen K, Coolsen MM, Slim K, et al;Enhanced Recovery After Surgery (ERAS) Society, for Perioperative Care; European Society for Clinical Nutrition and Metabolism

(ESPEN); International Association for Surgical Metabolism and Nutrition (IASMEN). Guidelines for perioperative care for pancreaticoduodenectomy: Enhanced Recovery After Surgery (ERAS®) Society recommendations. *World J Surg.* 2013;37:240-258.

10. Lassen K, Coolsen MM, Slim K, et al; ERAS® Society; European Society for Clinical Nutrition and Metabolism; International Association for Surgical Metabolism and Nutrition. Guidelines for perioperative care for pancreaticoduodenectomy: Enhanced Recovery After Surgery (ERAS®) Society recommendations. *Clin Nutr.* 2012;31:817-830.

11. Gerritsen A, Besselink MG, Gouma DJ, Steenhagen E, Borel Rinkes IH, Molenaar IQ. Systematic review of five feeding routes after pancreatoduodenectomy. *Br J Surg.* 2013;100:589-598.

12. Mortensen K, Nilsson M, Slim K, et al; Enhanced Recovery After Surgery (ERAS®) Group. Consensus guidelines for enhanced recovery after gastrectomy: Enhanced Recovery After Surgery (ERAS®) Society recommendations. *Br J Surg.* 2014;101:1209-1229.

13. Lassen K, Høye A, Myrmel T. Randomised trials in surgery: the burden of evidence. *Rev Recent Clin Trials.* 2012;7:244-248.

14. Han-Geurts IJ, Verhoef C, Tilanus HW. Relaparotomy following complications of feeding jejunostomy in esophageal surgery. *Dig Surg.* 2004;21:192-196.

15. Lassen K, Kjaeve J, Fetveit T, et al. Allowing normal food at will after major upper gastrointestinal surgery does not increase morbidity: a randomized multicenter trial. *Ann Surg.* 2008;247:721-729.

16. Vather R, Bissett IP. Risk factors for the development of prolonged post-operative ileus following elective colorectal surgery. *Int J Colorectal Dis.* 2013;28:1385-1391.

17. Vather R, Bissett I. Management of prolonged post-operative ileus:evidence-based recommendations. *ANZ J Surg.* 2013;83:319-324.

18. Adam MA, Lee LM, Kim J, et al. Alvimopan provides additional improvement in outcomes and cost savings in enhanced recovery colorectal surgery [published online ahead of print October 22, 2015]. *Ann Surg.* doi: 10.1097/SLA.0000000000001428.

19. Bragg D, El-Sharkawy AM, Psaltis E, Maxwell-Armstrong CA, Lobo DN. Postoperative ileus: Recent developments in pathophysiology and management. *Clin Nutr.* 2015;34:367-376.

14

15 Tubes, Drains, and Catheter Management

By Julie K Thacker, MD

Enhanced recovery protocols (ERPs) are presented as care pathways across the continuum of the patient's journey to and through an operation. Many individual elements of enhanced recovery have evidence independent of enhanced recovery science. This is particularly true of the individual elements of invasive monitoring and access common to traditional care.

Through the development of safe central access, routine Foley catheter use, and inexpensive, easy-to-use percutaneous drains, our traditional care model of care became fairly invasive. Most surgeons trained in the United States, especially before widespread adoption of enhanced recovery, have been trained to treat out of fear of possible complications: 15% of patients might get an ileus; therefore, we placed nasogastric tubes in all patients. Fewer than 10% of colon resection patients require intra- or postoperative blood transfusions, but we routinely placed central access. Anastomosis leak rates are <5% for colon operations, but we routinely placed intra-abdominal drains. Urinary retention after a colon operation is uncommon, yet we insisted on catheters to monitor output.

Concurrent to the evolution of enhanced recovery principles has been the evaluation of these monitoring practices. Uniformly, we have seen that the routine use of drains, tubes, and lines in routine abdominal and most pelvic operations causes more harm than good. This chapter is an overview of the evidence for avoidance and proper use of such practices when indicated.

Nasogastric Tubes

Nasogastric tube (NGT) decompression is routinely used to avoid aspiration in longer general anesthesia operations. Decompressing the stomach has been recommended to protect against stomach injury with blind Veress needle left upper quadrant entry in laparoscopy. However, neither of these indications carries over to postoperative care. *Our belief that decompressing the stomach was necessary until there is evidence of bowel function, at least flatus if not stool passage, has no evidence.* Postoperative NGT decompression was taught as necessary to prevent ileus by avoiding an early gastric challenge and to protect a colon anastomosis by keeping the bowel decompressed. Neither indication is backed by science.

Instead, we actually have good evidence that postoperative NGT decompression is potentially harmful. A 1995 review in the *Annals of Surgery* promoted selective vs routine use of NGT as the no-NGT group had fewer fevers, less atelectasis, and decreased incidence of pneumonia.[1] These conclusions were confirmed by a 2004 Cochran review, which further elucidated a decreased incidence of ileus and shorter length of ileus when it did occur in the no-NGT group.[2] A 2010 meta-analysis showed the same benefits, and reported an increased incidence of vomiting in the NGT group.[3] Perhaps the most convincing report is the Dutch study calling for the "Death of the NGT in the Netherlands," which reported a country-wide decrease of NGT use from 88% to 10% over a decade with no increased in anastomotic complications or ileus rate.[4]

This evidence is indication enough to avoid routine NGT decompression postoperatively. However, the recommendation is even stronger when combined with the enhanced recovery principles of early postoperative eating and ambulation. The evidence level of this recommendation is high, with a strong summary recommendation grade.[5,6]

When considering upper gastrointestinal resections, the evidence again supports the avoidance of NGTs. There are no convincing data of benefit to using NGT after hepaticopancreatic operations. There are reviews showing no harm in avoidance of NGT, and the same complications of NGT shown for colorectal surgery are reported for upper GI operations, including pulmonary and ileus complications. The only exception to the routine discontinuation of NGT in the OR recommendation is in an operation that disrupts the vagal control of the stomach or in a gastric resection where distention of the stomach in the early postoperative time would be detrimental to an anastomosis.[7,8]

It should be noted that the abandonment of the use of routine postoperative NGT for elective cases should not be confused with emergency cases that require NGT's pre- and postoperatively, or the therapeutic placement of NGT for symptomatic GI dysfunction (ileus and obstruction). Failure to recognized the need for and insert NGT in an obstructed patient can lead to lethal aspiration.

Abdominopelvic Drains

The idea that placing a drain next to a new gastrointestinal anastomosis to "clean up the area," drain blood, or detect an early postoperative leak is attractive. To detect or preemptively drain an anastomotic complication is the intent of abdominal drains; however, there is no evidence supporting this practice in colon operations. On the contrary, a 1999 meta-analysis showed there was no difference in the outcomes of drained or undrained colon anastomoses. And perhaps more importantly, the drains only detected 5% of anastomotic leaks, suggesting that leaks were identified by clinical signs and symptoms, not by routine drain use.[9] A 2004 Cochrane review further confirmed this observation by reviewing six randomized controlled studies of 1140 patients having colon operations. There was no difference in leak rates or other outcomes of interest in the drained vs undrained groups.[10]

While the evidence level for avoidance of abdominal drains in colon surgery is high, pelvic operations and some hepaticopancreatic operations may meet criteria for drainage. The evidence is equivocal for pelvic operations with the consensus of experts recommending drainage in procedures of high blood loss or creation of a space, such as total mesorectal excision without reconstruction. Proponents for drainage of the raw biliary bed of a hepatic resection report drain output as evidence supporting drainage, but there are not studies suggesting better outcomes in drained patients.[11]

Caution is recommended when interpreting recommendations regarding postoperative drains as evaluated for hepatic or colon operations as applicable to all abdominal surgeries. *Pancreatic resections may have the best outcomes with routine drainage as drains can detect pancreatic fistulae, which occur in up to 20% of patients.* The use of routine drainage after pancreaticoduodenectomy has been challenged recently, prompting a multicenter, randomized trial. The trial specifically evaluated outcomes relative to drain use and was stopped early for increased morbidity and mortality in the group without drains. The exact placement and duration of intraperitoneal drainage indicated for pancreaticoduodenectomy are not determined in the literature; however, drain use is recommended for this select population.[12,13]

Urinary Catheters

In the ambulatory, healing patient on an enhanced recovery pathway, a urinary catheter is not required. The ubiquitous use of urinary catheters aligns with the adage of bedrest for the postoperative patient. An ambulatory patient in 2016 can use the commode with a collection vessel to measure output. In-dwelling catheters have been recognized as infectious sources and are not recommended. Exceptions to this are for bed-bound or critically ill patients, and for patients who have had low pelvic resections with possible disruption or edema of pelvic nerves. Men with benign prostatic hypertrophy should be managed by clean intermittent catheterization.

Uniquely in multimodal pain management patients, sometimes ambulation is enabled with regional blocks, such as with an epidural in open hepatic, pancreatic, or rectal resections. The combination of general anesthesia and epidural anesthetic can lead to urinary retention, particularly in high-risk groups. Many centers using epidural catheters will use a urinary catheter until the first morning after general anesthesia with selective continuation based on risk factors. Continued use of urinary catheters is a known risk of increased urinary tract infection.[14]

Risk factors for urinary retention include:
- Male gender
- Prostatic hypertrophy
- Open approach for abdominal operations
- Preoperative pelvic radiation
- Resection of large or sidewall pelvic tumors
- Abdominoperineal resections
- Obesity

15

In addition to removing urinary catheters for avoidance of infection, interesting science is emerging regarding the definition of adequate urine output after surgery. Following the adoption of post-Korean War resuscitation algorithms, surgeons have mandated urine output after surgery to be 0.5 mL/kg true body weight per hour. In the first 48 to 72 hours following surgery, it is likely that the healthy, recovering patient may not make as much urine until antidiuretic hormone and other stress responses wane. Habitually, especially in training centers that require standards to guide less experienced trainees during overnight shift work, intravenous fluid is abundantly administered to the point of "pushing" the kidneys to a desired urine out. Such resuscitation in the patient not needing resuscitation results in bowel edema, renal calyx edema, and other adverse effects, before forcing the urine output to a desired mark.

We look forward to the work of Mattias Soop and others in redefining adequate urine output in the acute postoperative setting. In the meantime, permissive oliguria, allowing the healthy, otherwise normally recovering patient to have the lower than traditionally accepted urine output, tends to speed recovery, to avoid soft tissue edema and discomfort, and to result in the spontaneous higher urine output on postoperative days 3 to 4. Avoidance of fluid overload and associated worse outcomes and avoidance of the catheter merely to watch forced urine output are two difficult changes of practice for most surgeons. However, adopting these practices as part of enhanced recovery care can immediately improve outcomes with decreased complications and no increased risk to patients. Urinary catheter recommendations are shown in **Table 15.1**.

Central Venous Access

The evidence for minimizing the use of central venous access predates enhanced recovery, although it can be broadly applied. There are few colorectal or single-site hepatic resections that mandate the use of central access. For planned complex pelvic exenterations, advanced hepatic resections, and pancreaticoduodenectomies, central venous access is indicated for intraoperative blood resuscitation and more complicated medication administration. Recommendations for central venous access in abdominopelvic surgery include selective placement under sterile technique with removal within 24 hours of operation. Considerations in trying to avoid central access in patients with difficult routine peripheral access, which is common in elderly and preoperative chemotherapy patients, include the use of external jugular access for high-flow, non-central access, and

TABLE 15.1 — Urinary Catheter Recommendations

Abdominal Operations

• Summary and recommendation
  – None, if no epidural
  – Remove POD 1, if epidural
• Evidence level
  – Low (few studies, extrapolated data)
• Recommendation grade
  – Strong

Pelvic Operations
  • Summary and recommendation
  – Same, except for ultralow and combined urologic
    procedures
• Evidence level
  – Low
• Recommendation grade
  – Weak

Duke Surgery.

upper arm, deeper access obtained with ultrasound guidance.

In summary, fewer drains, tubes, and lines are better for patients undergoing surgery. The use of central venous access should be very intentional and discontinued as soon as the resuscitation is complete. Urinary catheters are to be used only when patients are not able to empty their bladders spontaneously or perform clean intermittent catheterization. Peritoneal drains have special application in pancreatic operations, but should otherwise be avoided. Pelvic drains are appropriate after significant intraoperative blood loss during pelvic operations and when an empty space is created in the pelvis by resection.

REFERENCES

1. Cheatham ML, Chapman WC, Key SP, Sawyers JL. A meta-analysis of selective versus routine nasogastric decompression after elective laparotomy. *Ann Surg*. 1995;221:469-476.

2. Nelson R, Edwards S, Tse B. Prophylactic nasogastric decompression after abdominal surgery. *Cochrane Database Syst Rev*. 2007;(3):CD004929.

3. Rao W, Zhang X, Zhang J, Yan R, Hu Z, Wang Q. The role of nasogastric tube in decompression after elective colon and rectum surgery: a meta-analysis. *Int J Colorectal Dis*. 2011;26:423-429.

4. Jottard K, Hoff C, Maessen J, et al; Dutch Perioperative Breakthrough Project; ERAS Group. Life and death of the nasogastric tube in elective colonic surgery in the Netherlands. *Clin Nutr*. 2009;28:26-28.

5. Gustafsson UO, Scott MJ, Schwenk W, et al; Enhanced Recovery After Surgery (ERAS) Society, for Perioperative Care; European Society for Clinical Nutrition and Metabolism (ESPEN); International Association for Surgical Metabolism and Nutrition (IASMEN). Guidelines for perioperative care in elective colonic surgery: Enhanced Recovery After Surgery (ERAS(®)) Society recommendations. *World J Surg*. 2013;37:259-284.

6. Nygren J, Thacker J, Carli F, et al; Enhanced Recovery After Surgery (ERAS) Society, for Perioperative Care; European Society for Clinical Nutrition and Metabolism (ESPEN); International Association for Surgical Metabolism and Nutrition (IASMEN). Guidelines for perioperative care in elective rectal/pelvic surgery: Enhanced Recovery After Surgery (ERAS(®)) Society recommendations. *World J Surg*. 2013;37:285-305.

7. Roland CL, Mansour JC, Schwarz RE. Routine nasogastric decompression is unnecessary after pancreatic resections. *Arch Surg*. 2012;147:287-289.

8. Kunstman JW, Klemen ND, Fonseca AL, Araya DL, Salem RR. Nasogastric drainage may be unnecessary after pancreaticoduodenectomy: a comparison of routine vs selective decompression. *J Am Coll Surg*. 2013;217:481-488.

9. Urbach DR, Kennedy ED, Cohen MM. Colon and rectal anastomoses do not require routine drainage: a systematic review and meta-analysis. *Ann Surg*. 1999;229:174-180.

10. Jesus EC, Karliczek A, Matos D, Castro AA, Atallah AN. Prophylactic anastomotic drainage for colorectal surgery. *Cochrane Database Syst Rev.* 2004;(4):CD002100.

11. Bretagnol F, Slim K, Faucheron JL. [Anterior resection with low colorectal anastomosis. To drain or not?]. *Ann Chir.* 2005;130:336-339.

12. Nitsche U, Müller TC, Späth C, et al. The evidence based dilemma of intraperitoneal drainage for pancreatic resection–a systematic review and meta-analysis. *BMC Surg.* 2014;14:76.

13. Van Buren G 2nd, Bloomston M, Hughes SJ, et al. A randomized prospective multicenter trial of pancreaticoduodenectomy with and without routine intraperitoneal drainage. *Ann Surg.* 2014;259:605-612.

14. Zaouter C, Kaneva P, Carli F. Less urinary tract infection by earlier removal of bladder catheter in surgical patients receiving thoracic epidural analgesia. *Reg Anesth Pain Med.* 2009;34:542-548.

15

16

Postoperative Pain Management:
Enhanced Recovery After Major Abdominopelvic Surgery

by Christopher L Wu, MD

Introduction

The increased interest in enhanced recovery pathways (ERPs) provides many opportunities and challenges for postoperative pain management. Uncontrolled postoperative pain results in detrimental physiologic and psychological effects that may delay patient recovery. The delivery of postoperative pain management in enhanced recovery patients (vs those receiving traditional care) needs to be modified to facilitate patient recovery. There are many options for postoperative pain management, and each analgesic drug or technique possesses advantages and disadvantages for the enhanced recovery patient.

Goals for Postoperative Pain Control in the Enhanced Recovery Patient

Control of postoperative pain in patients undergoing abdominopelvic surgery is an important component of any ERP. The overall goal is a multimodal analgesic approach to minimize the use of and side effects from opioids. In addition, there are certain physiologic benefits of analgesic options/techniques that may be especially beneficial to enhanced recovery patients.

Analgesic Options/Techniques

The goal for provision of postoperative analgesia for an ERP necessitates that the clinician optimizes the analgesic regimen for the patient undergoing major abdominopelvic surgery such that the physiologic and pharmacologic benefits are maximized and side effects minimized to facilitate patient recovery and return to baseline function (**Table 16.1**).

■ Regional Analgesic Techniques

Regional analgesic techniques for patients undergoing major abdominopelvic surgery are typically categorized as neuraxial (epidural and spinal) or peripheral (transversus abdominis plane, paravertebral, or wound infiltration) blocks/catheters.

Epidural Analgesia

Use of thoracic epidural analgesia (TEA) may be of great benefit for patients undergoing major abdominopelvic surgery. TEA (vs opioids) has been shown to provide superior postoperative analgesia, decrease some pulmonary/cardiac morbidity, and facilitate earlier return of gastrointestinal function.[1,2] The overall benefits of TEA in improving recovery or decreasing length of stay in ERPs or laparoscopic surgical procedures are uncertain.[3,4]

Common epidural analgesic regimens include both a local anesthetic (LA) (eg, bupivacaine or ropivacaine) and an opioid (eg, fentanyl or hydromorphone), although the clinician should consider using a LA-based regimen only because lipophilic epidural opioids may be absorbed systematically and theoretically contribute to decreased gastrointestinal function. Side effects from TEA are the result of the analgesic agents (LA: hypotension, sensory deficits, motor weakness, urinary retention; opioids: nausea, vomiting, pruritus, respiratory depression) or technique itself (catheter dislodgment/failure of technique, backache, headache, neurologic injury, epidural hematoma). The concurrent administration of anticoagulants in the presence of TEA should be performed with caution, and guidelines have been established.[5]

Neuraxial Opioids

Neuraxial opioids can be delivered either via the epidural or spinal (intrathecal) space. Commonly, neuraxial opioids are delivered as a single-shot spinal injection prior to surgery. Hydrophilic opioids (eg, morphine, hydromorphone) are typically used in a single-shot spinal injection as they have a longer duration of analgesia than lipophilic opioids (eg, fentanyl, sufentanil). Use of a single-shot spinal opioid is associated with significantly lower pain at rest/on movement and reduced opioid requirements.[6] The side effects of neuraxial opioids include opioid-related (nausea, vomiting, pruritus, respiratory depression) and technique-related (failure of technique, backache, headache, neurologic injury, epidural hematoma) complications.

Transversus Abdominis Plane (TAP) Blocks/Catheters

TAP blocks/catheters may be a valuable regional technique when neuraxial techniques have not been used. Use of TAP blocks/catheters (generally placed under ultrasound guidance) provides superior analgesia and decreases postoperative opioid consumption. For maximal analgesic coverage, bilateral subcostal and posterior TAP blocks are typically needed. Preoperative TAP block administration appears to have greater effects on early pain and opioid consumption compared with postoperative administration. There may be an association between TAP block LA dose and decreased late pain at rest and postoperative opioid consumption.[7] Side effects and complications may include failure of the technique, LA toxicity, and perforation of the peritoneum (damage to visceral structures).

Paravertebral Blocks/Catheters

Paravertebral blocks (PVBs) and catheters may be performed for patients undergoing major abdominopelvic surgery, although there is far less literature on the

TABLE 16.1 — Analgesic Options for Abdominopelvic Patients

Analgesic Agent/ Technique	Advantages	Disadvantages
Systemic opioids	No analgesic ceiling	Nausea, vomiting, pruritus, ↓ GI function, sedation, respiratory depression, immunosuppression, urinary retention
Neuraxial 0pioids	Less overall opioid use	Nausea, vomiting, pruritus, respiratory depression, urinary retention, technique failure, backache, PDPH, infection, hematoma
Neuraxial local anesthetics	↓ Pain; facilitates return of GI function; attenuates immunosuppression; ↓ some pulmonary/cardiac morbidity	Technique failure, hypotension, ↓ sensory/motor function, urinary retention, LA toxicity, backache, PDPH, infection, hematoma
Peripheral regional: TAP	↓ Pain; opioid-sparing effect; non-opioid analgesia	Technique failure, LA toxicity, perforation of peritoneum
Peripheral regional: paravertebral	↓ Pain; opioid-sparing effect; non-opioid analgesia	Technique failure, hypotension, vascular/pleural puncture, pneumothorax
Wound infiltration (LA)	Fast and simple technique; minimal risk	Duration of analgesia limited to duration of action of LA

Intravenous lidocaine	↓ Pain; facilitates return of GI function; ↓ LOS for open procedures	Optimal dosage regimen uncertain
Nonsteroidal anti-inflammatory agents	↓ Pain; opioid-sparing effect; non-opioid analgesia	Platelet dysfunction; GI irritation; renal dysfunction; ? anastomotic leakage
Acetaminophen	↓ Pain; opioid-sparing effect; non-opioid analgesia	Liver toxicity
Gabapentinoids	↓ Pain; opioid-sparing effect; non-opioid analgesia	Dizziness, sedation, peripheral edema; renally excreted
Glucocorticoids	↓ Pain; ↓ length of recovery room stay	↑ Serum glucose levels
Alpha-2 agonists	↓ Pain; opioid-sparing effect; non-opioid analgesia	Hypotension; bradycardia
N-methyl-D-aspartate antagonists	↓ Pain; opioid-sparing effect; non-opioid analgesia	Optimal dosage regimen uncertain
Tramadol	Opioid-sparing effect; minimal opioid analgesia	Seizures, possible serotonin syndrome with SSRIs

GI, gastrointestinal; LA, local anesthetic; LOS, length of stay; PDPH, postdural puncture headache; SSRI, selective serotonin reuptake inhibitor.

16

efficacy of this technique in this surgical population compared to others (eg, breast or thoracic surgery). PVBs/catheters are most often compared to epidural analgesia and both appear to provide comparable degree of analgesia. PVBs and catheters are generally associated with less hypotension, and concurrent use of anticoagulation appears to be less of an issue. Side effects and complications may include failure of the technique, hypotension (although to a lesser extent than epidural analgesia), vascular and pleural puncture, and pneumothorax.[8]

Wound and Peritoneal Infiltration/Catheters

Wound infiltration has been shown to be associated with a decrease in morphine consumption, need for opioid rescue, and significantly lower pain scores within the first hour, although there appears to be no analgesic benefit at 24 hours.[9] The analgesic efficacy of wound catheters for postoperative pain is uncertain as one of the latest meta-analyses found that wound catheters provided no significant analgesia at rest or on activity, except in patients undergoing gynecological and obstetric surgery.[10] Intraperitoneal instillation of LA after laparoscopic surgery is also associated with significantly lower pain scores up to 4 to 6 hours postoperatively, although there appeared to be no analgesic benefit at 24 hours.[11] Preliminary data suggest that use of longer-acting formulations of local anesthetic (eg, liposomal bupivacaine) may significantly reduce opioid consumption and opioid-related adverse events, and improve health economic outcomes in routine gastrointestinal surgery.[12] The role of these agents in ERPs will need to be investigated to determine if these outcomes can be replicated in these pathways.

■ Opioid Analgesics

Opioids have traditionally been a cornerstone of postoperative pain regimen; however, the goals of facilitating patient recovery in enhanced recovery colorectal patients necessitate a decrease in the utilization of opioids. Most clinically available opioids produce analgesia via mu receptors and may be administered via a variety of routes (intravenous [IV], intramuscular [IM], oral [PO], subcutaneous, neuraxial). There is no theoretical analgesic ceiling, but the dose of opioids that can be administered is clinically limited by the presence of side effects. Opioids are initially administered by IV patient-controlled analgesia (IV PCA) for patients who are unable to take an oral diet. For IV PCA, the use of a background/continuous infusion is discouraged in opioid-naïve patients, as there may be a higher risk for respiratory events.

Although opioids may provide adequate analgesia, the use of opioids is not conducive for enhanced recovery abdominopelvic patients due to the potential side effects from opioids, including nausea, vomiting, decreased gastrointestinal motility, urinary retention, pruritus, and respiratory depression/sedation. Minimizing opioid use via a multimodal analgesic approach is preferable. Regardless of potential side effects, opioids should not be withheld in patients experiencing moderate to severe pain or in those who are taking chronic opioids prior to surgery.

- **Nonsteroidal Anti-inflammatory Agents**
  (including COX-2 inhibitors)

Through inhibition of cyclooxygenase and prostaglandin synthesis, nonsteroidal anti-inflammatory agents (NSAIDs) are potent analgesics. Because of their analgesic potency, NSAIDs are an integral part of most ERPs and ideally should be administered on a scheduled basis. NSAIDS are preferably administered via the IV or PO routes. These agents have an analgesic ceiling and are associated with several side effects including platelet dysfunction, gastrointestinal irritation/bleeding, and renal dysfunction. Although NSAIDs may be withheld due to fear of perioperative bleeding, a recent meta-analysis suggests no increase in bleeding with ketorolac.[13] It is unclear whether the use of NSAIDs is definitively associated with an increase in anastomotic leakage; however, NSAIDs are an integral part of most multimodal analgesic regimens.[8]

16

■ Acetaminophen

Acetaminophen presumably exerts its analgesic action via inhibition of cyclooxygenase and, like NSAIDs, should be an integral part of most ERPs. Acetaminophen may be administered on a scheduled basis via IV/PO routes but preferably should not be administered per rectum (PR) due in part to the variable absorption. Addition of acetaminophen to NSAIDs will result in an additive if not synergistic analgesic effect. Due to the potential for liver toxicity, the maximum dosage of acetaminophen for a normal-sized adult is 4 g/day, although recent discussions suggest that a lower dose (3-3.25 g/day) may be warranted.

■ Gabapentinoids

These agents were originally designed as anticonvulsants but have demonstrated analgesic properties by interacting with the alpha 2-delta subunits of presynaptic calcium channels and decreasing excitatory neurotransmitter release. The two widely available drugs are gabapentin and pregabalin. Pooled estimates indicate that a single dose of gabapentin preoperatively is associated with a decrease in postoperative pain and opioid consumption at 24 hours but an increase in postoperative sedation.[14] Pooled estimates also indicate that pregabalin improves postoperative analgesia compared with placebo but with an increased risk of sedation and visual disturbances.[15] Typical doses for gabapentin and pregabalin when given as a single dose preoperatively range from 600-1200 mg and 75-300 mg, respectively. Gabapentin and pregabalin can be continued into the postoperatively period, although the precise dosing regimen and duration of administration are uncertain.

Several side effects of the gabapentinoids should be noted. These agents are renally excreted so the dose should be decreased (or even avoided) in patients with significant perioperative renal dysfunction. As noted, the gabapentinoids are associated with a higher risk of sedation, and as such, these agents should be used cautiously (if at all) in patients with a higher risk of sedation, and as such, these agents should be used cautiously (if at all) in patients with a higher risk of respiratory depression such as patients with obstructive sleep apnea. Other side effects include peripheral edema and dizziness.

Other Adjuvant Agents

■ Intravenous and Transdermal Lidocaine

In enhanced recovery patients, lidocaine may be administered either as an IV infusion or transdermal patch. Use of IV lidocaine in the perioperative period is associated with a reduction in acute pain (both at rest and with activity) and opioid consumption, earlier return of gastrointestinal function, and reduced hospital length of stay following open procedures.[16] Topical lidocaine may be effective for relief of pain, although it is not clear whether lidocaine patches may reduce postoperative pain[17]; however, lidocaine patches have a very favorable side effect (low risk) profile and may be considered as part of the multimodal analgesic regimen.

■ Tramadol

Tramadol produces analgesia via dual opioid (very weak mu receptor activation) and non-opioid (inhibits serotonin and norepinephrine reuptake) mechanisms of actions. Although not as potent as opioids or NSAIDs with regard to analgesia, tramadol produces analgesia with a relatively lower risk of addiction, less constipation, and less respiratory depression compared to that from opioids. However, tramadol should be used with caution in patients with a history of seizures and taking concurrent selective serotonin reuptake inhibitors (SSRi).

■ NMDA Antagonists

Perioperative inhibition of N-methyl-D-aspartate (NMDA) receptors may be desirable as these receptors are involved with nociceptive processing and development of chronic pain. Clinically available NMDA

16

antagonists include dextromethorphan, ketamine, and magnesium. Ketamine is typically administered as an infusion, and in subanesthetic doses, ketamine may reduce IV PCA morphine use and postoperative nausea/vomiting.[18] Systemic infusions of perioperative magnesium may reduce postoperative pain (at rest and with movement) and opioid consumption but did not decrease opioid-related side effects such as nausea and vomiting. There were no reports of clinical toxicity related to toxic serum levels of magnesium in these studies.[19]

■ Glucocorticoids

Glucocorticoids are used to reduce inflammation and may reduce acute pain. A recent meta-analysis examined the analgesic efficacy of a single perioperative dose of dexamethasone. Patients who received dexamethasone had lower pain scores, used less opioids, required less rescue analgesia for intolerable pain, had longer time to first dose of analgesic, and hadshorter stays in the post-anesthesia care unit.[20] Although there was no increase in infection or delayed wound healing with dexamethasone,[20] blood glucose levels were higher at 24 hours and the longer-term effects of perioperative administration of dexamethasone are uncertain.

■ Alpha-2 Agonists

Alpha-2 agonists may be useful as part of a multimodal analgesic regimen as they exhibit useful perioperative pharmacologic characteristics (sedation, hypnosis, anxiolysis, sympatholysis, and analgesia). Stimulation of alpha-2 receptors in the central nervous system produces analgesia. Use of systemic alpha-2 agonists (clonidine or dexmedetomidine) may reduce postoperative pain, opioid consumption, and some opioid-related side effects; however, there was an increased risk of perioperative hypotension (clonidine) and postoperative bradycardia (dexmedetomidine).[21]

■ Alternative/Complementary Therapy

There are many options for alternative/complementary therapy including acupuncture, aromatherapy, biofeedback, energy therapies, massage, meditation, music, reflexology, and transcutaneous electrical nerve stimulation (TENS). The overall efficacy of these therapies is uncertain; however, the risk of most of these therapies is minimal. If available, these therapies maybe offered to enhanced recovery patients as another method to decrease postoperative pain.

Summary

Control of perioperative pain is important for the recovery of enhanced recovery abdominopelvic patients. Although there are many options for analgesia, the optimal approach in these patients is typically a multimodal analgesic regimen that minimizes opioid use (**Table 16.2**).

REFERENCES

1. Pöpping DM, Elia N, Van Aken HK, et al. Impact of epidural analgesia on mortality and morbidity after surgery: systematic review and meta-analysis of randomized controlled trials. *Ann Surg*. 2014;259:1056-1067.

2. Block BM, Liu SS, Rowlingson AJ, Cowan AR, Cowan JA Jr, Wu CL. Efficacy of postoperative epidural analgesia: a meta-analysis. *JAMA*. 2003;290:2455-2463.

3. Hughes MJ, Ventham NT, McNally S, Harrison E, Wigmore S. Analgesia after open abdominal surgery in the setting of enhanced recovery surgery: a systematic review and meta-analysis. *JAMA Surg*. 2014;149:1224-1230.

4. Liu H, Hu X, Duan X, Wu J. Thoracic epidural analgesia (TEA) vs. patient controlled analgesia (PCA) in laparoscopic colectomy: a meta-analysis. *Hepatogastroenterology*. 2014;61:1213-1219.

5. Horlocker TT, Wedel DJ, Rowlingson JC, et al. Regional anesthesia in the patient receiving antithrombotic or thrombolytic therapy: American Society of Regional Anesthesia and Pain Medicine Evidence-Based Guidelines (Third Edition). *Reg Anesth Pain Med*. 2010;35(1):64-101.

16

TABLE 16.2 — Perioperative Multimodal Analgesic Regimen for Colorectal Patients at The Johns Hopkins Hospital (downtown campus)

Preoperative
- Gabapentin 600 mg PO ×1 (do not give to patients on hemodialysis, 300 mg for patients with decreased renal function, age >70)
- Acetaminophen 1 g PO ×1 (do not give to patients with liver failure or elevated liver enzymes)
- Celebrex 200 mg PO ×1 (do not give to patients with allergic-type reactions to sulfonamides)

Intraoperative
- Magnesium: 2 g/hr rate to a total of 4 g (2-h infusion) – start on induction
- For open surgical cases = epidural anesthesia + total IV anesthesia (TIVA):
  - TIVA: propofol infusion as needed; midazolam IV as needed on induction; titrate to BIS of 40-60
  - Epidural (T7-8): 2% lidocaine with 1:200,000 epinephrine as a test dose (3 mL) followed by a bolus to obtain T4 level. This is followed by an infusion of 2% lidocaine at 4-6 mL/hr. Consider giving an appropriate bolus (4-8 mL) of 0.25% bupivacaine via epidural at end of case depending on the clinical status of the patient
- For laparoscopic cases = general anesthesia + TAP block:
  - TIVA: propofol infusion as needed; midazolam IV on induction; titrate to BIS of 40-60.
  - IV lidocaine infusion: 1.5 mg/kg bolus on induction + 1.5 mg/kg/hr—stop at end of surgery
  - Opioid: hydromorphone IV as needed
  - TAP Block for laparoscopic cases/ileostomy reversals after completion of surgical procedure

Postoperative
- While patient is NPO:
  - Patient-controlled epidural analgesia: 0.0625% or 0.125% bupivacaine only (*no* fentanyl to start) at 5 mL/hr + 3 mL q10min prn–adjust as needed and continue for at least 1 full day after patient tolerating oral intake including oral analgesics

Continued

TABLE 16.2 — *Continued*

Postoperative (continued)
  – Adjuvant agents (assuming no contraindications):
    • Acetaminophen 1 g IV q6h
    • Ketorolac 30 mg IV q6h (decrease to 15 mg IV q6h for age >75; max 5 days total)
    • Lidoderm patch 1-2 patches q24h
    • Breakthrough pain: replace epidural if needed; hydromorphone IV q3h prn (if needed, order IV PCA hydromorphone for pain not controlled with above analgesic meds)
  • When oral intake resumes:
    – Tramadol 50 mg PO q4h prn (max dose: 400 mg/d or 300 mg/d age >75 y)
    – Acetaminophen 1 g PO q8h
    – Gabapentin 100 mg PO tid
    – Ibuprofen 400 mg PO q6h
    – Breakthrough pain (if tramadol fails): prn opioid (eg, hydromorphone 2 mg PO q4h prn breakthrough pain)

6. Meylan N, Elia N, Lysakowski C, Tramèr MR. Benefit and risk of intrathecal morphine without local anaesthetic in patients undergoing major surgery: meta-analysis of randomized trials. *Br J Anaesth.* 2009;102:156-167.

7. De Oliveira GS Jr, Castro-Alves LJ, Nader A, Kendall MC, McCarthy RJ. Transversus abdominis plane block to ameliorate postoperative pain outcomes after laparoscopic surgery: a meta-analysis of randomized controlled trials. *Anesth Analg.* 2014;118:454-463.

8. Tan M, Law LS, Gan TJ. Optimizing pain management to facilitate Enhanced Recovery After Surgery pathways. *Can J Anaesth.* 2015;62:203-218.

9. Bamigboye AA, Hofmeyr GJ. Local anaesthetic wound infiltration and abdominal nerves block during caesarean section for postoperative pain relief. *Cochrane Database Syst Rev.* 2009;3:CD006954.

10. Gupta A, Favaios S, Perniola A, Magnuson A, Berggren L. A meta-analysis of the efficacy of wound catheters for post-operative pain management. *Acta Anaesthesiol Scand.* 2011;55:785-796.

11. Marks JL, Ata B, Tulandi T. Systematic review and metaanalysis of intraperitoneal instillation of local anesthetics for reduction of pain after gynecologic laparoscopy. *J Minim Invasive Gynecol.* 2012;19:545-553.

16

12. Cohen SM, Vogel JD, Marcet JE, Candiotti KA. Liposome bupivacaine for improvement in economic outcomes and opioid burden in GI surgery: IMPROVE Study pooled analysis. *J Pain Res.* 2014;7:359-366.

13. Gobble RM, Hoang HL, Kachniarz B, Orgill DP. Ketorolac does not increase perioperative bleeding: a meta-analysis of randomized controlled trials. *Plast Reconstr Surg.* 2014;133:741-755.

14. Hurley RW, Cohen SP, Williams KA, Rowlingson AJ, Wu CL. The analgesic effects of perioperative gabapentin on postoperative pain: a meta-analysis. *Reg Anesth Pain Med.* 2006;31:237-247.

15. Mishriky BM, Waldron NH, Habib AS. Impact of pregabalin on acute and persistent postoperative pain: a systematic review and meta-analysis. *Br J Anaesth.* 2015;114:10-31.

16. Sun Y, Li T, Wang N, Yun Y, Gan TJ. Perioperative systemic lidocaine for postoperative analgesia and recovery after abdominal surgery: a meta-analysis of randomized controlled trials. *Dis Colon Rectum.* 2012;55:1183-1194.

17. Bai Y, Miller T, Tan M, Law LS, Gan TJ. Lidocaine patch for acute pain management: a meta-analysis of prospective controlled trials. *Curr Med Res Opin.* 2015;31:575-581.

18. Bell RF, Dahl JB, Moore RA, Kalso E. Perioperative ketamine for acute postoperative pain. *Cochrane Database Syst Rev.* 2006;1:CD004603.

19. De Oliveira GS Jr, Castro-Alves LJ, Khan JH, McCarthy RJ. Perioperative systemic magnesium to minimize postoperative pain: a meta-analysis of randomized controlled trials. *Anesthesiology.* 2013;119:178-190.

20. Waldron NH, Jones CA, Gan TJ, Allen TK, Habib AS. Impact of perioperative dexamethasone on postoperative analgesia and side-effects: systematic review and meta-analysis. *Br J Anaesth.* 2013;110:191-200.

21. Blaudszun G, Lysakowski C, Elia N, Tramèr MR. Effect of perioperative systemic $\alpha2$ agonists on postoperative morphine consumption and pain intensity: systematic review and meta-analysis of randomized controlled trials. *Anesthesiology.* 2012;116:1312-1322.

17

Patient Mobilization and Post Discharge Rehabilitation

by Sean Ryan, MD and
Sandhya Lagoo-Deenadayalan, MD

Introduction

The benefits of prehabilitation—optimizing function prior to encountering a physiologic stress such as surgery—are well documented.[1] Prehabilitation represents multiple arms of preparing for surgery including various exercises, inspiratory muscle training, dietary counseling, and strategies for anxiety control.[1] Therapy for 2 to 4 weeks preoperatively may contribute to a reduction in the length of hospital stay, as well as to decreased complications.[2]

Multiple trials for patients undergoing coronary artery bypass grafts and abdominal aortic aneurysm repair[2] have shown these benefits, as well as reduced pulmonary complications; however, other trials have had mixed results.[2,3] For patients undergoing major abdominal surgery, suboptimal preoperative level of function has been shown to increase the risk of complications after surgery and lengthen recovery time.[4] Preoperative activities as simple as increased physical movement and breathing exercises are correlated with improved ambulation and improved patient outcomes postoperatively.[4] The importance of patient mobilization postoperatively is directly related to this prehabilitation effort.

Surgery causes fatigue and postoperative pain, resulting in decreased mobility. Lack of physical activity suppresses the cardiopulmonary and musculoskeletal systems.[5] Movement must begin early in the postoperative period to minimize this suppression.[5,6] In addition, preventing deconditioning with early postoperative movement helps patients maintain flexibility, strength, and endurance. Randomized controlled trials of ERPs have been conducted in patients undergoing major abdominopelvic surgery (most notably colon surgery) and have shown a reduction in complication rates and length of hospital stay with implementation of the ERPs,[7-10] all of which include early mobilization.

Early mobility, a key component of the ERP, has been directly correlated with decreased atelectasis, pneumonia, ileus, thromboembolism, delirium, increased muscle strength and tissue oxygenation, decreased opioid use, and prevention of pressure ulcers.[2,7,11-14] The timing of mobilization is critical to the implementation of ERPs. One recent study showed a significant relationship between patient mobilization within 24 hours postoperatively and pulmonary infections,[7] while others recommend patients being mobilized for at least 2 hours on the same day as surgery and at least 6 hours on postoperative days 2 and 3.[12,13] In patients undergoing Enhanced Recovery following elective colon surgery in a study by Gillissen and colleagues,[9] patients had goals of being mobilized for 15 minutes on the day of surgery, and for 3 hours on postoperative day 1. Patients who were successfully mobilized early were subsequently discharged from the hospital sooner.

Ultimately, patient mobilization must be viewed as a spectrum, and rehabilitation should be adapted to meet the needs of each individual patient.[14] Nurses are at the forefront of this mobilization effort. With the help of physical therapists and the support of the multidisciplinary team involved in an ERP, nurses should continuously encourage patient activity.

Critical Information Prior to Surgery

Since mobility needs must be specific to each patient, it is vital to have a baseline assessment of the patient preoperatively (**Table 17.1**). Prior to surgery, patients must have a full medical history recorded,

TABLE 17.1 — Baseline Patient Preoperative Assessment

Initial Assessment	
Medical history	Chronic diseases, medications, chronic neuropathy
Surgical history	Hardware, chronic pain, prior limb-sparing surgeries or amputations.
Functional status	Activities of daily living (feeding, bathing, dressing, toileting, transferring), Instrumental activities of daily living, history of falls.
Social status	Origin prior to hospitalization: home (alone or with support) or skilled nursing facility.
Ambulation	Independent, use of mobility aids (cane, walker, wheelchair), physical therapy assessment
Goals of care	Work, fitness to return to work

looking at chronic medical conditions that may affect postoperative rehabilitation: medications, use of mobility gait aids including canes or walkers, history of falls, and need for an ostomy bag, urinary catheter, or drains. As part of this medical history, social history is another vital component: Does the patient live alone? Does he/she have home support? Did he/she come from a skilled nursing facility?

17

A realistic conversation with all patients about the goals of care directs the initial assessment (**Table 17.1**). Physical therapy and occupational therapy can help in developing goals of care and the input of these teams should be instituted to optimize the ERP. The patient's place of work, detail of activities at work, and fitness level required to return to work should be known when establishing these goals.

Barriers to Mobilization

The benefits of early mobilization are well studied and documented, yet the implementation has proven to be difficult. The common mentality of encouraging "bed rest" following surgery must be changed, and a balance of rest and mobility should be sought.[14] It was noted by Gillissen and associates that adherence to the ERP is highest before surgery and immediately perioperatively, but declines to between 60% to 70% in the early postoperative phase.[9] It is at this time that ambulation and patient rehabilitation are most critical. The multi-disciplinary nature of Enhanced Recovery requires all caregivers to adapt to new evidence and to discard old habits despite obvious barriers including patient fatigue, pain, postoperative drains, orthostatic hypotension, as well as other patient comorbidities including cognitive dysfunction and polypharmacy.

Intraoperatively, inflammatory cytokines including IL-6 are released, which contributes to patient pain and fatigue. According to Havey and coworkers,[14] this subsequently leads to decreased endurance, which can cause diminished drive to participate in rehabilitation activities. Consequently, this may cause further deconditioning, creating a pattern of inactivity. It is important to note, however, that minor stretching from passive and active range of motion (like ambulation) reduces the production of these inflammatory mediators, thereby reducing a patient's pain and fatigue and increasing future compliance with mobility.[14,15] Intraoperatively, it is critical to avoid skin shear during transfer, to keep adequate padding over bony prominences, and to be mindful of decreased mobility in certain joints.

Postoperative drains (nasogastric tubes, bulb suction, and negative pressure devices) are common following major abdominopelvic surgery. These drains often decrease mobility secondary to concern of displacement of the devices.[14] Nurses and physicians should be aware of the importance of securing the drains prior to ambulation and to examine the drains frequently to ensure proper function.[14]

Complaints of nausea, light-headedness, and dizziness caused by orthostatic hypotension are also prevalent barriers following surgery. This problem may be exacerbated postoperatively when epidural analgesia is used.[14] ERPs include transition from epidural analgesia,[7] as soon as oral medications are triaged minimizing orthostasis and early mobility. In cases of persistent orthostasis, baroreceptors can be retrained by slowly elevating the head of the bed, then placing the patient upright in a chair.[14] Blood pressure and patient symptoms should be continuously monitored throughout this process.

A final common obstacle to patient mobilization, especially in elderly patients, is escalation of medical comorbidities and polypharmacy. All patients must be medically optimized perioperatively to promote active participation in their rehabilitation. Geriatric medicine consults may be helpful to achieve this goal in the complex older patients.

ERP implementation truly requires multidisciplinary coordination at preoperative, intraoperative, and postoperative phases and includes the surgeon, anesthesiologist, intensive care physicians, nursing, therapists, case managers, and social workers.[7,9] Teams must be formed to include all participants so that obstacles at each healthcare facility can be overcome. Communication is critical, and surgeons must convey information about specific needs of the patient and concerns based on their preoperative functional status. They should share the discussions they have had with patients regarding their expectations after surgery and the need for involving caregivers in the rehabilitation process. Instructions to caregivers must be detailed with contact information and applicable resources.

17

Patients who use walkers or canes should have them at bedside, and physical therapy and occupational therapy should be readily available to assess the patient for any mobility needs (including lifts, swings, walkers, canes, or other assistive devices).[14] Patients should be counseled on the proper use of all assistive devices prior to and at the time of discharge.

Specifically following abdominopelvic surgery, abdominal binders can be a useful device to improve patient comfort, decrease wound dehiscence, and ultimately increase patient mobility.[14] Frequently, clinicians resist using binders due to a fear of suppressing pulmonary status secondary to restriction of the lung fields. There is no evidence, however, that properly worn elastic binders alter pulmonary function in either the sitting or lying positions.[16] Binders have been shown to provide patients with greater comfort in the early postoperative days and should be offered in cases where the use of a binder might encourage movement and recovery.[14,16]

Proper use of assistive devices can improve balance and increase mobility, and additionally prevent pain of movement.[17] Patients must be properly fit for these devices in order to receive the maximum benefit. For canes and walkers, a patient should have the height adjusted so that the top of the handle reaches the wrist when the patient is standing in a neutral position. This provides approximately 20 degrees of flexion of the elbows during use. Unfortunately, according to one study, only about 20% of patients were taught how to use their assistive device.[17] Improper use can increase the risk of falls; eg, pulling on the walker to help with rising to a standing position. Reluctance to use the device and excessive energy demands cause up to 50% of patients to discontinue use of the device.[17]

For patients who undergo abdominopelvic surgery, initiating mobility from a supine position while protecting the surgical site can be difficult with a single caretaker or for patients to perform independently on discharge. One way to overcome this is to use the log roll method. Have the patient bend their knees while supine with their feet on the bed and reach across their body with their ipsilateral arm. Have the patient roll toward the contralateral arm with the legs, hips, abdomen, and shoulders moving together. The patient's knees should now be at the edge of the bed, and as they push themselves up with their hands, their feet can slowly drop to the ground.[14] Teaching patients these types of maneuvers can decrease discomfort and complications following discharge from the hospital. An article by Havey and colleagues[14] entitled *Guarding the Gut: Early Mobility After Abdominal Surgery* cited multiple times in this text, provides an excellent resource for additional information on early mobilization.

Readiness for Discharge: Rehabilitation After Discharge

Not all patients will reach the same benchmarks prior to hospital discharge following major abdominopelvic surgery. In general, patients should be back to their baseline of movement and self-care. Except for in orthopedic cases, patients cared for on enhanced recovery protocols should not expected to refine new assist devices or skilled home care at discharge.

17

At discharge, rehabilitation should continue. In a recent study by Gillis and colleagues looking at patients undergoing colorectal resection for cancer,[1] about 50% of patients were >20 meters below their preoperative walking distance on the 6-minute walk test (6MWT) at 4 weeks postprocedure. This study further supported the implementation of prehabilitation, as only those patients with both pre- and postoperative rehabilitation were able to reach their baseline walking on the 6MWT at 8 weeks following surgery.[1] Other similar studies looking at patients undergoing abdominal surgery showed that about one third of patients complained of persistent fatigue at their 4-week follow-up, and two thirds of patients did not recover to their preoperative functional capacity by 9 weeks postoperatively.[4,18] Therefore, it is vital to stress to patients the importance of continued compliance with rehabilitation upon hospital discharge.

Patients requiring additional assistance with rehabilitation may be transferred to skilled nursing facilities (SNF), inpatient rehabilitation facilities (IRF), or may be provided with home health care (HHC). The need for these facilities implies decreased mobility at the time of discharge and is associated with poor patient outcomes. The need for additional care at the time of discharge is associated with increased risk of perioperative complications,[19] and efforts should be made to return patients to preoperative levels of function as soon as possible.

Conversely, successful enhanced recovery and rehabilitation programs have decreased the need for additional care at discharge. Determining which patients should be discharged home (with or without home health) vs to a care facility is a multifactional decision discussion with the patient, the family, and the multidisciplinary team. Several studies in spine and extremity surgery have explored patient characteristics associated with discharge needs.[20-22] The most significant determinants of discharge to home vs to a facility according to Kanaan and coworkers were distance walked during hospital stay, length of hospital stay, and patient age.[20] For patients who were discharged home, those who lived alone, had a low pre-admission level of function, and had longer hospital stays were significantly more likely to need home health.[20] Other factors affecting discharge planning include gender, history of nursing home residence, BMI, number of perioperative complications and comorbidities, and socioeconomic factors.[20-22] All of these factors should be used in conjunction to determine placement for patients undergoing major abdominopelvic surgery.

Coordination of Care and Communication

As with all aspects of ERPs, the multimodality, multidisciplinary approach must continue even after discharge. Follow-up should be arranged with the surgeon and with the patient's primary care provider. This allows for continued medical optimization and continued rehabilitation. The primary care provider and the surgeon should coordinate the patient's care in order to expedite recovery. Additionally, patients should have recommendations from and/or follow up with physical therapy in order to continue the rehabilitation process.

In enhanced recovery, goals of discharge care are clearly communicated to the patient. Discharge instructions in both verbal and written form contain all critical information. Discharge information should include but not be limited to nutritional recommendations including dietary restrictions (commonly for diabetics and patients with end-stage renal disease), medication changes, new anticoagulation, pain control, recommendations for glycemic control and blood glucose monitoring, contact information for the surgeon, and follow-up.

REFERENCES

1. Gillis C, Li C, Lee L, et al. Prehabilitation versus rehabilitation: a randomized control trial in patients undergoing colorectal resection for cancer. *Anesthesiology.* 2014;121:937-947.

2. Valkenet K, van de Port IG, Dronkers JJ, de Vries WR, Lindeman E, Backx FJ. The effects of preoperative exercise therapy on postoperative outcome: a systematic review. *Clin Rehabil.* 2011;25:99-111.

3. Hoogeboom TJ, Dronkers JJ, van den Ende CH, Oosting E, van Meeteren NL. Preoperative therapeutic exercise in frail elderly scheduled for total hip replacement: a randomized pilot trial. *Clin Rehabil.* 2010;24:901-910.

4. Carli F, Charlebois P, Stein B, et al. Randomized clinical trial of prehabilitation in colorectal surgery. *Br J Surg.* 2010;97:1187-1197.

17

5. Hoogeboom TJ, Dronkers JJ, Hulzebos EH, van Meeteren NL. Merits of exercise therapy before and after major surgery. *Curr Opin Anaesthesiol.* 2014;27:161-166.

6. Topp R, Ditmyer M, King K, Doherty K, Hornyak J 3rd. The effect of bed rest and potential of prehabilitation on patients in the intensive care unit. *AACN Clin Issues.* 2002;13:263-276.

7. Cakir H, van Stijn MF, Lopes Cardozo AM, et al. Adherence to Enhanced Recovery After Surgery and length of stay after colonic resection. *Colorectal Dis.* 2013;15:1019-1025.

8. Eskicioglu C, Forbes SS, Aarts MA, Okrainec A, McLeod RS. Enhanced recovery after surgery (ERAS) programs for patients having colorectal surgery: a meta-analysis of randomized trials. *J Gastrointest Surg.* 2009;13:2321-2329.

9. Gillissen F, Hoff C, Maessen JM, et al. Structured synchronous implementation of an enhanced recovery program in elective colonic surgery in 33 hospitals in The Netherlands. *World J Surg.* 2013;37:1082-1093.

10. Susa A, Roveran A, Bocchi A, Carrer S, Tartari S. [FastTrack approach to major colorectal surgery]. *Chir Ital.* 2004;56:817-824.

11. Patel BK, Hall JB. Perioperative physiotherapy. *Curr Opin Anaesthesiol.* 2013;26:152-156.

12. Nygren J, Thacker J, Carli F, et al; Enhanced Recovery After Surgery Society. Guidelines for perioperative care in elective rectal/pelvic surgery: Enhanced Recovery After Surgery (ERAS®) Society recommendations. *Clin Nutr.* 2012;31:801-816.

13. Nygren J, Soop M, Thorell A, Hausel J, Ljungqvist O; ERAS Group. An enhanced-recovery protocol improves outcome after colorectal resection already during the first year: a single-center experience in 168 consecutive patients. *Dis Colon Rectum.* 2009;52:978-985.

14. Havey R, Herriman E, O'Brien D. Guarding the gut: early mobility after abdominal surgery. *Crit Care Nurs Q.* 2013;36:63-72.

15. Winkelman C. Inactivity and inflammation in the critically ill patient. *Crit Care Clin.* 2007;23:21-34.

16. Olsen MF, Josefson K, Wiklund M. Evaluation of abdominal binder after major upper gastrointestinal surgery. *Adv Physiother.* 2009;11:104-110.

17. Bradley SM, Hernandez CR. Geriatric assistive devices. *Am Fam Physician.* 2011;84:405-411.

18. Christensen T, Kehlet H. Postoperative fatigue. *World J Surg*. 1993;17:220-225.

19. Sacks GD, Lawson EH, Dawes AJ, Gibbons MM, Zingmond DS, Ko CY. Which patients require more care after hospital discharge? An analysis of post-acute care use among elderly patients undergoing elective surgery. *J Am Coll Surg*. 2015;220:1113-1121.

20. Kanaan SF, Yeh HW, Waitman RL, Burton DC, Arnold PM, Sharma NK. Predicting discharge placement and health care needs after lumbar spine laminectomy. *J Allied Health*. 2014;43:88-97.

21. Fortington LV, Dijkstra PU, Geertzen JH. Determinants of discharge to long-term care after a lower limb amputation. *J Am Geriatr Soc*. 2013;61:298-299.

22. Dillingham TR, Yacub JN, Pezzin LE. Determinants of post-acute care discharge destination after dysvascular lower limb amputation. *PM R*. 2011;3:336-344.

17

18

Outcomes of Enhanced Recovery Protocols

by Stefan D Holubar MD, MS, FACS, FASCRS and Timothy Miller, MB, ChB, FRCA

The sine qua non of enhanced recovery protocols (ERPs) is optimal patient outcomes. In this chapter, we will first define and review categories of outcomes used to assess ERPs, so readers may critically interpret ERP literature and optimally assess and report their own ERP outcomes. We will then briefly review specialty-specific outcomes (colorectal, hepatobiliary, gynecology, and urology), focusing on the best available evidence.

Outcomes Defined and Explained

Postoperative outcomes can be defined in three broad categories:
- Clinical outcomes
- Patient-reported outcomes (PROs)
- Economic outcomes.

In general, all outcomes are short-term (30 days), although a recent trend includes reporting 60-day outcomes.[1]

■ Clinical Outcomes

Clinical outcomes relevant to ERPs include intraoperative variables, pain scores (also a PRO), length of stay (LOS), readmissions, complications, reoperation, and mortality.

Intraoperative variables relevant to ERPs include anesthesia parameters such as cumulative medication doses, intravenous fluids (IVF), urine output, and goal-directed therapy parameters/endpoints. Traditionally, variables such as volume of IVF are reported as total milliliters (mL, **Figure 18.1**, top panel), but given variation in operative length and body composition, reporting in mL/kg/hr is optimal statically as distribution curves will be tighter and trends can be more readily assessed (**Figure 18.1**, bottom panel).

LOS (in days), is a right-skewed variable with a non-parametric distribution (not bell-shaped) with most data points on the left (**Figure 18.2**) because most patients will be discharged within several days of surgery, but there will always be outliers with significantly longer lengths of stay. As medians and non-parametric tests are less influenced by outliers, optimally, both parametric (mean, standard deviation) and non-parametric (median, interquartile range) summary statistics and tests of significance (student t-test or linear regression vs log-rank test or logistic regression, respectively) should be reported. Furthermore, distribution analysis will reveal that the patient outliers with the longest LOS, specifically the top 2.5% or 5%, are defined as *statistical* outliers, and one may consider censoring those patients for LOS calculations, or capping LOS at the 95% or 97.5% of the distribution (**Figure 18.2**).

Readmission is traditionally reported as the 30-day readmission rate. Total length of stay (TLOS) is defined as the sum of the index admission LOS and the readmission LOS if readmitted within 30 days.[2] If both LOS and TLOS are tested for statistical significance, then Bonferroni's correction for multiple comparisons should be used to adjust the reported P value.

Postoperative complications have traditionally been reported by frequency (proportion) of individual complications (ie, ileus, acute renal failure). The shortcomings of this method are lack of severity and treatment implications. The Clavien-Dindo classification (www.surgicalcomplication.info), which also reports the grade of the complication based on the intervention required, is therefore recommended (**Table 18.1**).[3] For example, adhesive postoperative small bowel obstruction may only require intervention in the form of general medical care (grade 1) or TPN (grade 2); however, a small minority will require operative intervention under general anesthesia (grade 3c). Of note, these methods are not mutually exclusive, so both should be reported. Another strength of the Clavien classification is that it is not specific to any surgical specialty.

■ Patient-Reported Outcomes

PROs (ie, pain scores, quality of life [QoL], and satisfaction) are increasingly reported. Pain visual analog scores (VAS), as assessed on a finite numeric scale of 0-10 (**Figure 18.3**), and verbal rating scale (VRS) are widely used. QoL assessments traditionally have been global (SF-36 for overall health-specific QoL) or disease- or symptom-specific. In ERP literature, PROs, particularly post-discharge QoL, satisfaction, and functional status, are not commonly reported and represent an opportunity for future research.

Presently, no QoL instrument specific to enhanced recovery has been developed,[1] although the World Health Organization Disability Assessment Schedule (WHODAS) has recently been shown to be clinically acceptable and reliable for measuring postoperative disability in a diverse surgical population up to 12 months after surgery.[4]

■ Economic Outcomes

Economic outcomes are typically direct cost, although indirect cost and derivative concepts such as opportunity cost are especially suited to evaluating ERPs. Direct costs, not charges, should be reported as charges can vary greatly depending on how much an individual provider or institution somewhat arbitrarily requests from the payer. Costs are reported in median US dollars because costs too represent a right-skewed variable. Indirect costs are less commonly reported—examples include electricity, capital equipment, lost wages for time away from work, or child-care costs while hospitalized or recovering. Opportunity cost represents financial costs related to a missed opportunity.

18

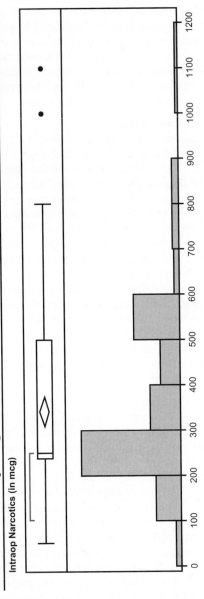

FIGURE 18.1 — Reporting and Distribution Analysis of Volume-Based (mL) Outcomes

Intraop Narcotics (in mcg)

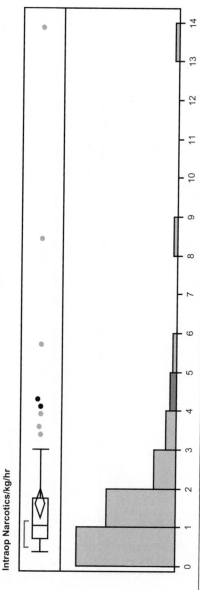

Intraop Narcotics/kg/hr

Note lack of any discernible pattern in top panel, which reports total intra-operative narcotic dose, adjusted for patient weight and operative duration, while in the bottom panel, a left-skewed distribution pattern emerges and outliers can be readily identified.

Figure courtesy of Stefan D. Holubar, MD.

18

FIGURE 18.2 — Length of Stay Distribution and Outlier Analysis

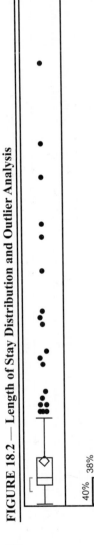

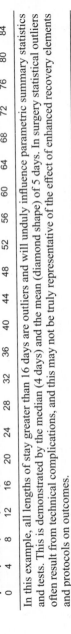

In this example, all lengths of stay greater than 16 days are outliers and will unduly influence parametric summary statistics and tests. This is demonstrated by the median (4 days) and the mean (diamond shape) of 5 days. In surgery statistical outliers often result from technical complications, and this may not be truly representative of the effect of enhanced recovery elements and protocols on outcomes.

Figure courtesy of Stefan D. Holubar, MD.

TABLE 18.1 — Clavien-Dindo Classification of Surgical Complications

Grade	Definition	Example Interventions	Example Complication
—	Any deviation from normal postoperative recovery …	—	—
I	… without need for intervention required by higher grade complications.	NPO, IVF, nasogastric tube, anti-emetics, anti-pyretics	Routine ileus
II	… requiring pharmacologic treatment.	Blood transfusion, TPN	Prolonged ileus, pulmonary embolism (PE) requiring anticoagulation
III	Requiring surgical, endoscopic, or radiological intervention…	—	
IIIa	… without general anesthesia	Interventional radiology drain placement	Contained anastomotic leak
IIIb	… requiring general anesthesia	Reoperation.	Free anastomotic leak
IV	Life-threatening complication (including CNS complications) requiring ICU management	Invasive hemodynamic monitoring, endotracheal intubation.	PE requiring intubation
V	Life-ending complications	NA	Lethal PE

18

FIGURE 18.3 — Patient-Reported Outcomes: Example of Pain Visual Analog Scale

How severe is your pain today? Place a vertical mark on the line below to indicate how bad you feel your pain is today

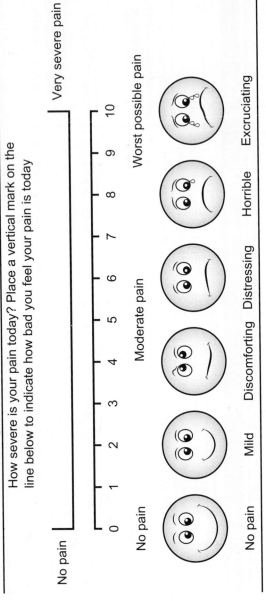

Given than LOS is a key performance measure of ERPs, in order to realize the full economic benefit, the unoccupied bed that results from an earlier discharge must be backfilled promptly. Value-based outcomes can be represented as the ratio of clinical outcomes to cost. High-value care, for ERP purposes, represents more efficient (shorter LOS) or safer (lower complication rate) care at a lower cost.

Specialty-Specific Outcomes

This section will briefly review outcomes from source literature, focusing on randomized controlled trials (RCTs) when available, stratified by sub-specialty and procedure within the broad category of abdomino-pelvic surgery. The authors strongly encourage interested readers to sign up for PubMed notifications (via My NCBI saved searches), as the number of reported ERP studies is growing asymptotically as this field quickly gains wider acceptance worldwide.

A single meta-analysis, spanning subspecialties, included 38 RCTs or quasi-RCTs.[5] Their results suggested that ERPs result in lower LOS (difference -1.14 days) and reduced risk of any complications (RR 0.7), with no difference in readmissions, major complications, or death. The findings of this study and the other below studies are summarized in **Table 18.2**.

Colorectal

Henrik Kehlet, MD, PhD, a Danish surgeon and the "father of enhanced recovery," reported the first outcomes of any ERP.[6] Fast-forward a decade later to the LAFA Study Group, which reported the results of a large multicenter RCT comparing traditional care vs ERP stratified by open and laparoscopic colectomy.[2] A total of 427 patients were randomized, and the LOS of 5 (lap/ERP), 6 (lap/standard), 6 (open/ERP), and 7 (open/standard), $P <0.01$, suggested that patients with colon cancer achieve optimal outcomes when lapa-

TABLE 18.2 — Summary of Meta-Analyses of Outcomes After ERPs for Different Abdominopelvic Surgical Procedures

Specialty or Procedure	No of Patients (# studies if meta-analysis)	LOS (WMD days. 95% CI)	Overall Complications (RR, 95% CI)	Readmissions	Mortality	Costs
Multiple	5099 (38)[a]	-1.14 (-1.45 to -0.85) $P < 0.0001$	0.71 (0.6-0.86), $P < 0.0001$	NS	NS	—
Colorectal	2376 (16)[a]	-2.28 (-3.09 to -1.47) $P < 0.0001$	0.60 (0.46-0.76), $P < 0.0001$	NS	NS	—
Gastric cancer	1676 (14)[b]	-1.10 (-1.56 to -0.65) $P < 0.001$[c]	NS	NS	—	—
Pancreatic resection	1558 (8)[b]	Varied from -6 to -2 days	Absolute risk difference 8.2 %, (2.0-14.4), P=0.008	NS	NS	Decreased
Liver surgery	723 (5)[a]	-2.77 (-3.87 to -1.66), $P < 0.001$	RR 0.66 (0.49-0.88), P=0.005	—	—	—

Key: WMD = weighted mean difference, RR = relative risk, — = not reported, NS = not significantly different, denoting safety.

[a] Meta-analyses of RCTs only.

[b] Systematic review including non-RCTs.

[c] Standardized mean difference now WMD.

roscopy is combined with ERP, and if open surgery is required, then ERP can result in benefit equivalent to laparoscopy.

A recent meta-analysis of 16 RCTs found ERPs to be associated with decreased LOS (-2.3 days, P <0.0001), fewer total complications (RR 0.60, P <0.0001), but no difference in surgical complications, readmissions, or mortality.[7] Thus ERPs have definitely been shown to be safe and effective in colorectal surgery, and represents high-value care.

Hepatobiliary

■ Gastric Resection

A systematic review and meta-analysis reported on the outcomes of ERPs compared with traditional recovery after gastric resection for gastric cancer. Fourteen studies were analyzed, and showed ERPs were associated with a decreased LOS (-1.1 days, P <0.001) and lower cost, although there was significant heterogeneity between studies.[8]

■ Pancreaticoduodectomy (PD, Whipple's procedure)

A meta-analysis of four studies focusing on PD found a significant reduction in complication rate favoring ERPs (absolute risk difference 8.2%, $P=0.008$).[9] Three of these studies also showed a reduction in LOS. However, there are no RCTs in PD, and as such, the available evidence is limited.

■ Hepatic Resection

A meta-analysis of five studies containing 723 patients showed a reduction in LOS (-2.77 days, P <0.00001) and overall complications (RR 0.66, $P=0.005$).[10] Four of these studies were conducted in China and one in the United Kingdom. ERPs appear to be safe and effective in liver resection surgery.

18

Major Gynecologic Surgery

One RCT and two nonrandomized pre-and post-intervention studies in major gynecologic surgery showed a reduction in LOS as well as other improvements, although there was significant variation between interventions.[11] The RCT showed multiple advantages after hysterectomy including less time in the recovery room (180 vs 237 minutes), less PONV (11% vs 50%), quicker PO intake (median 4 vs 5 hours), shorter time of Foley catheterization (9 vs 22 hours), and shorter LOS (2 vs 3 days).[12]

Urology

■ **Radical Cystectomy**

One RCT and two nonrandomized pre-and post-intervention studies have reported the outcomes of ERPs in radical cystectomy.[13,14] ERPs appear to be safe and feasible in this population. A multicenter RCT of alvimopan in this population showed a faster return of GI function, 5.5 vs 6.8 days; hazard ratio: 1.8; P <0.0001), and less ileus-related morbidity (8.4% vs 29.1%; P <0.001).[16]

■ **Nephrectomy**

A single RCT and three nonrandomized pre-and post-intervention studies have reported the outcomes of ERPs in renal surgery (open, laparoscopic, or partial nephrectomy).[13] The RCT of enhanced recovery vs standard of care for 45 patients undergoing radical nephrectomy showed a decreased LOS (5.8 vs 4.2 days, P <0.05) with no observed increase in morbidity.[17]

Conclusions

ERPs, which themselves are evidence-based, when compared with traditional recovery, have been shown to be associated with improved clinical, patient-reported, and economic outcomes. Nuances specific to statistical reporting of ERPs outcomes, including understanding data distribution (parametric vs non-parametric), proper unit reports (mL/kg/hr), total LOS, and grading of complications, can help readers to optimally interpret reported ERP data and studies. In abdominopelvic operations, ERPs have been shown to be associated with improved outcomes in colorectal, hepatobiliary, gynecologic, and urologic surgery.

REFERENCES

1. Neville A, Lee L, Antonescu I, et al. Systematic review of outcomes used to evaluate enhanced recovery after surgery. *Br J Surg*. 2014;101:159-170.

2. Vlug MS, Wind J, Hollmann MW, et al; LAFA study group. Laparoscopy in combination with fast track multimodal management is the best perioperative strategy in patients undergoing colonic surgery: a randomized clinical trial (LAFA-study). *Ann Surg*. 2011;254:868-875.

3. Clavien PA, Barkun J, de Oliveira ML, et al. The Clavien-Dindo classification of surgical complications: five-year experience. *Ann Surg*. 2009;250:187-196.

4. Shulman MA, Myles PS, Chan MT, McIlroy DR, Wallace S, Ponsford J. Measurement of disability-free survival after surgery. *Anesthesiology*. 2015;122:524-536.

5. Nicholson A, Lowe MC, Parker J, Lewis SR, Alderson P, Smith AF. Systematic review and meta-analysis of enhanced recovery programmes in surgical patients. *Br J Surg*. 2014;101:172-188.

6. Kehlet H, Mogensen T. Hospital stay of 2 days after open sigmoidectomy with a multimodal rehabilitation programme. *Br J Surg*. 1999;86:227-230.

7. Greco M, Capretti G, Beretta L, Gemma M, Pecorelli N, Braga M. Enhanced recovery program in colorectal surgery: a meta-analysis of randomized controlled trials. *World J Surg*. 2014;38:1531-1541.

8. Beamish AJ, Chan DS, Blake PA, Karran A, Lewis WG. Systematic review and meta-analysis of enhanced recovery programmes in gastric cancer surgery. *Int J Surg*. 2015;19:46-54.

9. Coolsen MM, van Dam RM, van der Wilt AA, Slim K, Lassen K, Dejong CH. Systematic review and meta-analysis of enhanced recovery after pancreatic surgery with particular emphasis on pancreaticoduodenectomies. *World J Surg*. 2013;37:1909-1918.

18

10. Ni TG, Yang HT, Zhang H, Meng HP, Li B. Enhanced recovery after surgery programs in patients undergoing hepatectomy: A meta-analysis. *World J Gastroenterol*. 2015;21:9209-9216.

11. Bauchat JR, Habib AS. Evidence-based anesthesia for major gynecologic surgery. *Anesthesiol Clin*. 2015;33:173-207.

12. Kroon UB, Rådström M, Hjelthe C, Dahlin C, Kroon L. Fast-track hysterectomy: a randomised, controlled study. *Eur J Obstet Gynecol Reprod Biol*. 2010;151:203-207.

13. Di Rollo D, Mohammed A, Rawlinson A, Douglas-Moore J, Beatty J. Enhanced recovery protocols in urological surgery: a systematic review. *Can J Urol*. 2015;22:7817-7823.

14. Daneshmand S, Ahmadi H, Schuckman AK, et al. Enhanced recovery protocol after radical cystectomy for bladder cancer. *J Urol*. 2014;192:50-55.

15. Jensen BT, Petersen AK, Jensen JB, Laustsen S, Borre M. Efficacy of a multiprofessional rehabilitation programme in radical cystectomy pathways: a prospective randomized controlled trial. *Scand J Urol*. 2015;49:133-141.

16. Lee CT, Chang SS, Kamat AM, et al. Alvimopan accelerates gastrointestinal recovery after radical cystectomy: a multicenter randomized placebo-controlled trial. *Eur Urol*. 2014;66:265-272.

17. Demanet J, Wattier JM, Colin P, Fantoni JC, Villers A, Lebuffe G. Feasibility of fast track strategy for patients undergoing radical nephrectomy: a prospective randomized trial. *Eur J Anaesthesiol*. 2011;28:120.

19

Overcoming Challenges— Anesthesiologists

by Joshua A Bloomstone, MD, CSSGB, CLS

"If they had figured out the BEST way to monitor intravascular volume status, don't you think that would be bigger news than simply a new Banner initiative? I'm all for hearing what a colleague has to say on the subject, but won't be coerced into using any modality I don't think will benefit my specific patient...Until the ASA comes out with a standard by which to measure volume status, they should allow the anesthesiologists to use the modalities at his/her disposal and INTERPRET the data, and act accordingly.... This comes dangerously close to dictating care."

System Anesthesiologist, May 2012

In 2010, our health system began its enhanced recovery pathway (ERP) for patients presenting for elective colorectal surgery. By 2014, we had collected data on 5000 patients demonstrating a 28.8% reduction in overall complications and a 17.5% reduction in readmissions.[1] In 2012, our goal-directed therapy work group received the above noted email, penned by one of our more prominent and influential anesthesiologists, shortly after our system-wide proposal to incorporate goal-directed fluid therapy (GDFT) into our existing, successful ERP. The anger, denial, frustration, fear, and closed-mindedness captured by these comments are emblematic of the barriers that are faced when departments and facilities attempt to change clinical practice, even when structured upon best evidence.

Uniform clinical practice development and standardization represent the foundation upon which quality improvement initiatives are built. Without standard practice, the well-proven Deming cycle cannot be realized.[2] Though belted in Lean Six Sigma, admittedly, I am neither an implementation scientist[3] nor certified in program or change management. I have, however, worked within, and have presided over, many quality improvement workgroups focused on defining, designing, and implementing evidence-based clinical practices covering a broad range of perioperative initiatives within a large and diverse multistate healthcare system.

Relative to the design and implementation of other complex clinical practices, such as perioperative glycemic control or reducing perioperative pulmonary complications, there are no *unique* barriers to the design and implementation of ERPs. However, there are fundamental steps and concepts required to bring this sort of initiative to full and successful implementation, and of greater import, program sustainability. Any initiative that either enhances patient safety or modifies institutional care delivery will require organizational change. It is the goal of this section to review and define the necessary tools, both structural and psychological, which will be required within a facility or health system to successfully implement, and more important, to sustain an enhanced recovery program.

The quality journey begins with the recognition that clinical implementation gaps (CIGs) may exist within one's department. That is, there are evidence-based practices and protocols that are known to improve outcome, that are not routinely applied to patients (**Figure 19**.1). It is known that, on average, 17 years will elapse between the identification of an evidence-based clinical practice known to improve outcomes, and its widespread implementation.[4,5] It is the charge of every clinical department to identify these gaps and to formulate clinical practices to eliminate them. For most perioperative departments nationwide,

FIGURE 19.1 — The Clinical Implementation Gap

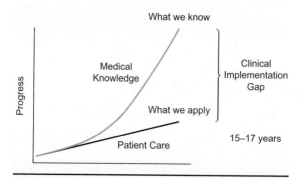

Once an important CIG has been identified, the challenge of closure will, in many cases, require both multidisciplinary clinical expertise (eg, physicians, nurses, pharmacists, PhDs) and organizational support (eg, program management, business intelligence, IT, supply chain management, educators) that is capable of leveraging change management principles.[6] Initiatives such as enhanced recovery implementation only succeed when organizations recognize the importance of the initiative and provide the necessary support structure. Unfortunately, upwards of 60% of healthcare organizations fail to implement evidence-based clinical practices due to failure of their ability to implement change.[7] It is imperative that organizations recognize the significance of incorporating change management principles into the process of clinical practice development if they, and their patients, are to realize the benefits of clinical practice implementation (**Table 19.2**).

the evidence-based enhanced recovery components represent CIGs that must be closed if we are to truly enhance perioperative care. While it is not the charge of this chapter to address all of the enhanced recovery components, the anesthesiology-specific CIGs are reviewed in **Table 19.1**.

19

TABLE 19.1 — Anesthesia Enhanced Recovery—Specific Clinical Implementation Gaps

Pre-operative
• Patient and carer education relative to their roles and expected milestones within the ERP
• Individualized patient risk assessment
• Optimize medical management
• Optimize nutritional status
• Assure 12.5% carbohydrate beverage loading within 2 hours of surgery
• Assure adherence to ASA NPO guidelines allowing for clear liquid consumption until 2 hours prior to surgery[a]

Intraoperative
• Assure multimodal, narcotic-sparing analgesia including regional anesthesia
• Assure multimodal PONV prophylaxis
• Assure goal-directed fluid therapy including goal-directed hemostasis management
• Assure that appropriate SCIP measures have been completed including maintenance of normothermia.

Postoperative
• Assure pain management is adequate to allow for early ambulation
• Assure continued PONV management to allow for early alimentation
• Postoperative patient follow-up including the post acute care phase
• Audit all steps for compliance, review and process improvement

[a] Supported by ASA guidelines in healthy patients.

While this chapter does not focus on change management per se, no discussion of change management would be complete without mentioning two key philosophies underlying this field of study: John Kotter's Change Management Model and William Bridges Transitional Model. It is essential that team leaders charged with designing and implementing clinical practices recognize that "change is both situational and

TABLE 19.2 — Key Healthcare Change Management Principles

- Assess and address local culture for its ability to accept change. Perform a stakeholder analysis early in the project and include experts with ALL points of view.

- Obtain top leadership team support from project start. This includes *all* members of the C-Suite.

- Involve all staff levels touched by the project, from project start.

- Create an emotional case for change that is supported by a robust business model.

- Program leaders must own the program and take full responsibility for its success.

- Communicate the message, do not assume that everyone involved in the project or the people that the project touches, understands either the necessity for change, the issues involved, or the project's direction.

- Involve grassroots leaders ("culture ambassadors") early in the project. These are individuals who are trusted by staff for their knowledge, skill, and experience but who do not hold formal leadership roles.

- Leverage formal solutions. Defining, designing, and implementing new clinical practices require formal program management strategies. A new practice must have structure, training, and clear roles and responsibilities.

- Leverage informal solutions. In spite of a clear formal structure, culture can always undermine change success. Stakeholders and "culture ambassadors" will play a key role, as will positive reminders of the project's benefit.

- Continuously address individual concerns.

- Audit results. Prepare for the unexpected, assess, and adapt (P-D-C-A).

19

Adapted from 10 principles of change management tools and techniques to help companies transform quickly. In: Jones J, Aguirre D, Calderone M. *Strategy and Business.* Summer 2015.

psychological," and that "ignoring either or both" will likely result in project failure.[8]

While Kotter's model has been addressed in detail elsewhere,[8] teams charged with clinical practice design and implementation should recognize the importance of incorporating Kotter's model early in the process of clinical practice design (**Figure 19.2**). Two key ideas dominate his work. First, change is not well received by those who are not involved with its design and implementation. Negative emotions often felt by those who must endure practice change, as exemplified by my colleague's email, can derail the good work that clinical practice design teams accomplish. Kotter's model provides the necessary skills to turn these negative emotions into positive ones; thus, incorporating his principles early in the design process enhances the likelihood of implementation success. Second, Keynote and Power Point presentations complete with convincing analytics rarely change how people behave, however, "when behavior is fueled by emotion, it is more likely to last longer."[8] Thus, in order to initiate and maintain momentum before and after clinical practice implementation, it is critical that the goals of a new clinical practice be described with both a sense of urgency and with a clear vision of how this practice change will enhance the lives of our patients.

Simply building a protocol or pathway and having all the necessary tools available is often not enough to claim change success. One must understand *and take into account* the psychological aspects of the change experience (William Bridges *Transitional Model*)[8,9] if one is to realize its full potential. To this point, obtaining "buy-in" from all perioperative personnel who are touched by a new clinical practice must be obtained. Compared with pathway development, "buy-in" is a far greater challenge and represents a key barrier to enhanced recovery implementation.

Practice changes that involve protocols, pathways, and multidisciplinary teamwork are often difficult for physicians to accept. Anesthesia care providers who are used to providing care their way "because it has always worked" are no exception. The transition from an autonomous practitioner to team member, and from a relatively independent decision maker to one that complies with evidence-based pathways, care sets, and best-practice guidelines is challenging.[10] To this point, trusted facility champions from each department affected by the practice change must be identified early in the process, they must become intimately familiar with the goals of the proposed practice change, and they must also understand how transitions in the care process are experienced by clinicians. Once facility champions have been identified and educated, a careful stakeholder analysis should be performed.[11] The goal here is to assure that all individuals who have the ability to either propel or repel the project are identified, brought to the table as early in the project as possible, and that consensus as to practice change is obtained.

Given the high-volume, fast pace, and focus on efficiency within today's perioperative space, it is critical that enhanced recovery implementation not be perceived as negatively impacting either perioperative efficiency or effectiveness. To this point, we have found that leveraging electronic medical record care sets and scheduling systems is an important step in assuring compliance and enhancing efficiency. That is, the more that happens without the requirement for constant clinician input, the greater is the likelihood of success. In our system, when a patient is scheduled for an elective open colon or small bowel resection, the acronym IGDT (intraoperative goal-directed fluid therapy) automatically prints next to the case on the final schedule. This alerts supply chain to have all of the necessary equipment to provide GDFT available within the case carts. Furthermore, it alerts the anesthesiology technicians to set up the equipment so that the anesthesia provider need not specifically order the equipment. Finally, it alerts the anesthesia provider that the scheduled procedure may require GDFT and to review the protocol (**Figure 19**.3 and **Figure 19**.4).

FIGURE 19.2 — Kotter's Model of Change Management

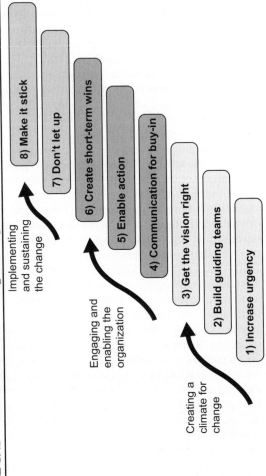

1) Increase urgency
2) Build guiding teams
3) Get the vision right
4) Communication for buy-in
5) Enable action
6) Create short-term wins
7) Don't let up
8) Make it stick

Creating a climate for change

Engaging and enabling the organization

Implementing and sustaining the change

1. Acting with or creating urgency
2. Form an influential workgroup
3. Develop and/or create a vision for change
4. Communicate the vision with emotion
5. Remove obstacles to empower broad-based actions
6. Generate short-term wins
7. Build on changes and gain momentum

http://marioborgerding.blogspot.com/2011/05/dr-john-kotters-8-steps-for-leading.html. Accessed February 25, 2016.

19

FIGURE 19.3 — Automated GDFT Scheduling

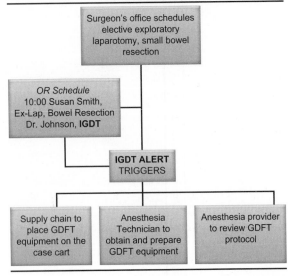

Although not yet implemented within our facilities, we are soon to change the IGDT alert to enhanced recovery, thus signaling the inclusion of regional anesthesia equipment into the case carts, in addition to GDFT equipment. Applying lean principles by leveraging one's scheduling system and one's EMR to automate the process is an important step in combating the "efficiency" argument and to enhancing pathway and protocol compliance. Furthermore, the adoption of standardized ordering systems reduces unwanted care variability.

As David Urbach and Nancy Baxter so aptly wrote in 2005, "the immediate challenge to improving the quality of surgical care is not discovering new knowledge, but rather how to integrate what we already know into practice.[12] The components of a facility-based enhanced recovery initiative are no exception. Not only do evidence-based guidelines exist[13] but so does the evidence that compliance with these guidelines enhances surgical outcomes.[14-16] Although the evidence supporting enhanced recovery implementation is striking, barriers and concerns relative to the anesthesia specific enhanced recovery components exist.

First, while allowing patients to consume clear liquids until 2 hours prior to surgery enhances patient satisfaction without an increase in aspiration risk[17] and may itself improve outcomes by maintaining hydration in the face of volume depleting bowel preparations, it may also reduce flexibility in surgical scheduling, should there be a need to alter the operative time. The anesthesiology department should reach consensus on a time that seems reasonable. Allowing patient to consume clear liquids until 4 hours prior to surgery may allow for such flexibility and is still better than starvation from midnight.

Second, regional anesthesia will necessarily add time to the surgical schedule, especially when a facility pain service capable of placing an epidural catheter preoperatively does not exist. In addition, regional catheters will require hospital follow-up and management, a luxury that is not often available outside of teaching facilities. Furthermore, other modalities, such as the transversus abdominus plane (TAP) block, require additional training and equipment if it is to be performed by anesthesia care providers.[18] Having facilities agree to compensate both travel and education for their anesthesia providers will assuredly improve compliance and will also demonstrate a facility's commitment to vision and goals of enhanced recovery.

Third, GDFT requires near continual assessment and management of fluid responsiveness. It is unsurprising that GDFT lags in compliance compared with other enhanced recovery elements, especially when cases are of significant magnitude and the burden of work is high. It is hoped that the development of closed-loop fluid systems will greatly ease the additional workload that GDFT presents.[19]

Fourth, although evidence exists that implementation of an ERP reduces cost,[20] relative to GDFT specifically, cost savings will depend upon whether a facility

19

FIGURE 19.4 — GDFT Sample Protocol

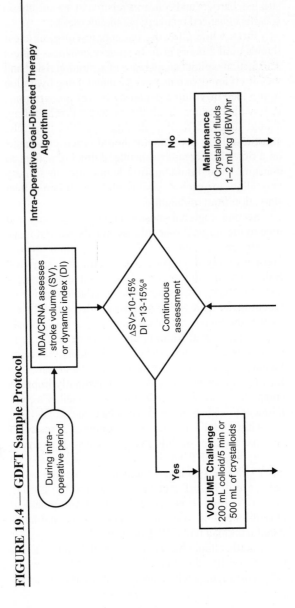

Intra-Operative Goal-Directed Therapy Algorithm

During intra-operative period

MDA/CRNA assesses stroke volume (SV), or dynamic index (DI)

ΔSV>10-15%
DI >13-15%[a]
Continuous assessment

Yes

No

VOLUME Challenge
200 mL colloid/5 min or 500 mL of crystalloids

Maintenance
Crystalloid fluids 1–2 mL/kg (IBW)/hr

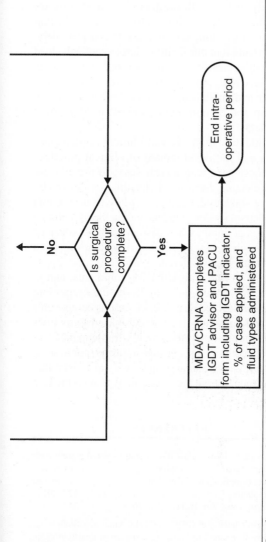

No ←

Is surgical procedure complete?

Yes ↓

MDA/CRNA completes IGDT advisor and PACU form including IGDT indicator, % of case applied, and fluid types administered

End intra-operative period

<hr>

[a] For those patients whose tidal volume (TV) is <8 mL/kg (ARDSNET), if the DI is <13%, the patient may still be volume responsive. Consider increasing the TV to 8 mL/kg for 3 minutes and reassess DI.

Banner Health Intra-Operative Goal-Directed Therapy Clinical Practice. May 2012.

19

already has the necessary equipment to perform GDFT and upon the number of cases performed per annum.[21] Implementing an ERP within a facility or system is completely in-line with the Institute for Healthcare Improvement's Triple Aim.[22] There is no doubt that as perioperative clinicians and anesthesia providers, we must assure that our facilities implement enhanced recovery strategies so as to provide our communities with the very best, evidence-based care. Clinical practice design and implementation requires both top-down leadership and commitment from all perioperative stakeholders.

The identification of local clinical implementation gaps and the development of clinical practices to close these gaps with a clear sense of urgency are critical. Selecting department champions followed by aggressive stakeholder analysis is key to design and implementation success. Understanding the psychology of change is of import when designing one's enhanced recovery implementation strategy. Local customs and practices must be considered.

Finally, in line with Urbach's comments, and in relation to my colleague's email, the data regarding enhanced surgical recovery and its various components is clear and convincing. Evidence-based guidelines exist and should be systematically implemented. As perioperative clinicians, anesthesiologists, nurse anesthetists, and anesthesia assistants, we must insist that our departments serve their communities with the best possible care.

REFERENCES

1. Loftus TJ, Stelton S, Efaw BW, Bloomstone J. A system-wide enhanced recovery program focusing on two key process steps reduces complications and readmissions in patients undergoing bowel surgery [published online ahead of print April 22, 2015]. *J Healthc Qual*. doi: 10.1111/jhq.12068.

2. Plan-Do-Check-Act (PDCA) Cycle. American Society for Quality Web site. http://asq.org/learn-about-quality/project-planning-tools/overview/pdca-cycle.html. Accessed February 25, 2016.

3. Nilsen P. Making sense of implementation theories, models and frameworks. *Implement Sci.* 2015 Apr 21;10:53. doi: 10.1186/s13012-015-0242-0. 10:53. http://www.implementationscience.com/content/pdf/s13012-015-0242-0.pdf. Accessed February 25, 2016.

4. Morris ZS, Wooding S, Grant J. The answer is 17 years, what is the question: understanding time lags in translational research. *J R Soc Med.* 2011;104:510-520. http://jrs.sagepub.com/content/104/12/510.full.pdf+html. Accessed February 25, 2016.

5. Banner Health. New Territory: The Journey Continues. Clinical Performance Report 2013. http://www.banner-health.com/NR/rdonlyres/EDB7233F-227B-4A5C-A9D0-F569E0A4E877/69305/ClinicalPerformanceReport2013.pdf. Published April 24, 2013. Accessed February 25, 2016.

6. Ramanujam R, Keyser DJ, Sirio CA. Making a case for organizational change in patient safety initiatives. In: Henriksen K, Battles JB, Marks ES, Lewin DI, editors. *Advances in Patient Safety: From Research to Implementation.* (Vol 2: Concepts and Methodology). Rockville, MD: Agency for Healthcare Research and Quality (US); 2005. http://www.ncbi.nlm.nih.gov/books/NBK20490/. February 25, 2016

7. Burnes B. Emergent change and planned change-competitors or allies?: The case of XYZ construction. *Int J Oper Prod Man.* 2004;24:886-902.

8. Campbell RJ. Change management in health care. *Health Care Manag* (Frederick). 2008;27:23-39.

9. Bridges W. Navigating the transitions of change. Strategies for Managing Change Web site. http://www.strategies-for-managing-change.com/william-bridges.html. Accessed February 25, 2016.

10. Sonnenberg M. Chief Medical Officer: Changing Roles and Skill Sets. American Association for Physician Leadership Web site. http://www.physicianleaders.org/news/plj-articles/2015-january-february/2015/01/01/chief-medical-officer-changing-roles-and-skill-sets. Published January 2015. Accessed February 25, 2016.

11. Schmeer K. Section 2. Stakeholder Analysis Guidelines. http://www.who.int/workforcealliance/knowledge/toolkit/33.pdf. Accessed February 25, 2016.

12. Urbach DR, Baxter NN. Reducing variation in surgical care. *BMJ.* 2005;330:1401-1402.

13. Gustafsson UO, Scott MJ, Schwenk W, et al; Enhanced Recovery After Surgery (ERAS) Society, for Perioperative Care; European Society for Clinical Nutrition and Metabolism

19

(ESPEN); International Association for Surgical Metabolism and Nutrition (IASMEN). Guidelines for perioperative care in elective colonic surgery: Enhanced Recovery After Surgery (ERAS(®)) Society recommendations. *World J Surg*. 2013;37:259-284.

14. Miller TE, Thacker JK, White WD, et al; Enhanced Recovery Study Group. Reduced length of hospital stay in colorectal surgery after implementation of an enhanced recovery protocol. *Anesth Analg*. 2014;118:1052-1061.

15. Loftus TJ, Stelton S, Efaw BW, Bloomstone J. A system-wide enhanced recovery program focusing on two key process steps reduces complications and readmissions in patients undergoing bowel surgery [published online ahead of print April 22, 2015]. *J Healthc Qual*. doi: 10.1111/jhq.12068.

16. Pędziwiatr M, Kisialeuski M, Wierdak M, et al. Early implementation of Enhanced Recovery After Surgery (ERAS®) protocol - Compliance improves outcomes: A prospective cohort study. *Int J Surg*. 2015;21:75-81.

17. Brady M, Kinn S, Stuart P. Preoperative fasting for adults to prevent perioperative complications. *Cochrane Database Syst Rev*. 2003;(4):CD004423.

18. Baeriswyl M, Kirkham KR, Kern C, Albrecht E. The analgesic efficacy of ultrasound-guided transversus abdominis plane block in adult patients: a meta-analysis. *Anesth Analg*. 2015;121:1640-1654.

19. Rinehart J, Liu N, Alexander B, Cannesson M. Review article: closed-loop systems in anesthesia: is there a potential for closed-loop fluid management and hemodynamic optimization? *Anesth Analg*. 2012;114:130-143.

20. Miller TE, Thacker JK, White WD, et al; Enhanced Recovery Study Group. Reduced length of hospital stay in colorectal surgery after implementation of an enhanced recovery protocol. *Anesth Analg*. 2014;118:1052-1061.

21. Bloomstone JA, Loftus T, Hutchison R. ERAS: enhancing recovery one evidence-based step at a time. *Anesth Analg*. 2015;120:256.

22. IHI Triple Aim Initiative. Institute for Healthcare Improvement Web site. http://www.ihi.org/engage/initiatives/tripleaim/Pages/default.aspx. Accessed February 25, 2016.

20 Overcoming Challenges— Surgeons

by Amit Merchea, MD and
David W Larson, MD, MBA

Introduction

Enhanced Recovery Protocols (ERPs) have become the standard of care for elective colorectal surgery. Despite widespread evidence of its various elements, adoption of these protocols has been variable. Given the multimodal and multidisciplinary approach, successful implementation is dependent upon a multitude of caregivers (eg, surgeons, anesthesiologist, nurses, pharmacists, physiotherapists, dietitians, and non-clinical caregivers) during different phases of care (preoperative, intraoperative, and postoperative). Poor compliance or failure of the pathway has been attributed to a perception of lack of resources and persistence of individual practice variability and autonomy despite care that is not supported by best practice.

Barriers and Facilitators to Implementation

Surgeons remain integral to the success of ERPs given their involvement in all phases of care and as the natural leaders of the care team. Previous qualitative studies have examined barriers and facilitators to implementation of enhanced recovery.[1-3] Barriers to implementation are often related to patient-specific factors, provider-specific factors, practice-related issues, and institutional resource availability.[2]

Use of educational materials and interventions to outline patient expectations are essential to success. Patients and their families must understand

20

their expected postoperative course, activity, diet, and criteria for discharge. Structured verbal and written educational materials with consistent messaging have generally been viewed positively.

Providers (surgical and nonsurgical) must also have appropriate and consistent education, expectations, and behaviors. Identification of key stakeholders to act as champions of the pathway can help foster multidisciplinary relationships within the institution to ensure compliance and feedback. Furthermore, there must be sufficient flexibility of the providers to alter the care they provide to align with the pathways. Providers have reported resistance to implementation when specific interventions were seen as a significant practice change. Often this resistance is founded in surgical dogma rather than evidence-based care.

Crucial to implementation is building a "community of practice" across disciplines and providers.[4] Creating this system requires commitment of resources, both personnel and financial. Allocation of hospital and discharge resources ultimately should be prioritized to expedite patient care. Patients requiring out of hospital interventions, such as home-health assistance, postoperative physical therapy, or rehabilitation services, should have these needs anticipated and planned. These activities are ideally initiated prior to hospitalization.

Each of these interventions facilitates successful implementation of an ERP. Creating the environment within the institution to allow for this is best achieved through stable and systematic organizational design. Furthermore, building a loyal care team that is fully interested in the success of the program is essential to increasing the likelihood of success of implementation and sustaining that success over time.

Organizational Design

Organization architecture is paramount to ensuring optimal resources and environment exist for success. The integral elements of organizational architecture and design are delegation of decision-making authority, evaluation of the performance of the individual, and a structure of rewards or penalties for compliance or noncompliance, respectively. These elements are each equally important and are dependent upon each other; this has been referred to as the "three-legged stool" of organizational design.[5]

■ Decision-Making Authority

Decision-making authority is generally delegated to the team leader or champion of the process. Four steps make up this process:
- Formulating potential decisions
- Approval of the selected decision
- Execution of the decision
- Evaluation of outcomes.

These steps comprise elements of decision management and decision control. Development of organizational hierarchies can allow for delegation of various tasks and decisions. This decentralization of care allows for some independence of care and also encourages direct input of the providers. Ultimately, the elements of decision control should be held by the champions of the cause.

■ Evaluating Performance

This process allows for reflection and feedback on whether the decisions being made are in fact increasing value for the organization. Furthermore, this allows for justification of resource use and appropriate allocation of future resources.

As applied to enhanced recovery pathways, monitoring the level of compliance or noncompliance of the elements allows for timely and directed feedback and intervention to the unit that is not meeting expectations. As an example, it may be critical to measure all levels of a decision made from the order that is written, to the timing of the execution of that order by nursing and pharmacy, to the level of acceptance and satisfaction of that executed order by the patient. Performance may

20

also be evaluated by measuring changes in complication rates, readmission rates, and length of stay, all of which are expected to decrease with enhanced recovery pathways.

■ Incentives

Incentives or rewards can be utilized to motivate caregivers from all elements of the team to continue to pursue the goals of the organization—in this case, enhanced recovery. Public recognition of the team members for their contribution to the success of the pathway has demonstrated success in helping to build a willing and loyal team. Team participants often find the availability of relevant and recent data on the pathway to be effective in demonstrating the results of their efforts.[4]

Achieving Consensus— The Golden Circle

Building a team of caregivers to implement the mission of the institution may be the most difficult aspect of initiating an ERP. Often this task is the responsibility of the surgeon champion and underscores why as a leader they must inspire loyalty and engagement in the process.

"The Golden Circle," as described by Simon Sinek (**Figure 20.1**), outlines a thought process and ideals by which leaders can inspire action.[6] The elements of this circle, from the outside in, are *what, how,* and *why*. These are relatively easily defined — *what* describes the exact product, service, or process; *how* generally refers to the precise process by which the *what* is achieved; *why* is perhaps the most difficult to identify, refers to the underlying motivation, purpose, or belief. Most leaders or organizations lead or act from the outside of the circle in, describing *what* they do, then *how* they plan on doing it, and occasionally *why* they intend to do it. However, the most inspiring and successful leaders function in the opposite direc-

FIGURE 20.1 — The Golden Circle

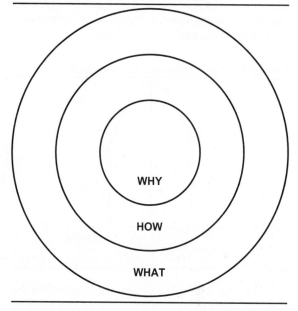

tion—starting with *why*. Thus, the most effective way to build a loyal and engaging team that will follow the surgeon champion is to identify people who believe in the mission first and why enhanced recovery is important. Ultimately, the care team and patients will be more likely to buy into the process not because of what it is, but why it is being completed.[6]

Diffusion of Practice

Building a team with common philosophies of care is important in order to ultimately achieve penetration and acceptance of the care pathway. The Law of Diffusion of Innovations, described by Everett Rogers, explains processes by which innovation is disseminated and integrated.[7] He describes four elements that influence the diffusion of a new idea: the innovation itself, communication of the innovation, time for adoption,

20

and a social system (organization mandates, colleague relationships, etc). Adopters of the innovative idea are categorized as innovators, early adopters, early majority, late majority, and laggards (**Figure 20.2**).

FIGURE 20.2 — Diffusion of Innovation

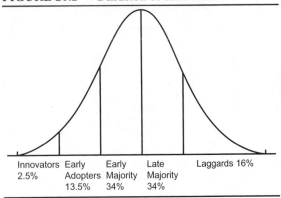

| Innovators 2.5% | Early Adopters 13.5% | Early Majority 34% | Late Majority 34% | Laggards 16% |

The rate of adoption is generally defined by the time for people to accept the innovation into practice. At some point of inflection, the innovation achieves a critical point when the number of adopters rapidly increases and the innovation becomes self-sustaining. Numerous strategies exist to help innovations increase the rate of adoption and include providing feedback/reactions of the early adopters to the non-adopters, or having a visible and influential person within the social system adopt the practice. Typically, the point of inflection on this diffusion curve occurs when around 15% of the population has adopted the practice, largely due to the fact that the early majority generally will not adopt a new practice or technology unless someone else has trialed it first. Thus, the most expeditious way to reach the early majority is to ensure that the innovators and early adopters maintain the same beliefs and motivations as the initial champions of the cause.

Summary

There are numerous potential barriers to successful implementation of ERPs. Adherence to the elements generally increases with time and continued exposure of the caregivers to the pathway.[8]

Creating the optimal institutional architecture, leadership teams, and feedback mechanisms can ease the implementation of a new clinical pathway and should be developed up front rather than in a post hoc manner.

20

REFERENCES

1. Pearsall EA, Meghji Z, Pitzul KB, et al. A qualitative study to understand the barriers and enablers in implementing an enhanced recovery after surgery program. *Ann Surg*. 2015;261:92-96.

2. Lyon A, Solomon MJ, Harrison JD. A qualitative study assessing the barriers to implementation of enhanced recovery after surgery. *World J Surg*. 2014;38:1374-1380.

3. Kahokehr A, Sammour T, Zargar-Shoshtari K, Thompson L, Hill AG. Implementation of ERAS and how to overcome the barriers. *Int J Surg*. 2009;7:16-19.

4. Gotlib Conn L, McKenzie M, Pearsall EA, McLeod RS. Successful implementation of an enhanced recovery after surgery programme for elective colorectal surgery: a process evaluation of champions' experiences. *Implement Sci*. 2015;10:99.

5. Brickley JA, Smith CW Jr., Zimmerman JL. Corporate Governance, Ethics, and Organizational Architecture. *J Appl Corp Finance*. 2003;15:34-45.

6. Sinek S. *Start with Why: How Great Leaders Inspire Everyone to Take Action*. New York, NY: Penguin Group; 2009.

7. Rogers EM. *Diffusion of Innovations*. 5th ed. New York, NY: A Division of Simon & Schuster, Inc.; 2003.

8. Larson DW, Lovely JK, Cima RR, et al. Outcomes after implementation of a multimodal standard care pathway for laparoscopic colorectal surgery. *Br J Surg*. 2014;101:1023-1030.

21
Overcoming Challenges—
Nurses and Support Staff

by Robin Anderson, RN, BSN and
Debbie Watson, RN, MN and

Enhanced recovery protocols (ERPs) challenge traditional practice such as reducing the amount of postoperative rest, instituting multimodal pain regimens, and facilitating earlier GI motility. Working with an interdisciplinary team to create evidence-based protocols is a fundamental part of an enhanced recovery program, but it takes more than protocols to succeed and achieve positive outcomes. Nurses play a crucial role in the creation, implementation, and sustainability of an ERP. Once a protocol is in place, there will undoubtedly be a knowledge deficit within workgroups, institutional limitations, and resistance to overcome. Understanding these barriers prior to implementation is vital in order to strategize ways to reduce obstacles and facilitate the implementation.

In this chapter, we define barriers to implementation and elaborate on some of the factors that can enable an ERP. Obstacles can be categorized into four main groups[1]:

- Practice change
- Care providers
- The practice setting
- The organization.

21

Under each category, concrete examples of barriers to implementation of an ERP can be identified along with ideas to overcome these challenges. Throughout the entire spectrum of perioperative care, frontline health care providers, including nurses, are key stakeholders in ERPs and hence facilitators for overcoming challenges in each area.

301

Barriers to implementation can be described as factors that may inhibit or cause obstacles to a process.[1] To help in identifying these factors, a new ERP should be drafted, then compared to current institutional practice. The multidisciplinary team, including nursing representatives, should assess for specific challenges or hurdles that may be faced with a new protocol. Recognizing these barriers requires a collaborative approach with frontline staff. Some obstacles may not be identified until the practice change has been initiated. For example, some institutions may realize a shortage of assistive personnel to help with early and frequent ambulation as indicated in an ERP. These and other challenges are specific and unique to each institution based on its resources available, size, leadership support, physician engagement, and organizational culture.

The Practice Change

Successful protocol implementation will likely involve significant changes in practice and culture. The creation of an ERP may be a result of influences outside the institution (ie, reimbursement, quality mandates) or the work of an advocate within (surgeon or anesthesiology champion). Regardless of the strength or direction of the program creation, engagement from all levels of staff needs to occur. This involvement will be much more likely if staff is motivated by belief in the concept rather than if it is imposed by a top-down approach. It is believed that "70% of change projects fail because of the failure to engage staff at all levels before, during, and after a change and/or to embed the new processes into everyday practices."[2] Thus, a protocol is not enough to implement and sustain an ERP. An ERP requires engagement from team members as well as ongoing communication from the champions leading this change.

The multidisciplinary team should include nursing leadership, managers, and staff nurses from all phases of perioperative care. Nurse representatives should participate in the development of protocols, in the identification of barriers, in the communication to team members, and in the frequent review of outcomes and compliance with protocol elements. Enhanced recovery elements may create a change in routine nursing practices. Early postoperative ambulation is a common and expected postsurgical practice for nurses, but expecting the nurse to get their patients out of bed on the evening of surgery is a challenge. Being more specific with progressive ambulation orders may increase adherence. A written order specifying patients be out of bed in a chair for all meals or out of bed for at least 6 hours each day may be more likely adhered to than "out of bed beginning today."

Patient Preparation

Educating patients about the elements of enhanced recovery is essential in order to provide information and establish realistic expectations for postoperative recovery. Preoperative education should include informing patients how to prepare for surgery, what to expect after surgery, and ultimately what they need to do to continue recovery at home. Ideally, the surgeon will initiate the conversation about expectations and benefits of Enhanced Recovery, but it is often the nurse who is tasked with ensuring the patient understands the entire perioperative journey. These educational sessions may create a change in routine in the clinic or outpatient setting but are at the foundation for success in engaging the patient. Interestingly, Taylor and Burch concluded that enhanced recovery programs require a change to the surgical nursing role by an increase in the emphasis on teaching and information sharing with patients throughout the entire perioperative period.[3] Unfortunately, there is usually not additional time allotted for this. Rather, there is likely less time and fewer nurses available. As patients experience shorter hospital stays, it is imperative that nurses work creatively to ensure patients are prepared for all aspects of their recovery.

21

Patient expectations or perceptions of what their recovery should entail can sometimes create challenges for staff. A patient's beliefs about what is meant to recover after surgery can be influenced by culture, past surgical experiences for themselves or others, insufficient knowledge, and their readiness for surgery. If a patient has had previous colorectal surgery, they may have preconceived notions about their recovery based on past experience. Comprehensive patient preparation including verbal information followed by written material to reinforce the verbal teaching, may have a significant impact on the patient's anxiety and satisfaction levels. By informing patients of the realistic and specific expectations around their surgical procedure and recovery, they might be more engaged in reaching recovery goals.

The role of the family or the patient's support system should not be overlooked as these individuals also bring prior knowledge and experience that may influence the patient. For instance, patients are informed that they may drink clear liquids up until 2 hours before surgery. Their friends or family members may not be aware this is safe, evidence-based practice and may suggest the patient not follow these instructions. Involving family members or caregivers in the preoperative education early on will help to ensure that everyone is aware of the institutional policies, such as the fasting guidelines, and that everyone understands the expectations around surgery and recovery.

Staff Education

Providing staff education related to the evidence behind a new practice will likely help to engage and alter attitudes of the team.[4] For example, evidence suggests that a preoperative carbohydrate drink can assist in improving a patient's recovery by decreasing preoperative thirst and hunger and reducing postoperative insulin resistance.[5] Informing staff about the advantages of carbohydrate loading, may help them to articulate this change effectively to the patient, be more supportive of this practice change, and be more likely to accurately document this protocol element. Providing evidence and rationale for goal-directed fluid management, minimizing opioids, early diet, and early mobilization related to gastric motility may help staff to understand the basis of multimodal practices in Enhanced Recovery. Emphasizing the safety and efficacy of certain Enhanced Recovery elements might be one way to overcome resistance to change. The task of assessing current practices, educating front-line staff, and communicating these challenges is not insignificant. Creating a program that involves the widespread involvement of nursing staff, all care providers, and hospital leaders contributes greatly to successful implementation of an ERP.

Care Providers

Although this chapter focuses on challenges for nurses, it is important to discuss the obstacles inherent for all disciplines and the effect these obstacles can have on nursing care. It is widely known that lack of education related to protocol elements is one of the biggest barriers for all care providers. Prior to implementation, everyone involved should be knowledgeable about the specific details of the ERP. Involving the care providers from the beginning is likely to decrease resistance to change. Staff meetings, grand rounds, and informal unit-based teaching sessions are just a few suggestions for engaging staff and care providers. One factor to keep in mind is that staff members are ever changing as hospitals or nursing units deal with staff turnover and mixed specialty units where certain patient populations are seen only on occasion, or the consistent throughput of surgery resident staff in teaching institutions. Another potential challenge may include how to create the educational resources used in each institution and keep them updated and accurate as protocols change, the ERP grows, and the care providers vary.

21

Reaching consensus among the surgeons prior to implementation creates consistency, decreases variability, and strengthens surgeon engagement. It also may result in less confusion for nursing staff. One way to improve consistency of care is through the standardization of preoperative and postoperative order sets, whether electronic or in paper form. The establishment of standardized guidelines in addition to the order sets are critical steps in facilitating consistent practice.[6] Although creating consistency with order sets is crucial in all programs, it is especially relative in academic medical centers with resident staff who are heavily involved in the postoperative management of surgical patients. Deviations from ERP guidelines tend to occur in the postoperative period and are often most difficult to overcome and provide the biggest opportunity for improvement.[6,7] Increasing consistency and decreasing variability among surgeons should be highlighted as having a potential positive effect on nursing practice during education sessions with frontline staff.

Practice Setting

The practice setting refers to the individuals who care for patients (care team), the types of patients, and the resources available in the local setting.[1] Within the practice setting, the role of the ERP "champion" is invaluable. Champions are facilitators or enablers to implementation and can come from any level or discipline. At the very least, a surgeon, anesthesia, and nursing champion should be identified who, together, will review the literature, develop the protocol, educate team members, and report on various outcomes. At our organization, it was significant not to impose an ERP but to create it with support and engagement of frontline staff and surgeons. A bottom-up approach might improve clinical staff engagement and can be driven by unit-based champions.[8] To be most successful, the ERP champions of each unit should evolve as informal leaders who play an active role in improving adherence to the various elements, thus improving perioperative outcomes. Champions should be volunteers rather than be assigned to the role, as this will likely increase their participation and engagement.[8] These informal leaders will be invaluable as mentors, educators, resources, and communicators in their work areas to help disseminate the ERP information, assist with implementation, and help to drive change on the unit.

ERPs incorporate a combination of many elements that implemented together improve patient outcomes. Collecting information and understanding the level of compliance with each of the protocol elements can be resource intensive. Taking action when compliance is low with certain protocol elements should be a priority as we know that outcomes will improve with higher rates of compliance.[9] Auditing and providing feedback related to compliance and outcomes is imperative to keep staff engaged and energized and to demonstrate the impact they are having on patient care. Positive outcomes and even small successes should be highlighted and celebrated. These small victories can often be a catalyst to gain new interest or recognition from staff, physicians, or organizational leadership.

Organization

There may be several motivating factors for an institution to create an ERP, but one key objective is to adapt these protocols to your organization. There is no standard method or no "one size fits all" approach for implementing a new program. Processes will need to be adapted relative to the policies, resources available, and culture while still translating knowledge using evidence-based medicine. For example, resource limitations can include surgical equipment, specific drug availability, clinical policies, or staffing models. Institutional leadership support becomes critical as staffing resources, financial resources, and organizational engagement are required for change. Another example of financial support needed from the organi-

21

zation is funding to hire a full-time ERP coordinator to help lead this initiative. The Enhanced Recovery coordinator may help with auditing, coordinating meetings, facilitating discussions, providing ongoing education, as well as collaborating and communicating with key stakeholders. These functions, among others, are essential in order to create, implement, and sustain a program. Formalized data collection and analysis resources are needed not only to demonstrate improved outcomes but to provide frontline staff with necessary feedback related to compliance with protocol elements. This feedback will most likely be the stimulus for continuously engaging staff and promoting compliance. In order to have a more collaborative approach and facilitate problem solving, the creation of a network for ERP coordinators should be explored and developed more formally across the United States.

A few other resources should be considered for program success. Specialized staff such as enterostomal therapy (ET) nurses, nutritionists, physical therapists, pharmacists, and case managers can all participate in creating protocols, implementing practice change, and positively influencing protocol compliance. Since patients are often discharged sooner after ERP implementation, ET nurses should collaborate in early proactive discharge planning for a smoother transfer to home. Some institutions have learned that not having these resources available daily has impacted their ability to discharge patients when they meet discharge criteria.[4]

Finally, expanding the ERP to other patient populations or across institutional entities can be an organizational challenge in itself. With the use of data to provide evidence of improved outcomes, institutions will want to ensure the program expands to other services where patients will continue to benefit. The challenges will likely be similar to those seen with early implementation, and organizational leadership will continue to be needed. As variations among teams, protocols, and/or institutions within the organization begin to occur, there will be an increased need for consistent communication and teamwork among groups.

Conclusion

After reviewing many of the challenges and complexities, it is clear that there will be a learning curve associated with implementation of an ERP at any institution. More importantly, no two programs will be exactly the same. The multidisciplinary team is at the core of the process and will be dynamic in the roles, needs, and expectations of the program. Patience, determination, and continued staff support are vitally important to ensure we can help patients to meet their recovery goals and ensure program success. As with any new program, the final challenge becomes sustainability while realizing it will be ever-changing and will require ongoing and real-time review. Although there may be roadblocks, missed deadlines, and staff resistance, the ultimate goal is to reduce the stress of surgery and improve patient recovery.

21

REFERENCES

1. Castiglione SA, Ritchie JA. Moving into action: we know what practices we want to change, now what? An implementation guide for health care practitioners. Canadian Institutes of Health Research Web site. http://www.cihr-irsc.gc.ca/e/documents/lm_moving_into_action-en.pdf. Published March 2012. Accessed February 25, 2016.

2. Parsons ML, Cornett PA. Leading change for sustainability. *Nurse Lead.* 2011;9:36-40.

3. Taylor C, Burch J. Feedback on an enhanced recovery programme for colorectal surgery. *Br J Nurs.* 2011;20:286-290.

4. Lyon A, Solomon MJ, Harrison JD. A qualitative study assessing the barriers to implementation of enhanced recovery after surgery. *World J Surg.* 2014;38:1374-1380.

5. Jones C, Badger SA, Hannon R. The role of carbohydrate drinks in pre-operative nutrition for elective colorectal surgery. *Ann R Coll Surg Engl.* 2011;93:504-507.

6. Nadler A, Pearsall EA, Victor JC, Aarts MA, Okrainec A, McLeod RS. Understanding surgical residents' postoperative practices and barriers and enablers to the implementation of an Enhanced Recovery After Surgery (ERAS) Guideline. *J Surg Educ.* 2014;71:632-638.

7. Maessen J, Dejong CH, Hausel J, et al. A protocol is not enough to implement an enhanced recovery programme for colorectal resection. *Br J Surg.* 2007;94:224-231.

8. Gotlib Conn L, McKenzie M, Pearsall EA, McLeod RS. Successful implementation of an enhanced recovery after surgery programme for elective colorectal surgery: a process evaluation of champions' experiences. *Implement Sci.* 2015;10:99.

9. Gustafsson UO, Hausel J, Thorell A, Ljungqvist O, Soop M, Nygren J; Enhanced Recovery After Surgery Study Group. Adherence to the enhanced recovery after surgery protocol and outcomes after colorectal cancer surgery. *Arch Surg.* 2011;146:571-577.

22

Business Case for Enhanced Recovery

by Anthony J. Senagore, MD, MBA, FACS, FASCRS

Introduction

The specific processes of care and the associated patient benefits of enhanced recovery protocols (ERPs) after surgery protocols are described elsewhere in this publication. This chapter will seek to frame the benefits of ERPs that support the business case for adoption at the hospital and health system level. The two major sources of organizational benefit are related to reductions in resource consumption, the incidence of potentially avoidable complications, and a structured approach to manage common complications effectively. A structured ERP, therefore, reduces unnecessary and expensive variation around the care of common surgical procedures.

There is often concern regarding the complexity and cost of adoption, but in reality, the principal components of care should be readily available and actually less expensive compared with standard care. The real complexity is how to effectively drive change in management based upon specific outcome data. The slow adoption of ERP strategies confirms the difficulties in transforming traditional approaches in health care systems, even in the face of simple, evidence-based processes of care that benefit both patients and providers. The majority of the evidence presented in this chapter will focus on colorectal surgery simply because the greatest depth of assessment has been in this area.

ERP Impact on Length of Stay

The increasing pressure on cost control faced by health care systems is being driven by both payer demands for lower cost of care and the development of expanded episodes of care, which place greater economic risk on the provider. Because most colorectal pathology has a predictable incidence and prevalence of disease burden within a population, the only option to control costs at the provider level is to redesign the processes of care, reduce variability of care, decrease the rate of truly preventable complications, and refine the care of typical complications.

It is interesting that since the 2000s, ERPs have been adopted broadly and the result has been consistent improvements in outcomes, a reduction in the duration of hospital stay, and institutional productivity gains and cost savings. At a basic level, safely reducing the length of stay allows for either greater access for patients within the constraints of fixed resources (hospital beds and nursing staff) or, alternatively, a reduction in staffing in a predictable fashion if patient volumes are stable. This benefit has been consistently demonstrated across all studies and accrues to both open and laparoscopic approaches. Therefore, the data consistently demonstrate and confirm a reduction in length of stay by 2 to 5 days, depending on the original process of care and the adoption of laparoscopic techniques.

Adoption of Laparoscopic Colectomy

After the initial delay in adoption of laparoscopic colon resection related to concerns regarding the adequacy of oncologic resection, the growth has been logarithmic with significant outcome benefits associated simply due to smaller wounds for access. These studies also confirmed a reduced length of stay compared to open colectomy in the absence of a structured ERP, while simultaneously questioning many of the traditional tenets of patient care. One of the first lessons of ERP transition is that increasing the case mix in favor of laparoscopic resection is an important component of providing significant system benefits even within an ERP.

The data are clear that laparoscopic surgery is a key enabler within a system to safely and consistently reduce the length of stay and other outcomes. Archibald and colleagues showed clearly demonstrated that even a 10% shift toward laparoscopic colectomy, in addition to adoption of an ERP, was an important component of reducing system length of stay. Similarly, Bosio and associates showed in a case matched study that this combination of laparoscopy and ERP resulted in a 5-day reduction in length of stay. Yet there remains large geographic variability in uptake of laparoscopic colectomy for colon cancer in the United States, from 0% to 67%. Given the breadth of data and the increased training opportunities for advanced laparoscopic techniques, the data support a broader adoption of laparoscopic colectomy whenever possible.

Specific Components of ERPs

It is difficult to tease out the relative benefits of laparoscopic colectomy vs ERP components; however, the evidence does suggest a reduction in specific complications related to simple components of care. Cakir and colleagues assessed multiple ERP components and determined that laparoscopic surgery, removal of nasogastric tube before extubation, mobilization within 24 hours after surgery, starting nonsteroidal anti-inflammatory drugs at day 1, and removal of thoracic epidural analgesia at day 2 were independent predictors of length of stay.

A frequently misunderstood opportunity is the **22** reduction in the incidence of postoperative ileus because it is the most common cause for unnecessary delay in discharge and a significant source of increased cost of care. The causes of postoperative ileus are multifactorial, with two of the major causes being excess administration of postoperative intravenous fluids and the dosing and type of opioids used for analgesia. Most patients undergoing laparoscopic colectomy rarely need intravenous fluids beyond postoperative day 2.

The detrimental effect of opioids can be addressed by using narcotic-sparing multimodal analgesia and prophylaxis with a peripheral opioid antagonist such as alvimopan. Although alvimopan is not routinely mentioned as part of ERPs, there are data to suggest that use of this agent is associated with a reduction in both ileus rates and length of stay in patients where opioids are the primary form of analgesia after surgery. Implementation is often denied due to the silo phenomenon of hospital cost assessment, where the pharmacy assumes the maximal use of the drug (7 days) rather than demonstrated improvement in contribution margin for the entire at-risk population. However, it should be understood that each team should assess the care plan used because the relative benefit of extended use (other than preoperative prophylaxis for intraoperative narcotic exposure) of alvimopan is dependent on the amount of narcotic used subsequently as ileus risk appears to be dose dependent.

Effective multimodal analgesia is a major component of ERPs because it not only reduces ileus risk, but allows for early ambulation due to improved analgesia, which conveys its own particular advantages. The various components vary by institution; however, commonly invoked strategies included epidural analgesia, TAP, nonsteroidal anti-inflammatory agents, gabapentin, and acetaminophen. In laparoscopic colectomy, epidural analgesia is clearly not advantageous as an important adjunct for the care of the patient within an ERP. Therefore, the data suggest that inexpensive, oral analgesia combined with surgeon-delivered TAP blocks provides for a very efficient means of perioperative analgesia. For open colectomy, there are more data in support of the role of epidural analgesia within a structured ERP.

Surgical site infection (SSI) is probably the second most common complication associated with colectomy and results in patient morbidity, mortality, increased cost of care, and prolonged length of stay. Once again, laparoscopic colectomy appears to be associated with a relative reduction in SSI compared with open colectomy. A major issue in the ERP Society guidelines is the recommendation that mechanical bowel preparation be avoided, at least for open colon surgery. This recommendation is based on systematic reviews finding no decrease in SSI rate with the use of mechanical bowel preparation vs no preparation, but a major limitation is that the bowel preparation groups did not include the use of oral antibiotics. This gap has been exposed by studies that document higher SSI rates after abandoning the oral antibiotic/mechanical preparation strategy and lower rates after its re-introduction.

The issue of appropriate intravenous prophylactic antibiotics has been well studied, and the appropriate options are evidence based. These data support the role of inexpensive strategies to effectively reduce the risk of SSI following colectomy, and one should give strong consideration to adding these measures to their ERP protocol.

Cost Benefits of ERPs

The data associated with ERP clearly demonstrate many potential sources of cost containment with adoption of these inexpensive strategies. In fact, other than the often and unnecessarily cumbersome process of adoption of ERPs, the individual components are relatively inexpensive and readily available even in cost-constrained environments. Sammour and co-workers identified an adoption cost of NZ$ 102,000 for an ERP that produced an excellent rate of return of NZ$6900 per patient. Delaney and colleagues demonstrated 22 similar benefits and highlighted a variety of sources of cost reduction related to shortened length of stay, lower complication rates, and lower utilization of laboratory, imaging, and pharmaceutical resources. These cost benefits can be considered within the construct of a warranty process that allows providers to assess the financial risks associated with internal processes of care and the population managed.

Summary

Adoption of an ERP, particularly when combined with a laparoscopic approach, has consistently demonstrated efficient cost reduction while producing superior clinical outcomes. There is little excuse for failing to demand implementation of a "bundle" of inexpensive highly effective processes of care. Successful adoption requires the team to define a metric for outcome evaluation and then regularly assess and evaluate further opportunities guided by actual experience for further protocol modification.

These assessments should include both clinical and financial analyses, as well as the potential cost of risk mitigation. This practical approach to operational management will allow maximal innovation, which should produce higher quality and lower cost of care for colorectal surgical patients.

Key take-home messages include:

- Introduction of an ERP will consistently and safely reduce the length of hospital stay by focusing on the use of proven components of the care plan that positively impact recovery. Variance in length of stay is also reduced. Compliance to ERP elements is key to see these benefits.
- The transition to a broader use of minimally invasive colorectal resection will be necessary for a system to see significant improvement even with the introduction of an ERP.
- Prophylaxis for postoperative ileus is an important adjunct because this factor disproportionately accounts for many unnecessary days of care within a colectomy population.
- A multimodal, narcotic-minimized analgesic program is highly effective in managing post-

operative pain while avoiding opioid-related adverse events.
- The standardization of care and adoption of effective, inexpensive care components will yield a significant cost of care for the provider within an ERP.

SELECTED READINGS

Archibald LH, Ott MJ, Gale CM, Zhang J, Peters MS, Stroud GK. Enhanced recovery after colon surgery in a community hospital system. *Dis Colon Rectum*. 2011;54:840-845.

Asgeirsson T, El-Badawi KI, Mahmood A, Barletta J, Luchtefeld M, Senagore AJ. Postoperative ileus: it costs more than you expect. *J Am Coll Surg*. 2010;210:228-231.

Asgeirsson T, Jrebi N, Feo L, Kerwel T, Luchtefeld M, Senagore AJ. Incremental cost of complications in colectomy: a warranty guided approach to surgical quality improvement. *Am J Surg*. 2014;207:422-426.

Englesbe MJ, Brooks L, Kubus J, et al. A statewide assessment of surgical site infection following colectomy: the role of oral antibiotics. *Ann Surg*. 2010;252:514-519.

Keller DS, Stulberg JJ, Lawrence JK, Delaney CP. Process control to measure process improvement in colorectal surgery: modifications to an established enhanced recovery pathway. *Dis Colon Rectum*. 2014;57:194-200.

Reames BN, Sheetz KH, Waits SA, Dimick JB, Regenbogen SE. Geographic variation in use of laparoscopic colectomy for colon cancer. *J Clin Oncol*. 2014;32:3667-3672.

Senagore AJ, Duepree HJ, Delaney CP, Brady KM, Fazio VW. Results of a standardized technique and postoperative care plan for laparoscopic sigmoid colectomy: a 30-month experience. *Dis Colon Rectum*. 2003;46:503-509.

Vlug MS, Wind J, Hollmann MW, et al; LAFA study group. Laparoscopy in combination with fast track multimodal management is the best perioperative strategy in patients undergoing colonic surgery: a randomized clinical trial (LAFA-study). *Ann Surg*. 2011;254:868-875.

Wind J, Polle SW, Fung Kon Jin PH, et al; Laparoscopy and/or Fast Track Multimodal Management Versus Standard Care (LAFA) Study Group; Enhanced Recovery after Surgery (ERAS) Group. Systematic review of enhanced recovery programmes in colonic surgery. *Br J Surg*. 2006;93:800-809.

23

Ensuring Success and Sustainability: Audit, Compliance, and Sustainability

by Robert R. Cima, MD, MA

Introduction

Enhanced recovery is a collection of guiding principles to accelerate a patient's recovery.[1] Such programs are described extensively in the literature across nearly every surgical subspeciality.[2] The elements and interventions that comprise enhanced recovery protocols (ERPs) are distributed across the surgical care continuum and vary from general topics such as patient education to specific detailed areas such as modern pain management. Although the elements comprising different ERPs even within the same surgical discipline may be quite different, the outcomes are strikingly similar. Thus successful implementation of an ERP depends on the successful implementation of a defined *system of care* rather than deployment of individual protocol elements.

A "system of care" is conceptually important to understand to implement a successful ERP. A simplistic view is that developing a long and detailed set of guidelines or care paths will ensure success of the enhanced recovery system. Unfortunately, as is often the case, the simplest view is not correct. In the complex healthcare setting, a system is comprised of a series of interacting components that have defined functions or behaviors and have multiple interconnections, interactions, and interdependencies.[3] Further complicating healthcare systems is the fact that they are comprised of often extremely complex socio-technical systems interfacing with clinical microsystems. One needs to account for the interaction or inaction of innumerable people starting with the patient all the way through different providers with whom the patient interacts. Appreciating the complexity of delivering surgical care within a microsystem is essential for designing, implementing, monitoring, and sustaining an ERP. It is these last two critical areas, monitoring and sustaining, that will be reviewed in this chapter.

Issues With Measurement of Quality

There continues to be a debate about the best way to measure quality in health care. Each measurable element, structure, process, and outcome as described by Donabedian, has an important role depending upon the specific goal that is being assessed.[4] Measuring a directly observable outcome, which is frequently favored by clinicians, seems perfectly reasonable as it reflects the ultimate purpose of the intervention or process. However, just measuring the output of the process or system of care may be profoundly deficient in fully describing the *efficiency or quality* of care. **Table 23.1** describes how a simple but important outcome measure may not be the best measure of clinical quality. Clearly, Patient A had a very different hospital course and experience than Patient B. The same can be said for the use of process measures (**Table 23.2**). As the examples highlight, a single measure, either process or outcome, is not a reliable indicator of the efficacy or success of a complex system. Monitoring of an ERP requires regular tracking of both intermediate and final outcome measures as well as specific process measures.

■ Temporal Issues

Ideally, collection of such data elements should occur close in time to the actual event occurring and in an automated fashion. For an ERP, collection of milestone data for an individual patient on a daily basis might give providers a chance to intervene and get the

TABLE 23.1 — Example Outcome Measures, "Discharged Alive"

	Hospital Course	Discharged Alive
Patient A	Admitted for an esophagectomy with a 6-day hospital stay on the general care floor	Yes
Patient B	Admitted for an esophagectomy complicated by reoperation for bleeding on POD 1, development of acute renal failure requiring initiating dialysis on POD 4, and development of a wound infection on POD 11. Dismissed to a rehabilitation facility on POD 16	Yes

TABLE 23.2 —Example Process Measures, "Use of NSAIDs"

	Hospital Course	Use of NSAIDs for Postoperative Pain Control in the ERP Colectomy Pathway
Patient A	A healthy 45-year-old woman underwent a laparoscopic colectomy and had an average postoperative pain score of 3	Yes
Patient B	A 45-year-old chronic narcotic user with Crohn's disease underwent a laparoscopic colectomy and had an average postoperative pain score of 9.	Yes

patient "back on the pathway." Furthermore, high-level pathway performance data on a biweekly or monthly basis are essential for a multidisciplinary enhanced recovery team to identify changes in outcomes, investigate the causes, and implement interventions to correct any problems. Timely collection and review of the system data is important as infrequent review allows for more potential "drift" of the microsystem away from the desired outcome and thus a lost opportunity for providing optimal care. Additionally, if an investigation of the data is required to determine a cause for a change, there is simply more information to analyze, and the passage of time may make it more difficult to clearly identify contributing factors to the outcome change during that time period.

■ System Dynamics

Successful and actionable system measurement requires identification of discrete data elements representing both process and outcomes within the system. As system complexity increases, collection of intermediate measures is essential to better understand how subsystems/processes contribute to the ultimate system output. Additionally, having access to subsystem performance data allows for quicker identification of areas that might be influencing change in the final system output thus accelerating investigation and correction of any problems within the specific subsystem.

Information Management

As discussed above, collection of both process and outcomes data is essential for monitoring the impact of any clinical system especially an ERP. In an information-rich environment, the tendency is to collect as much data as possible, which can lead to information overload and paralysis. This is especially true in the clinical setting as more institutions transition to integrated electronic medical records, which make data collection easier. While having data on every aspect of an ERP allows a deeper analysis of the program and practices, it does not help in the daily management and sustainability of an ERP. It is unrealistic to believe that every enhanced recovery element will be completed on every patient for a multitude of very appropriate clinical or process reasons. If every element is tracked and displayed, the lack of some information increases the "noise" in the data especially in ERPs because the exact contribution of each element to the outcome is unknown.

A best practice approach to the *information overload dilemma* is to use a surrogate data element that reflects a composite of other elements. For example, a patient's reported pain score on postoperative day 1 could be a marker for the overall compliance with the ERP day of surgery pain control plan (multimodal non-narcotics) and goal (VAS ≤4) (**Figure 23.1**). Using this approach, it can translate to all providers their performance on an important patient-specific outcome that is an aggregate for a number of interdependent elements. This approach is especially useful for the development of performance dashboards, as discussed below.

FIGURE 23.1 — Use of a Composite Outcome Representing a Complex Set of Process Measures as a Surrogate for Multiple Individual Data Points

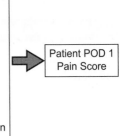

Pre-operative phase
1. Oral acetaminophen
2. Oral gabapentin

Operative phase
1. Epidural catheter placement
2. IV ketorolac
3. IV acetaminophen

Postoperative phase
1. Oral narcotics in PACU
2. Scheduled IV ketorolac
3. Scheduled oral acetaminophen

Patient POD 1 Pain Score

Information Analysis

Unlike standardized manufacturing processes, traditional clinical surgery care had so much variability in the processes of care that only very high-level performance metrics were available. However, the development of ERPs based upon standardized care processes permits use of analytical methods developed for the manufacturing industry to measure process. These types of tools known as *statistical process control (SPC)* charts are used to monitor process data in a way that can identify trends and performance, accounting for the natural variability in most processes.[5]

The most commonly used tool is a control chart that displays how a process changes over time. The basic elements of a control chart are:

- A center line representing the average performance of the process
- Upper and lower control limit lines that describe the variability of the process.

Most commonly, the upper and lower control limits are three standard deviations from the average based upon historical data. By comparing current data to these lines, one can draw conclusions about whether the process variation is predictable and consistent (in control, with only common cause variation) or is unpredictable or in flux (out of control, or changing due to special cause variation). When a process is out of control that indicates that the "standard" process is no longer performing as expected and warrants an indepth investigation to determine what elements or factors are disrupting it (unless it is due to an intentional change in the process). There are also a number of statistical rules based upon the distribution of data points that can provide insight into the status of the process being measured.[6]

An example of a control chart tracking a practice's surgical site infection (SSI) rate is shown in **Figure 23.2**. In this practice, there was a bundle of interven-

23

FIGURE 23.2 — A Control Chart Reflecting a Practice Change, SSI Reduction Bundle, Implementation, and the Impact on the Rate of SSI

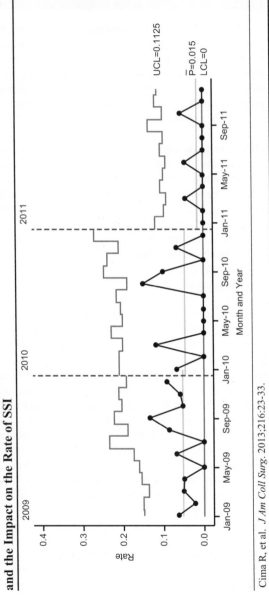

Cima R, et al. *J Am Coll Surg.* 2013;216:23-33.

tions aimed at reducing SSIs (the outcome of the process) that is reflected in the change of the centerline and control limits. The changes reflected in the control chart demonstrate a significant change in the average SSI rate; in addition, a decrease in the upper control limit indicates there is significantly less variability in the SSI rate over time.

Maintaining the Gains

As discussed, ERPs represent a defined system of care. The system is composed of multiple elements/interventions that contribute to the desired outcome(s). Up to now, we have reviewed principles of how to measure clinical processes in a way to provide actionable data to teams. Unfortunately, all too often clinical processes are implemented and data is tracked, but over time, performance changes, frequently in the undesired direction, for unclear reasons. The process owners are left wondering why.

To avoid this situation, there are two important concepts that need to be built into the monitoring of any ERP. The first is auditing the performance of a specific element in the ERP at regularly predetermined time intervals, ie, quarterly. For unclear reasons, sometimes documentation and the reality of what occurred differ. It is important to ensure that what is supposed to happen is actually happening. The audits should be of a reasonable size and cut across the breadth of the practice involved in the ERP. The second key concept is that of element adherence and compliance. Not all elements will be appropriate for every patient. However, in aggregate, the goal is to ensure that as many enhanced recovery elements are completed in every patient. The importance of high compliance with an ERP should not be underestimated as the level of compliance is directly correlated with achieving the goals of decreased length of stay (LOS, in days) in ERPs.[7,8]

23

In a detailed analysis of compliance with the enhanced recovery elements during implementation, Pedziwiatr and colleagues showed a direct inverse relationship between LOS and compliance with higher compliance with enhanced recovery elements resulting in consistently decreased LOS[8] (**Figure 23.3**). This relationship between adherence to performing as many of the ERP elements and improved outcomes is consistent throughout the literature despite the fact that the elements included in the pathways are frequently different.[9,10] While it is clear that adhering to the elements of enhanced recovery, whichever ones are implemented at a specific institution, it is equally clear that without continued performance monitoring of adherence to those elements the benefits of enhanced recovery will be lost[10] (**Figure 23.4**).

FIGURE 23.3 — Graphical Representation of a Direct Inverse Relationship Between Length of Stay and Increased Level of Compliance With Higher Levels of Compliance

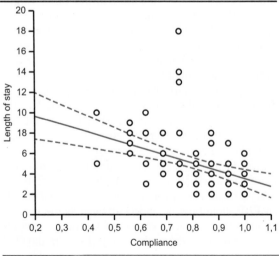

Pedziwiatr M et al. *Int J Surg.* 2015;21:75-81.

FIGURE 23.4 — Decline in Adherence to ERPs Without Continued Performance Monitoring

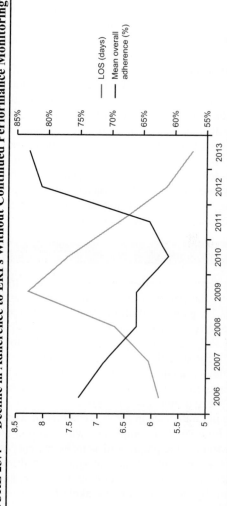

As adherence to ERP elements declines over time the primary outcome, length of stay increases. However, recommitment to element compliance results in a return to an improved outcome.

Bakker N, et al. *Surgery*. 2015;157:1130-1136.

23

In order to sustain an ERP's results, it requires continued monitoring of the primary outcomes of interest but also intermediate outcomes and process measures that the team believes significantly contribute to the overall desired outcome. As a multidisciplinary team effort, key data points need to be shared regularly, perhaps weekly but certainly monthly, with all stakeholders. The best tool for this purpose is a *dashboard*. Dashboards provide stakeholders a quick view of the current and historical state of performance on specific outcomes of interest such as LOS or adherence to total elements. The most important rule about dashboard construction is to only provide a limited number of data points that are tied to an actionable, meaningful, and value-added objective as it relates to the overall enhanced recovery system of care. More granular dashboards for specific phases of care such as the intraoperative phase would only focus on those metrics that are meaningful and actionable to those team members as opposed to a postoperative floor dashboard.

Summary

ERPs represent well-defined systems of care. They are characterized by specific interventions and milestones for patients. With the standardization of practice across a population, the planned interventions can be tracked and analyzed in a systematic fashion. Using different statistical tools designed for system analysis allows stakeholders to quickly identify trends, opportunities for improvement, and potential areas where there is a decline in performance.

Optimum outcomes in ERPs are achieved when there is a high level of compliance with meeting as many elements of the program in as many patients as possible. Like any socio-technical system, ensuring compliance and outcomes success requires vigilant monitoring by the leaders and stakeholder of the process. There needs to be frequent feedback regarding performance to those involved in the process. The feedback should be comprised of timely, relevant, and actionable data tailored to the viewer according to their position or role.

REFERENCES

1. Gustafsson UO, Scott MJ, Schwenk W, et al; Enhanced Recovery After Surgery (ERAS) Society, for Perioperative Care; European Society for Clinical Nutrition and Metabolism (ESPEN); International Association for Surgical Metabolism and Nutrition (IASMEN). Guidelines for perioperative care in elective colonic surgery: Enhanced Recovery After Surgery (ERAS(®)) Society recommendations. *World J Surg*. 2013;37:259-284.

2. Nicholson A, Lowe MC, Parker J, Lewis SR, Alderson P, Smith AF. Systematic review and meta-analysis of enhanced recovery programmes in surgical patients. *Br J Surg*. 2014;101:172-188.

3. de Weck OL, Roos D, Magee CL. *Engineering Systems: Meeting Human Needs in a Complex Technological World*. Cambridge, MA: Massachusetts Institute of Technology; 2011.

4. Donabedian A. *An Introduction to Quality Assurance in Health Care*. New York, NY: Oxford University Press; 2003.

5. Carey RG, Lloyd RC. *Measuring Quality Improvement in Healthcare: A Guide to Statistical Process Control Applications*. Milwaukee, WI: American Society for Quality; 1995.

6. Joshi MS, Ransom ER, Nash DB, Ransom SB, eds. *The Healthcare Quality Book: Vision, Strategy, and Tools*. 3rd ed. Chicago, IL: Health Administration Press; 2014.

7. ERAS Compliance Group. The impact of enhanced recovery protocol compliance on elective colorectal cancer resection: results from an international registry. *Ann Surg*. 2015;261:1153-1159.

8. Pędziwiatr M, Kisialeuski M, Wierdak M, et al. Early implementation of Enhanced Recovery After Surgery (ERAS®) protocol - Compliance improves outcomes: a prospective cohort study. *Int J Surg*. 2015;21:75-81.

9. Gustafsson UO, Hausel J, Thorell A, Ljungqvist O, Soop M, Nygren J; Enhanced Recovery After Surgery Study Group. Adherence to the enhanced recovery after surgery protocol and outcomes after colorectal cancer surgery. *Arch Surg*. 2011;146:571-577.

10. Bakker N, Cakir H, Doodeman HJ, Houdijk AP. Eight years of experience with Enhanced Recovery After Surgery in patients with colon cancer: impact of measures to improve adherence. *Surgery*. 2015;157:1130-1136.

24 Protocols

The following example protocols represent the current "state of the art" in enhanced recovery as seen through the eyes of the editors. However, they should be reviewed with several caveats.

First, an ERP is much more than any written protocol or document; the written protocol can be conceptualized as the embodiment of the authors' desire for each and every patient to achieve their individual best outcome. Protocols form the framework, but individual patients and teams of healthcare providers must walk the pathway together, navigating a complex, constantly changing modern healthcare system. It is the editors' experience that in the final analysis, the sine qua non of success in ERP is effective leadership (ie, enthusiastic champions) and interpersonal communication between team members, physicians, and nurses, most importantly the core anesthesiologist-patient-surgeon triad. Communication and education is the glue which keeps the patient and team adhered to the pathway; the protocol is only the scaffolding.

Secondly, successful ERPs are always local. What works at Duke, Dartmouth, or in Europe will not necessarily be applicable to individual hospitals in disparate settings across North America. Local (individual) hospital culture and policies will form the most significant barriers, and thus opportunities, for improvement and successful implementation. Champions must think globally but act locally.

Finally, a successful ERP is not static, but a living, breathing thing; ERP is a high-maintenance creature, and requires ongoing care, feeding, and nurturing. Planned quarterly updates. Annual didactic updates. Occasional amputations and facelifts. Regular upgrades. Continuous quality improvement.

Thus, do not view these protocols as the end-all-and-be-all. View them as a starting points for discussion. We wish you, your programs, and your patients the best of luck in achieving the best possible outcome for each individual patient in their perioperative journey.

24

TABLE 24.1 — Radical Cystectomy Protocol

Preoperative Phase

Education in Surgical Clinic

- **Define Expectations**: preoperative counseling and training
  - Exercise daily until surgery
  - Quit smoking
  - Quit drinking alcohol
  - Healthy diet and nutritional supplements (as recommended)
- **Label** the patient as enhanced recovery in procedure description of the case request
- **Provide** instructions for individual care pathway and expected hospital stay
- **Define discharge** criteria
  - Medical criteria that the MD and team will monitor daily
  - Ambulating and self-care
  - Tolerating liquids enough to stay hydrated and to tolerate PO pain regimen

Confirmation of Optimization and Readiness-Pre Anesthesia Testing (PAT)

- **Identify** the patient as enhanced recovery
- **Screen** for anesthetic risk and **optimizing** opportunities
- **Distribute** carbohydrate drink (Clearfast 12 oz) and instructions
- **Distribute** CHG sponges and instructions
- **Provide** written reinforcement of fasting guidelines. No food after midnight prior to surgery. Clear liquids until 1 hour before scheduled arrival time at the hospital
- CHO drink to be drunk 1 hour before scheduled arrival time at the hospital

Day of Surgery, Preop Holding

- **Identify** the patient as enhanced recovery and initiate protocol
- **Document** CHO drink was taken and document time
- **Document** if bowel prep completed or not

continued

TABLE 24.1 — *Continued*

- **Administer** and **document** multimodal drugs in **Preop Holding**
  - Alvimopan 12 mg PO
  - Acetaminophen 975 mg PO
  - Gabapentin 600 mg PO
  - Thoracic epidural (T10-12) unless contraindicated

Intraoperative Phase

- **Administer VT prophylaxis**
  - Heparin 5000 Units SC
  - SCD's in place
- **Administer antibiotic prophylaxis**
  - Give within 1 hour prior to incision
  - First-line Cefazolin 2 g IV (3 g for >120 kg). Re-dose in 4 hr
  - Beta-lactam allergy: Clindamycin 600 mg IV (re-dose 6 hr)
- Give within 1 hour prior to incision.
- **Administer Multimodal Pain MGT** during surgery
  - Hydromorphone 0.4 mg-0.8 mg (epid) before induction of anesthesia
  - Run infusion of 0.125% bupivacaine/hydromorphone 10 mcg/mL after bladder has been removed and hemostasis achieved. (3-6 mL/hr epidural) as tolerated
  - **Goal is to avoid IV opioids**. No intraoperative IV opioids after induction without discussion with attending anesthesiologist.
  - 15 mg IV ketorolac towards the end of the case if ok with surgeons
  - In chronic pain patients, consider adding IV ketamine infusion 4 mcg/kg/min during surgery
- Goal-directed fluid therapy (GDFT)
  - LR infusion 3 mL/kg/hour based on **ideal body weight** (available to EPIC main screen under vitals)
  - GDFT with boluses of colloid to optimize SV/SVV using a CO monitor
  - Record initial stroke volume (SV)
  - After incision give a 250-mL colloid bolus over <15 min (can omit if SVV < 12%)
    ○ If SV increases by >10% repeat bolus
    ○ If SV increases by <10% patient does not require a further bolus
    ○ Record peak value achieved

24

continued

TABLE 24.1 — *Continued*

- ∘ If still hypotensive, consider phenylephrine bolus or infusion
- ∘ Give a further colloid bolus when SV drops 10% from peak value
- ∘ Repeat cycle
- **Maintain** normothermia (temp >36)
- **Minimize** tubes, lines, and drains
  - Foley out except for neobladder cases
  - Pelvic drains at pelvic surgeon's discretion
  - Maintain ureteral stents as ordered
  - Remove orogastric tube prior to transfer to PACU

Postoperative Phase

- **Identify** the patient as enhanced recovery
- **Enforce** continuous SCD usage from PACU arrival until discharge
- **Continue** epidural use from intraop through PACU toward
- **Allow** a diet immediately–postsurgical bland
- **Ambulate** immediately and four times daily until discharge
- **Hob** elevated at 30 degrees at all times
- **Out** of bed at least 6 hr daily in addition to walks
- **Minimize** IVF to less than 1L/POD 0-1, then none thereafter.
- **Initiate** VT prophylaxis at 8 AM POD 1
- Remove JP drains and stents after POD 5
- **Transition** from epidural/block to oral narcotics once diet is tolerated.
- **Enforce** multimodal, non-narcotic pain management as first line
- **Maintain** euglycemia. 24h q6H BS, with intervention and on-going surveillance if >150
- **Encourage** incentive spirometry
- **Continue** appropriate alvimopan until first BM, then D/C
- **Continue** laxative for all non-stoma patients until first BM
- **Enforce** defined discharge criteria
  - Discuss from POD 0 with patient, family, resident team, and nurse staff
  - Reinforce expectations and discuss regularly with **patient**, RN staff, PRM, and family
  - Anticipate discharge needs
    - ∘ HHN for stoma/urostomy care
    - ∘ Enoxaparin for VT prophylaxis for 30 days.
    - ∘ Follow-up appointments with Oncology/GU.

TABLE 24.2 — Liver Resection:
Open and Laparoscopic Protocol

Preoperative Phase

Education in Surgical Clinic

- **Define Expectations**: preoperative counseling and training
  - Exercise daily until surgery
  - Quit smoking
  - Quit drinking alcohol
  - Healthy diet and nutritional supplements (as recommended)
- **Label** the patient as enhanced recovery in procedure description of the case request
- **Provide** instructions for individual care pathway and expected hospital stay
- **Define discharge** criteria
  - Medical criteria that the MD and team will monitor daily
  - Tolerating liquids enough to stay hydrated and eating solid foods
  - Pain control with oral analgesia-multimodal

Confirmation of Optimization and Readiness: Pre-Anesthesia Testing (PAT)

- **Identify** the patient as enhanced recovery
- **Screen** for anesthetic risk and **optimizing** opportunities
- **Distribute** carbohydrate drink (Clearfast 12 oz) and instructions
- **Distribute** CHG sponges and instructions
- **Provide** written reinforcement of fasting guidelines. No food after midnight prior to surgery. Clear liquids until 1 hour before arrival to hospital
- CHO drink to be drunk 1 hr before scheduled arrival time at the hospital

Day of Surgery, Preop Holding

- **Identify** the patient and enhanced recovery and initiate protocol
- **Document** CHO drink was taken and document time

continued

24

337

TABLE 24.2 — *Continued*

- **Administer** and **document** multimodal drugs
  - Gabapentin 600 mg PO
  - Naproxen 500 mg PO
  - Scopolamine patch for high-risk PONV patients
  - Thoracic epidural (T7-9) unless contraindicated
  - Heparin 5000 units SC immediately after epidural placement

Intraoperative Phase

- **Place** arterial line and 2 large Bore peripheral IVs. Consider no A-line for small resections
- **VT Prophylaxis**
  - SCD's in place
- **Administer antibiotic prophylaxis**
  - Give within 1 hr prior to incision
  - First-line Cefazolin 2 g IV (3 g for >120 kg). Re-dose in 4 hr
  - Add metronidazole 500 mg IV if biliary involvement. No metronidazole re-dose.
  - Beta-lactam allergy: Ciprofloxacin 400 mg IV (No re-dose) + Clindamycin 600 mg IV (re-dose 6 hr)
- **Administer Multimodal Pain MGT** during surgery-per anesthesia protocol
  (A) Thoracic epidural in situ
  - Hydromorphone 0.4 mg-0.8 mg (epid) before induction of anesthesia
  - Run infusion of epidural 0.125% bupivacaine /hydromorphone 10 mcg/mL throughout case (3-6 mL/hr) as tolerated
  - **Goal is to avoid IV opioids**. No intraoperative IV opioids after induction without discussion with attending anesthesiologist. If patient is frail, this may be achieved with epidural hydromorphone alone, especially in laparoscopic cases
  - 15 mg IV ketorolac towards the end of the case if good hemostasis (confirm with surgeon)
  - In chronic pain patients consider adding pre-incision IV ketamine 0.3-0.5 mg/kg and infusion 4 mcg/kg/min during surgery

continued

TABLE 24.2 — *Continued*

(B) Thoracic epidural unsuccessful or contraindicated
- IV ketamine pre-incision bolus 0.3-0.5 mg/kg and infusion 4 mcg/kg/min
- IV lidocaine pre-incision bolus 1 mg/kg and infusion 0.5-1 mg/kg/hour
- Hydromorphone boluses as needed
- 15 mg IV ketorolac towards the end of the case if good hemostasis (confirm with surgeon)
- **Fluid Therapy**
  Part 1: Until liver specimen removed, run patient 'dry'
  - LR infusion 3 mL/kg/hour only based on **ideal body weight**.
  - Goal is to run the patient 'dry' with permissive hypovolemia. Albumin to replace blood loss 1:1 if hypotensive. Phenylephrine infusion as needed.
  Part 2: Once liver specimen removed, optimize with goal-directed fluid therapy
  - Continue LR infusion 3 mL/kg/hr
  - GDFT with boluses of colloid to optimize SV/SVV using a CO monitor
  - Record stroke volume (SV)
  - Give a 250-mL colloid bolus over <15 min (can omit if SVV <10%)
    ○ If SV increases by >10% repeat bolus
    ○ If SV increases by <10% patient does not require a further bolus
    ○ Record peak value achieved
    ○ If still hypotensive consider phenylephrine bolus or infusion
    ○ Give a further colloid bolus when SV drops 10% from peak value
    ○ Repeat cycle
- **Low flow anesthesia** with isoflurane at flows ≤1 l/min
- **Gastric tube**–orogastric tube to be removed at the end of surgery
- PONV prophylaxis–dexamethasone 4 mg IV at start of case, ondansetron 4 mg IV when closing
- **Maintain** normothermia (temp >36)
- **Ventilation/oxygenation**
  - Maintain TV 6-8 mL/kg IBW
  - If oxygenation OK, consider no PEEP until after liver specimen removed

24

Continued

TABLE 24.2 — *Continued*

- **Minimize** tubes, lines, and drains
  - JP drain(s) as indicated
  - Remove OG at end of surgery
  - Foley–remove if no epidural in place

Postoperative Phase

- **Identify** the patient as enhanced recovery
- **Enforce** continuous SCD usage from PACU arrival until discharge
- **Continue** epidural use through PACU to ward
- **Continue** PONV medications
  - Ondansetron 4 mg IV q8h prn
  - Phenergan 6.25 mg IV q6h prn
- **Allow** Clear liquids on POD 0, with no carbonation
- **Allow** Postsurgical bland diet on POD 1
- **Encourage** gum chewing at least 3 times per day
- **Hob** elevated at 30 degrees at all times
- **Sit** on side of bed or in chair on day of surgery at least one time
- **Out of bed** for all meals and at least 6 hr daily in addition to walks beginning POD 1
- **Ambulate** 4 times daily until discharge beginning POD 1
- **Maintain** optimal fluid status
  - Maintenance IVF at 50 mL/hr until POD 1 at 0600
- **Remove** Foley on POD 1 at 0600. Keep Foley if high risk for urinary retention.
- **Remove** JP drain if JP bili is less than or equal to 3 times serum bili- POD 3
- **Initiate** VT prophylaxis POD 1 (AM)
  - Heparin SC if Epidural in place
  - Enoxaparin SC when epidural removed
- **Enforce** multimodal, non-narcotic pain management as first line
  - Naproxen 500 mg PO BID scheduled
  - Acetaminophen 650 mg PO q6h scheduled–not for major resections per surgeon
  - Continue Gabapentin 100 mg PO q8h scheduled
- **Transition** from epidural/block to oral narcotics once diet is tolerated
  - Tramadol 25-50 mg PO q6h prn

continued

TABLE 24.2 — *Continued*

- **Monitor** lab work:
  – Hgb/Hct, LFT, CMP – POD 1
  – Hgb/Hct, LFT - POD 2,3
  – JP Bilirubin POD 3
- **Maintain** euglycemia. Blood sugar monitoring
  q6h × 24 h, with intervention and on-going surveillance
  if >150
- **Consult** to endocrine if blood glucose >180 × 2
- **Encourage** incentive spirometry every hour ×10 while
  awake
- **Continue** laxative until first BM
  – Senna-S 2 tabs BID beginning POD 1
  – Miralax qd
- **Enforce** defined discharge criteria
  – Discuss from POD 0 with patient, family, resident
    team, and nurse staff
  – Reinforce expectations and discuss regularly with
    patient, RN staff, PRM, and family
  – Anticipate discharge needs
    ◦ Enoxaparin for VT prophylaxis ×14 days post
      discharge
    ◦ Senna-S BID while taking narcotics
    ◦ Miralax qd if no BM the previous day
    ◦ Naproxen BID scheduled
    ◦ Tramadol prn
    ◦ Follow-up appointments, staple removal,
      oncology–2-3 weeks

24

TABLE 24.3 — Gyn-Oncology Surgery Protocol

This section is to be used as a prompt for compliance with the patient pathway and an audit tool. It does not replace medical notes.

Pre-Assessment
- Enhanced recovery discussed with patient
- Length of stay discussed (EDD 5 days post op)
- Patient given ERP booklet and patient diary
- Patient given information sheet regarding spinal/epidural
- Patient given carbohydrate pre-load drinks and information

Admission
- Admitted to ESU/Ward
- Carbohydrate loading drink taken (9 PM day before surgery, plus by 6 AM if on AM list or 10:30 AM if on PM list)
- Prescribe phosphate enema if required

Anesthesia
- Routine epidural
- Goal-directed fluid management as per protocol for duration of operation and for 6 hours following (send card to ICU)
- Give stat dose of IV antibiotics
- Prescribe/sign for dalteparin
- Prevention of hypothermia

Day of Surgery Surgical Procedure
- Patients to be sat up in cardiac chair position within 4 hr of return to ICU
- Encourage free fluids—aim for 1 L
- Commence light diet

Step One—Postoperative
- Discontinue IV fluids
- Normal diet
- Chest assessment by a physiotherapist
- Sit out 2 hr per session
- Commence oral analgesia and NSAID (minimal use of opiates)
- Mobilize twice (PT/NS)
  - Time____
  - Time____

Continued

TABLE 24.3 — *Continued*

Step Two—Postoperative
- Normal diet
- Aim pain free on oral analgesics and NSAID
- Remove epidural
- Remove catheter
- Mobilize three times (PT/NS)
  – Time___
  – Time___
  – Time___
- Sit out total of 4 hr over the day

Step Three—Postoperative
- Normal diet
- Aim pain free on oral analgesics and NSAID
- Remove epidural (if not removed on POD 2)
- Remove catheter (if not removed on POD 2)
- Mobilize four times (PT/NS)
  – Time___
  – Time___
  – Time___
  – Time___
- Sit out total of 8 hr over the day
- Begin self-administration of dalteparin for patients requiring extended DVT prophylaxis
- Start discharge process
- Accurate and appropriate EDD
- TTOs

Step Four—Postoperative
- Normal diet
- Aim pain free on oral analgesics and NSAID
- Mobilize four times (PT/NS/independently)
  – Time___
  – Time___
  – Time___
  – Time___
- Sit out total of 8 hr over the day
- Self administration of dalteparin if appropriate
- Continue with discharge process
- Accurate and appropriate EDD
- TTOs

Continued

24

TABLE 24.3 — *Continued*

Step Five—Postoperative (Day of Discharge)

Discharge Checklist

- Good pain control with oral analgesia
- Eating and drinking a normal diet
- Patient passed flatus (no need to wait for bowels open)
- Independently mobile (or back to pre-operative baseline)
- Discharge advice given
- Nursing staff
- Physiotherapist
- TTOs, including dalteparin and sharps bin
- Patient aware to contact if any problems on discharge
- All of the above met and patient able to go home

Follow-up

- Telephone call 24 to 48 hr post discharge

TABLE 24.4 — Colorectal Surgery Pathway Protocol

A priori cohort definition: *"exclude elements, not patients"*

- All anticipated (*elective*) abdominopelvic cases with need for at least 1 hospital overnight
- Contraindications to ERP
  - Absolute: eg, organ system failure (frank CNS, cardiovascular, or pulmonary)
  - Relative: eg, emergency (imminently life-threatening) indication/situation
  - Nonapplicable: outpatient/same-day (eg, anorectal) surgeries?
  - Hypothetical/moral: refusal

Pre-hospital (At Home) Phase

- Patient optimization
  - Dedicated multiple media (ie, >1 mode) general perioperative safety and procedure-specific patient education, ie, in-person, booklets, e-booklets, videos
  - Alcohol and smoking cessation
  - Nutritional optimization:
    - Daily multivitamins with minerals supplement
    - High-protein supplements
    - Nutrition consult if BMI >30, recent unintentional weight loss >10 lb, or hypoalbuminemia
- Prehabilitation
  - Increased physical activity from baseline, eg, exercise >20 min 3× per week
  - Create incentives: "Many local gyms offer a free 1-month trial membership"
  - Physical therapy consult in frail patients (use a frailty assessment)
- Medical optimization
  - Anemia: if Hgb <10, then "FIVe" therapy: folate, iron + vitamin C
  - Diabetes: screen all patients, especially diabetics, for HbA1c–treat accordingly
  - Steroid-dependency vitamin supplements: MVI, vitamin C, vitamin A, zinc (all to optimize collagen synthesis)
  - Pre-op medical subspeciality consultations as needed, eg, anesthesia, cardiology, endocrinology, pulmonary

Continued

24

TABLE 24.4 — *Continued*

- **Preoperative Analgesia**
  - Preop Acute Pain Service (APS) consult for chronic pain patients
  - Prescriptions–consider preoperative prescriptions to ease discharge (some may require prior authorization)
    - Acetaminophen 1 g PO q6 ×16 days, 2 refills, begin at home 48 hours preoperatively
    - Lovenox 40 mg SC once daily × 28 days, begin postoperatively
    - Ibuprofen 600 mg PO q6 × 14 days, 2 refill, begin postoperatively
    - *Either* Gabapentin 300 mg q8 PO q12 × 2 weeks, 2 refills, begin postoperatively
    - *or* Pregabalin 75 mg PO q12 × 2 weeks, 2 refills, begin postoperatively
- **PONV prophylaxis**
  - Risk assessment (female, nonsmoker, prior PONV, planned postoperative opioid each 1 point). See PONV prophylactic protocol.
  - Scopolamine-Transdermal patch if >1 point
- **Carbohydrate loading**
  - 1 to 3 bottles (355 mL) of ClearFast, Gatorade, Nutricia, or other (last dose 2.5 hours prior to surgery)
- **Antibiotic-cathartic bowel prep**
  - Cathartic: Milk of magnesia for small bowel cases, MiraLax + DulcoLax for large bowel cases
  - Antibiotics: Neomycin 2 g twice, metronidazole 2 g twice; Cipro-flagyl if neomycin allergy

Pre-operative (In Same Day) Phase

- Encourage clears/Gatorade/Carbohydrate drink up to 2 hours prior to surgery
- Saline lock IV prior to OR
- Alvimopan PO 12 mg, unless chronic opioid user or opioid-free anesthesia pathway
- Multimodal opioid-sparing analgesia
  - Medications in preop holding area:
    - Acetaminophen, eg, 1000 mg PO or IV, at induction of anesthesia or at end of case
    - Neuropathic pain medications: eg, Gabapentin 600 mg q8h or Pregabalin 150 mg PO q12h (hold if age >70)

Continued

TABLE 24.4 — *Continued*

- ▫ NSAIDs: eg, Celecoxib 400 mg PO (hold if age >70 or renal insufficiency)
- Regional or neuraxial (all patients receive one of the below):
  - TAP block
    - ▫ By Block Team under ultrasound guidance, laparoscopic if Block Team not available
    - ▫ Liposomal bupivacaine 266 mg mixed in 100 cc injectable saline; 60 cc for block, 40 cc to surgeon for infiltration
    - ▫ Contraindication in pregnancy, pediatrics, cirrhotic, allergy to bupivacaine
  - Epidural—mid-thoracic, placed by APS under fluoroscopy
    - ▫ If planned laparotomy (open) incision or increased risk of conversion to supra-umbilical laparotomy incision), some centers use routinely for lap cases
    - ▫ Patients identified by surgeon in clinic
    - ▫ Patients secondarily identified by night-before screening by APS
    - ▫ 1/16th% (0.0625%) bupivacaine with hydromorphone after epidural placement to be continued in the OR

Intra-operative Phase

- Analgesia
  - Avoid intraoperative opioids
  - Ketamine 0.5 mg/kg at induction with infusion (10-20 mcg/kg/min) during case
  - Propofol 20-50 mcg/kg/min (to minimize inhaled anesthesia/reduce PONV)
  - Sevoflurane 0.5-0.7 MAC
  - See TAP block section above
  - APS to initiate 1/16th% bupivacaine with hydromorphone after epidural placement to be continued in the OR
  - IV acetaminophen 1000 mg in the PACU upon arrival, but no sooner than 6 hours after last dose
- PONV prophylaxis
  - Dexamethasone 8 mg IV
  - Ondansetron 4 mg IV at the end of the case

Continued **24**

TABLE 24.4 — *Continued*

- Fluid management: restrictive protocol vs goal-directed therapy (GDT)
  - Restrictive protocol (ASA 1 and 2 patients having uncomplicated surgery)
    - Continuous crystalloid infusion (do not use normal saline, prefer dextrose-containing, eg, D5LR or D5Normosol): laparoscopic surgery—3 mL/kg/hr or open surgery—4 mL/kg/hr
    - For MAP <65, administer fluid bolus of 250 mL crystalloid (not NS) and repeat once if concern for fluid responsive hypovolemia. If no response to 2 boluses, initiate phenylephrine infusion prior to more fluid. For continued hypotension, use your clinical judgment.
    - Replace EBL 1:1 with crystalloid, administer albumin or hetastarch (250 mL) for EBL over 500 mL or known hypoalbuminemia
    - *Note intraoperative oliguria is a normal physiologic response to surgery*
  - GDT (for ASA 3 and 4 or complicated surgery)—utilize noninvasive cardiac output monitor
  - Remove orogastric tube intraoperatively
  - Oxygen therapy: Keep FiO$_2$ >0.60
  - VTE prophylaxis
- S/Q heparin 5000 units prior to incision, ideally prior to induction
- Hold Lovenox for 12 hr before or after insertion or planned removal of epidural; *Lovenox 9 pm dosing allows no dose to be held, while still allowing morning removal the next day*
  - Stress-dose steroids—recent literature suggests intraoperative stress-dose steroids not necessary in colorectal; monitor for signs of Addisonian crisis
  - Infection prevention (see CRS Infection Prevention Bundle protocol)
    - Foley—routinely secure to inner thigh, do not let Foley fall between anus in lithotomy patients;
      - Foley out in OR for small bowel, right colon, and select other abdominal cases
      - Do not remove in OR for pelvic cases, colovesical fistula/exenteration cases
    - Routine upper ± lower body warmer
    - Antibiotic protocol

Continued

TABLE 24.4 — *Continued*

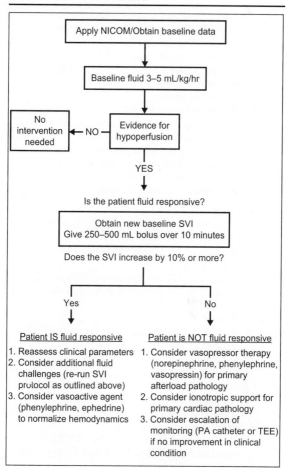

Continued

24

TABLE 24.4 — *Continued*

□ 2 g Ancef, re-dose 1 g every 3 hr *and* 1 g metronidazole, re-dose 500 mg every 6 hr
□ If anastomosis planned, then
  · Zosyn 3.375 g q6h *or*
  · Levaquin 750 mg if PCN allergy or planned anastomosis, re-dose at 6-12 hr
– Chlorhexadine scrub
– Routine wound protector use
– Triple antibiotic (Bacitracin, neomycin, polymixin) cavity and wound irrigation for >3 min
– Change gloves after bowel work and prior to closing
– Closing tray with clean Bovie and suction tips
– No routine abdominal drains
– Avoid closed-suction pelvic drains

Postoperative
• Labs—minimize labs; Hgb, K in PACU and POD 1; low threshold to trend CRP
• Foley management: for most patients, removed at end of case or at 6 AM on POD 1
– Prior to removing Foley in a patient with an epidural, make sure it is mid-thoracic and that they do not have a "low level"
– *Keep Foley if:*
  □ Urine bloody (darker than fruit punch) from cysto/ureteral stents
  □ Urine output inadequate (<20 cc per hour averaged over 4 hours)
• Fluid: D5 ½ NS+ 20KCl at 42 cc/hour (= 1 L in 24 hr *or* 0.5 cc/kg/hr)
– Daily weights at 6 AM
– Saline lock as soon as possible
– Fluid bolus: permissive oliguria, ie, UOP 20 cc averaged over 4 hr acceptable *(0.2 cc/kg/ hr)* (it takes several hours after laparoscopy and/or anesthesia to wear off before urine output will pick up)
– Low threshold for albumin, hetastartch, and/or Lasix to aid in obtaining optimal fluid balance and UOP
– When indicated, *use physiologic boluses (10 cc/kg) of balanced crystalloid* (LR or PlasmaLyte)
  □ Permissive hypotension if epidural present and patient asymptomatic

Continued

TABLE 24.4 — *Continued*

- Relative indications are
  - Persistent and fluid responsive oliguria
  - Hypotension (if no epidural); in addition needs Hgb recheck STAT
- Analgesia
  - Routine:
    - Heating pad to bedside, encourage use
    - Acetaminophen 1 g q6h (not prn), alternate with ketorolac q3h; avoid if cirrhotic
    - Ketorolac 15-30 mg IV q6h (not prn); avoid if renal dysfunction, age >70
    - Gabapentin 300 mg PO q8h or Lyrica 75 mg PO q12h; avoid in age >70
    - Tramadol 50-100 mg PO q6 hr prn
  - Selective/restricted narcotic use:
    - Oxycodone 2.5-5 mg PO q4h for breakthrough or non-narcotic naïve
    - Fentanyl 50-100 mcg or fentanyl PCA for breakthrough or refractory pain
    - Ketamine infusion (APS)
    - Lidocaine infusion (APS)
    - Epidural management per APS
- Diet/Ileus
  - Resume diet in PACU as soon as awake and not nauseous
  - Regular diet vs low residue if new ileostomy
  - Goal = 800 mL of oral fluid intake before morning; avoid carbonated drinks
  - Nutritional supplements three times daily
  - Milk of magnesia 10 cc (concentrate) every 12 hr; hold after first BM, patients should anticipate loose stools
  - Alvimopan 12 mg PO q12h if taking narcotics, DC upon first BM
  - Encourage chewing gum
- Activity
  - Incentive spirometer 10 ×/hr while awake
  - Out of bed (OOB) to chair the night of surgery + 1 walk
  - OOB to chair 6 AM, OOB > 6-8 hr, >4 walks
  - All meals in chair/bed for sleeping only
  - PT consult if not OOB by 9 AM POD 1 or if age >70

24

TABLE 24.5 — Duke Enhanced Recovery Distal Pancreatectomy Procedure (Lap and Open) Protocol

Preoperative Phase

Education in Surgical Clinic

- **Define Expectations**: preoperative counseling and training
  - Exercise daily until surgery
  - Healthy diet and nutritional supplements; Impact AR 1 box TID every day for 5 days prior to surgery
  - Nutrition consult for all patients
- **Label** the patient as "Enhanced Recovery" in procedure description of the Case Request
- **Complete** preop orders via Maestro Order Set
- **Provide** instructions for individual care pathway and expected hospital stay
- **Define discharge** criteria
  - Medical criteria that the MD and team will monitor daily
  - Ambulating independently and self-care
  - Tolerating liquids enough to stay hydrated and eating
  - Pain control with oral analgesia-multimodal

Confirmation of Optimization and Readiness— Pre-Anesthesia Testing (PAT)

- **Identify** the Enhanced Recovery patient
- **Screen** for anesthetic risk and **optimizing** opportunities
- **Distribute** carbohydrate drink (Clearfast 12 oz) and instructions
- **Distribute** CHG sponges and instructions
- **Provide** written reinforcement of fasting guidelines. No food after midnight prior to surgery, clear liquids until 1 hour before arrival to hospital, and CHO drink prior to arriving at hospital

Day of Surgery, Preop Holding

- **Identify** Enhanced Recovery patient and initiate protocol
- **Document** CHO drink was taken and document time
- **Administer** and **document** multimodal drugs
  - Gabapentin 600 mg PO
  - Tylenol 975 mg PO
  - Naproxen 500 mg PO

Continued

TABLE 24.5 — *Continued*

– Scopolamine patch for high-risk PONV patients
– Aprepitant for patients with history of PONV
– Thoracic epidural (T7-10) unless contraindicated
TEAM STEPPS with discussion of ERP preop and intraop elements

Intraoperative Phase
- **Obtain** U/A with Foley insertion
- **Administer VT prophylaxis**
  – Heparin 5000 Units SC after epidural placement. If no epidural, give before skin incision
  – SCD's in place
- **Administer antibiotic prophylaxis**
  – First-line Cefazolin 2 gm IV + Metronidazole 500 mg IV
  – If allergic, Clindamycin 900 mg IV + Ciprofloxacin 400 mg IV
- **Prevent** PONV–dexamethasone at start of case and ondansetron at end
- **Administer** multimodal analgesia per anesthesia protocol
- **Administer multimodal pain management** during surgery per anesthesia protocol
- **Avoid** intraoperative IV opioids (attending anesthesiologist approval required)
- **Optimize** intraoperative fluids with **goal-directed fluid therapy** per anesthesia protocol
- **Maintain** normothermia (temp >36)
- **Minimize** tubes, lines, and drains
  – JP drains
  – Remove OG
  – Foley remains

Postoperative Phase
- **Identify** patient as Enhanced Recovery
- **Enforce** continuous SCD usage from PACU arrival until discharge
- **Continue** PONV medications
  – Ondansetron 4 mg IV q8h prn–first-line
  – Phenergan 12.5 mg IV q6h prn–second-line
- **Encourage** gum chewing at least 3 times per day
- **Allow** sips of water only on POD 0 with max 250 mL q8h

24

Continued

TABLE 24.5 — *Continued*

- **Encourage** Impact AR 1 box TID + clear liquids- POD 1
- **Continue** Impact AR 1 box TID and advance to postsurgical bland diet POD 2
- **HOB** elevated at 30 degrees at all times
- **Sit** on side of bed or up in chair at least one time on day of surgery
- **Out of bed** for all meals and at least 6 hours daily in addition to walks
- **Ambulate** at least 4 times daily until discharge beginning POD 1
- **Maintain** optimal fluid status
  - Maintenance IVF w/LR based on IBW POD 0
  - Maintenance IVF D51/2 + KCL (IBW) with goal to HL POD 1
  - Saline lock
- **Remove** Foley on POD 1 at 0600 if no hx BPH
- **Remove** JP drain if drain amylase is less than 5000 and serous; POD 3 if attending agrees
- **Weigh** patient daily
- **Initiate** VT prophylaxis POD 1 (AM)
  - Heparin 5000u SC q8h if epidural in place
  - Lovenox 40 mg SC daily after epidural removed
- **Initiate** aspirin 81 mg PO daily (vein graft or cardiac risk) POD 1
- **Enforce** multimodal, non-narcotic pain management as first-line
  - Begin Tylenol 600 mg PO q6h when taking sips POs
  - Begin Gabapentin 100 mg PO q8h when taking POs
  - Begin Naproxen 500 mg BID when eating meals
- **Transition** from epidural/block to oral narcotics once diet is tolerated
  - Tramadol 25-50 mg PO q6h prn–first-line
  - Oxycodone prn–second-line
- **Maintain** euglycemia. Check BS q6h × 24 hrs, with intervention and on-going surveillance if >150.
- **Consult** endocrine if random BS >180 on 2 separate occasions
- **Encourage** incentive spirometry every 1 hour × 10 while awake
- **Continue** laxative until first BM
  - Senna-S beginning POD 1
  - Miralax qd when PSB diet begins

Continued

TABLE 24.5 — *Continued*

- **Begin** pantoprazole 40 mg IV/PO daily beginning POD 1
- **Monitor** lab work daily
  - CBC, CMP, Mg, drain amylase POD 1
  - Drain amylase POD 2
- **Enforce** defined discharge criteria
  - Discuss from POD 0 with patient, family, resident team, and nurse staff
  - Reinforce expectations and discuss regularly with patient, RN staff, PRM, and family
  - Anticipate discharge needs
    - Lovenox for VT prophylaxis × 28 days after surgery
    - Senna S and Miralax while taking narcotics
    - Prilosec OTC or pantoprazole 40 mg qd
    - Gabapentin × 2 weeks
    - Tylenol 600 mg PO q 6h prn
    - Naproxen OTC 220 mg BID
    - Tramadol prn, oxycodone prn if needed
    - Follow-up appointments w/MD, NP, or PA in 1 week after discharge

24

TABLE 24.6 — Duke Enhanced Recovery Whipple Procedure Protocol

Preoperative Phase

Education in Surgical Clinic

- **Define Expectations**: preoperative counseling and training
  - Exercise daily until surgery
  - Healthy diet and nutritional supplements–Impact AR 1 box TID every day for 5 days prior to surgery
  - Nutrition consult
- **Label** the patient "Enhanced Recovery" in procedure description of the Case Request
- **Complete** preop orders via Maestro Order Set
- **Provide** instructions for individual care pathway and expected hospital stay
- **Define discharge** criteria
  - Medical criteria that the MD and team will monitor daily
  - Ambulating independently and self-care
  - Tolerating liquids enough to stay hydrated and eating
  - Pain control with oral analgesia-multimodal

Confirmation of Optimization and Readiness—Pre-Anesthesia Testing (PAT)

- **Identify** the Enhanced Recovery patient
- **Screen** for anesthetic risk and **optimizing** opportunities
- **Distribute** carbohydrate drink (Clearfast-12 oz) and instructions
- **Distribute** CHG sponges and instructions
- **Provide** written reinforcement of fasting guidelines. No food after midnight prior to surgery, clear liquids until 1 hour before arrival to hospital, and CHO drink prior to arriving at hospital

Day of Surgery, Preop Holding

- **Identify** Enhanced Recovery patient and initiate protocol
- **Document** CHO drink was taken and document time
- **Administer** and **document** multimodal drugs
  - Gabapentin 600 mg PO
  - Tylenol 975 mg PO
  - Naproxen 500 mg PO
  - Scopolamine patch for high-risk PONV patients
  - Aprepitant for patients with history of PONV
  - Thoracic epidural (T7-10) unless contraindicated

Continued

TABLE 24.6 — *Continued*

TEAM STEPPS with discussion of Enhanced Recover preop and intraop elements

Intraoperative Phase

- **Obtain** U/A with Foley insertion
- **Administer VT prophylaxis**
  – Heparin 5000 Units SC after epidural placement. If no epidural, give before skin incision
  – SCD's in place
- **Administer antibiotic prophylaxis**
  – First-line–Cefazolin 2 g IV + Metronidazole 500 mg IV
  – If allergic, Clindamycin 900 mg IV + Ciprofloxacin 400 mg IV
- **Prevent** PONV–dexamethasone at start of case and ondansetron at end
- **Administer multimodal analgesia** per anesthesia protocol
- **Administer multimodal pain management** during surgery per anesthesia protocol
- **Avoid** intraoperative IV opioids (attending anesthesiologist approval required)
- **Optimize** intraoperative fluids with **goal-directed fluid therapy** per anesthesia protocol
- **Maintain** normothermia (temp >36)
- **Minimize** tubes, lines, and drains
  – JP drains
  – NG tube remains unless surgeon states otherwise
  – Foley remains

Postoperative Phase

- **Identify** patient as Enhanced Recovery
- **Enforce** continuous SCD usage from PACU arrival until discharge
- **Continue** PONV medications
  – Ondansetron 4 mg IV q8h prn–first-line
  – Phenergan 12.5 mg IV q6h prn–second-line
- **NPO** POD 0
- **NG** to LCWS
- **Remove** NG on POD 1 if output less than 700 mL for 12 hours
- **Encourage** gum chewing at least 3 times per day
- **Allow** sips of water POD 1 (max 250 mL q8h)
- **Encourage** Impact AR 1 box TID + clear liquids POD 2

Continued

24

TABLE 24.6 — *Continued*

- **Continue** Impact AR 1 box TID and advance to postsurgical bland diet if no DGE-POD 3
- **HOB** elevated at 30 degrees at all times
- **Sit** on side of bed or up in chair at least one time on day of surgery
- **Out of bed** for all meals and at least 6 hours daily in addition to walks
- **Ambulate** at least 4 times daily until discharge beginning POD 1
- **Maintain** optimal fluid status
  - Maintenance IVF w/LR based on IBW until POD 1 at 0600
  - Maintenance IVF D51/2 + KCL based on IBW POD 1
  - Goal to saline lock on POD 2
- **Remove** Foley on POD 1 if no hx BPH
- **Remove** JP drain if drain amylase is <5000 and serous POD 3 if attending agrees
- **Weigh** patient daily
- **Initiate** VT prophylaxis POD 1 (AM)
  - Heparin 5000 Units SC q8h if epidural in place
  - Lovenox 40 mg SC daily after epidural removed
- **Initiate** aspirin 81 mg PO daily (vein graft or cardiac risk)
- **Enforce** multimodal, non-narcotic pain management as first line
  - IV Tylenol × 4 doses beginning POD 0
  - Begin Tylenol 600 mg PO q6h when taking sips POs
  - Begin Gabapentin 100 mg PO q8h when taking sips POs
- **Transition** from epidural/block to oral narcotics once diet is tolerated
  - Tramadol prn–first-line
  - Oxycodone prn–second-line
- **Maintain** euglycemia. Check BS q6h × 24 hrs, with intervention and on-going surveillance if >150.
- **Consult** endocrine if random BS >180 on 2 separate occasions
- **Encourage** incentive spirometry every 1 hr × 10 while awake
- **Continue** laxative until first BM
  - Senna-S beginning POD 1
  - Miralax qd when diet begins

Continued

TABLE 24.6 — *Continued*

- **Begin** pantoprazole 40 mg IV/PO daily beginning POD 1
- **Monitor** lab work daily
  - CBC, CMP POD 0
  - CBC, CMP, Mg, drain amylase POD 1
  - CBC, CMP, drain amylase POD 2
  - CBC, CMP POD 3,4
- **Enforce** defined discharge criteria
  - Discuss from POD 0 with patient, family, resident team, and nurse staff
  - Reinforce expectations and discuss regularly with patient, RN staff, PRM, and family
  - Anticipate discharge needs
    - Lovenox for VT prophylaxis × 28 days after surgery
    - Senna-S and Miralax while taking narcotics
    - Prilosec OTC or pantoprazole 40 mg qd–lifetime medication
    - Tylenol 600 mg PO q 6h prn
    - Gabapentin × 2 weeks
    - Naproxen OTC 220 mg BID
    - Tramadol prn, oxycodone prn
    - Follow-up appointments w/MD, NP, or PA 1 week after discharge

24

TABLE 24.7 — ASER Anesthetic Checklist

Pre-operative
- Patient's health status optimized (anemia, diabetes)
- Patient education performed
- Oral carbohydrate drink 800 mL night before, 400 mL morning of surgery; if not available, allow free fluids up to 2 hours preoperatively
- Avoid sedative premedication

Intra-operative
- Antibiotic prophylaxis prior to surgery
- Avoid nasogastric tubes (if needed to decompress stomach, remove at end)
- PONV prophylaxis (two different class of drugs)
- Short-acting anesthetic agents
- Maintenance (if necessary) and monitoring of neuromuscular block
- Depth of anesthesia monitoring where appropriate
- Protective ventilation strategy (5-8 mL/kg) with optimal PEEP
- Maintain normoglycemia
- VTE prophylaxis—TEDS, calf compression device, chemoprophylaxis
- Maintenance of normothermia—warming device/fluid warming
- Consider analgesic technique (neuroaxial block/TEA/TAP/truncal blocks) to reduce opioid need postoperatively
- Goal-directed fluid therapy where appropriate to optimize the cardiac output, maintain normovolemia, but avoid fluid excess.
- Aim for normovolemia and maintain MAP with vasopressors
- Maintain optimal hemoglobin for the patient/procedure

Postoperative
- Rapid awakening from anesthesia
- Controlled extubation to reduce risk of microaspiration with full return of neuromuscular function
- Optimize analgesia as necessary while minimizing intravenous opioids
- Optimize fluid therapy as necessary during the period of maximal fluid shifts immediately after surgery

Continued

TABLE 24.7 — *Continued*

- Intravenous fluids and salt load should be minimized to the amount necessary to maintain normovolemia prior to adequate oral intake
- Start oral feeding and mobilization
- Ensure multimodal analgesia, antiemetics, and VTE prophylaxis are prescribed

Your patient should be able to drink, take a light diet, and mobilize the morning after surgery.

ASER Anesthetic Checklist. Scott MJ, Gan TJ, Miller TE. www.aserhq.org.

24

25 Abbreviations/Acronyms

1RM	one repetition maximum
6MWT	6-minute walk test
ABG	arterial blood gas
ACC	American College of Cardiology
ACCP	American College of Chest Physicians
ACE	angiotensin-converting enzyme
AHA	American Heart Association
AHRQ	Agency for Healthcare Research and Quality
AKI	acute kidney injury
APACHE II	Acute Physiology and Chronic Health Evaluation II
ASA-PS	American Society of Anesthesiologists physical status [score]
ASER	American Society for Enhanced Recovery
AT	anaerobic threshold
ATII	angiotensin II
ATP	adenosine triphosphate
BMI	body mass index
CI	confidence interval
CIGs	clinical implementation gaps
CO	cardiac output
COPD	chronic obstructive pulmonary disease
CPET	cardiopulmonary exercise testing
CrCl	creatinine clearance
CrI	credible interval
CRNA	certified registered nurse anesthetist
CVP	central venous pressure
CWI	continuous wound infiltration
DASI	Duke Activity Status Index
DVT	deep vein thrombosis
ED	esophageal Doppler

EDM	esophageal Doppler monitor
ER	enhanced recovery
ERAS	enhanced recovery after surgery
ERP	enhanced recovery protocol
ET	enterostomal therapy
FTc	corrected aortic flow time
GDFT	goal-directed fluid therapy
GDT	goal-directed therapy
GI	gastrointestinal
HbA1C	hemoglobin A1C
HDU	high dependency unit
HHC	home health care
HR	heart rate
HRR	heart rate reserve
hsCRP	high-sensitivity C-reactive protein
IBD	inflammatory bowel disease
ICD	International Classification of Diseases
ICU	intensive care unit
IGDT	intraoperative goal-directed fluid therapy
IM	intramuscular
IPPV	intermittent positive pressure ventilation
IQR	interquartile range
IRF	inpatient rehabilitation facilities
ISWT	Incremental Shuttle Walk Test
IV	intravenous
IVF	infusion of intravenous fluid
LA	local anesthetic
LMWH	low molecular-weight heparin
LOS	length of stay
LVNX	enoxaparin
MAP	mean arterial pressure
MBP	mechanical bowel preparation
MET	Metabolic Equivalent of a Task
MI	myocardial infarction
N_2O	nitrous oxide
NA	not available
NICE	National Institute for Health and Care Excellence

NIH	National Institutes of Health
NMB	neuromuscular block
NMDA	N-methyl-D-aspartate
NPO	nothing by mouth
NRI	nutritional risk indicator
NRS	nutritional risk screening
NSAID	nonsteroidal anti-inflammatory drug
OMBP	oral mechanical bowel preparation
OR	odds ratio
PAC	pulmonary artery catheter
PACU	post-anesthesia care unit
PCA	patient controlled anesthesia
PDPH	postdural puncture headache
PE	pulmonary embolism
PEEP	peak end expiratory pressure
PEG	polyethylene glycol
PO	oral
POD	postoperative day
PONV	postoperative nausea and vomiting
POSSUM	Physiological and Operative Severity Score for the Enumeration of Mortality and Morbidity
PPG	photoplethysmograph
PPN	peripheral parenteral nutrition
PPV	pulse pressure variability
PRO	patient-reported outcome
PUFA	polyunsaturated fatty acid
PVB	paravertebral block
PVI	pleth variability index
QoL	quality of life
RCT	randomized controlled trial
RNA	ribonucleic acid
ROM	range of motion
ROS	reactive oxygen species
RPE	rate of perceived exertion
RR	relative risk
SC	subcutaneous
SCIP	Surgical Care Improvement Project
SGA	subjective global assessment
SIRS	systemic inflammatory response syndrome

25

SNF	skilled nursing facilities
SPC	statistical process control [chart]
SQH	subcutaneous heparin
SSI	surgical site infection
SSRI	selective serotonin reuptake inhibitor
SV	stroke volume
SVV	stroke volume variability
TAP	transversus abdominus plane
TBI	traumatic brain injury
TCI	target-controlled infusions
TEA	thoracic epidural anesthesia
TEE	transesophageal echocardiography
TENS	transcutaneous electrical nerve stimulation
TIVA	total intravenous anesthesia
TLOS	total length of stay
TnT	troponin T
TOF	train of four ratio
TPN	total parenteral nutrition
VAS	visual analog scale
VISION	Vascular Events in Noncardiac Surgery Patients Cohort Evaluation
VRS	verbal rating scale
VTE	venous thromboembolism
WHODAS	World Health Organization Disability Assessment Schedule
WMD	weighted mean difference

Note: Page numbers in *italics* indicate figures.
Page numbers followed by a "t" indicate tables.

26

26

26

26

26

26

26

26

26